Colorado
Cooks for Education

A Celebrity cookbook dedicated to the
education of Colorado's children, all funds raised will
go to Colorado's schools.

Cover designs and illustrations by
Colorado's Elementary School students.

Front cover by: Tom McChesney Wellington, CO
Back cover by: Kelley Smith Mancos, CO

published by Eyestone PTO

TABLE OF CONTENTS

Tabitha Peter, Wellington, Co.

"COLORADO COOKS FOR EDUCATION"

Thank You to Our Recipe Submitting Celebrities

Sports Teams -
The Denver Nugget's (Dan Issel)   The Denver Bronco's (Pat Bowlen, Wade Phillips, D. Smith, J. Fassel)
C.U. Golf Team (Mark Simpson)   The Colorado Rockies (David Nied, Gary Wayne)
                                     C.U. and C.S.U. Womens Basketball teams (Ceal Barry and Lisa Parker)
Supreme Court Justice -   Byron White
T.V. and Radio Personalties -
Bob Palmer (Channel 4)   Cynthia Hessin (Channel 7)   Willard Scott (Today Show)
Katie Stapleton (KOA)   Pat Miller (The Gabby Gourmet)   Pete MacKay (KBPI)
Nancy Richards (Radio KMJî 100) Ed Greene (Channel 4)   Sherry Sellers (Channel 9)
Bill Kuster (Channel 9)   Mark Koebrich(Good After. CO)   Keith Weinman (KOA)
Rick Crandall (KOSI & KEZW)   Kim Christiansen (Channel 9)   Kathy Walsh (Channel 4)
Paula Woodward (Channel 9)   Beverly Weaver (Channel 2)   Pam Daale (Channel 7)

Newspaper -   Marty Meitus (Rocky Mt. News)
Magazine Food Editors -   Southern Living Magazine: Peggy Smith, Judy Feagin,
                                Diane MoatsHogan, Jane Cairns, Patty Vann and Kaye M. Adams

Politicians -
Governor Roy Romer   Mayor Ann Azari   State Treasurer Gail Schoettler
Sen Ray Powers   Attorney General Gale Norton   Sen. Tom Blickensderfer
Congressman Dan Schaefer   Sen. Jeff Wells   Senator Hank Brown
Dick and Dottie Lamm   Senator Ben Nighthorse Campbell   Rep. William Kaufman
Vice President Al Gore   Sen. Pres. Tom Norton   Congressman Wayne Allard
Rep. Jeane Faatz   Congressman Scott McInnis   Rep. Mike Coffman
Congressman Joel Hefley   Rep. Tim Foster   Rep. Moe Keller
Rep. Lewis Entz   Rep. Robert Shoemaker   Rep. Vi June
Sen. Lloyd Casey   Sen. Linda Powers   Rep. Mary Morrison
Rep. Gloria Tanner   Sen. Steve Ruddick   Sen. Tillie Bishop
Rep. Peggy Reeves   Rep. Norma Anderson   Rep. Don Armstrong
Nancy Reagan   Lady Bird Johnson
Actors -
Tim Allen (Home Improvement)   Barney   Clint Eastwood
Oprah Winfrey
Artists -   Mary Weiss
Musicians/Dance -   Doug Kershaw (The Ragin'Cajun) Martin Fredman (Dir. Co. Ballet)
Authors -
Will Hobbs   Baxter Black   Dr. Seuss
Educators -
C.U. President Judith Albino   C.U.Teaching Hosp. (Dennis Brimhall) Tom Sutherland (Iran Hostage)
Brig. Gen. Patrick K. Gamble   C.S.U. President Dr. Yates   C.S.U. Dr. Michael Charney
Fire Prevention Educators:
Elnora McCloughan   Cheryl Poage   Carol E. Small

Top CEO's and Comp. -

Tom Flanagan (Key Bank)	Coors Brewing Company	John Kelly (Pak Mail)
Rex Ulster (The Grease Monkey)	7-UP/Dr. Pepper (Coke)	Colo. Dept. of Health (Pat Nolan)
Dept. Child Food (Kathy Brunner)	Dr. Suzanne Barcher(Children's Mus.)	Laurie Mathew (Co. State Parks)
Hershey's (Cheryl A. Reitz)	Kraft (Lisa Balingit)	Marvel Entertainment (G. White)
Pillsbury (Rebecca Erdahl)	Fred Turner (Sr. Chair. McDonald's)	Dave Thomas (Wendy's)
M & M/Mars	Sonia Danielson (Eastwood Printing)	B. Hirschfeld (Hirschfeld Press)

Top Colorado Restaurants -

The Scanticon-Ronald Pehoski	The Buckhorn Exchg.-George Carlberg	The Fort - Samuel P. Arnold
The Left Bank - Liz & Luc Meyers	The Black Forest Inn - Lisa Arts	The Buckingham Broker-S. Carter
Furr's Cafeteria - William Hyde Jr.	The Olive Garden - Brad Kirby	Godfather's Pizza - Sue Gano
TCBY - Sara Wilson	D.J. McCadams - Kevin Harper	Tante Louise
The Denver Salad - Robert Riley	El Rancho Restaurant	Silverheels - Robert Starekow
Bernardi's Italian Rest. - Ed Bigg	Gussies - Kevin Young	Cherry Creek Inn - S. Kleinman
Henry's Rest. - Steve Coakley	The Castaway's - Van Dyke & Fabeck	
The Black Bear Inn - Hans J. Wypple		Alfalfa's Market - Paul Gingerich

Cooking Competitions Winners -

National Beef Cookoff - 25 winning recipes:

Armetta Keeney - 1992 Best Cook in the Country

1992 & 1993 CO State Fair winners: Dolores Vaccaro, Linda & Lindsey Holzrichter , C. &T. Schoenmaker, Nancy Horton

1993 Colorado Beef Cookoff winner: Tonya D. Sarina

1993 Hi Country Lamb Cook-off   1st Place - Nancy Rundel

                                        2nd Place - Tim Sebald and Gary Schrecongost (Monfort)

                                        3rd Place –Jim Dalton Family

Also Mrs. Harold Harper, Ruth Gjelsness, Rusti Ruth and Darlene Miller

Colorado Associations –

American Sheep Council (John M. Olson)	Co. Wheat Council(B. Witte)
Assoc. Educ. of Young Children(Dona Kelley)	Beef Prom. - Monte Reese
National Watermelon Prom. Board Western Dairy Farmers	Wash. Apple Growers - K. Bruno
Amer. Heart Assoc. of Colo. (R. Brennan)	Junior League of Denver
Colorado Corn Administration Committee	

Top-Athletes -

Hale Irwin	Arnold Palmer	Chris Evert
Billy Kidd	Wendy Lucero (Olympic diver)	Danny Schayes (past Nugget)
Jesse Clay (4x Karate World Champion)		

Museums and Historians -

Sam'l P. Arnold	Mrs. Eveitte Swanson	Charlotte Ortega Van Horn
Molly Brown House	Gilpin County Historical Society (Francis Beyer)	
Hiwan Homestead Museum (Sue Ashbaugh)	Cripple Creek District Museum (Erik Swanson)	
Boulder Museum of History (Wendy Gordon)		

Celebrity Donations without recipes -

Roseanne Arnold	James Michener	Sesame Street's Big Bird

A Special Thank-you to: Frank T. Pierz for the CSU agriculture statistics

Office Depot	Target	Anheuser-Busch
OEA Aerospace	Travel Connection	Walgreens
Colorado School of Mines	Hardee's	Sally Fox (The Square mall)

IDedication

All Coloradoans will surely agree that our children will face a much more challenging world than any past generation. To do this successfully, they will need to benefit from the very best and most comprehensive education our schools can provide. This is the challenge and responsibility of the current generation, made even more difficult by waning funds for education and it is toward the complete fulfillment of this challenge that this book is dedicated.

By purchasing this book you're joining our celebrity cooks (and contributing parents and teachers) in saying to children:

"Learn well; we're waiting for you to join us and show us the way to a better world."

Thank You,
Eyestone PTO

Tom McChesney, Wellington, Co.

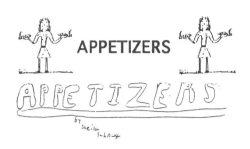

APPETIZERS

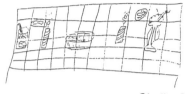

by Sheila Schnug

Sheila Schnug, Wellington, Co.

Powers Apple Rings

4 large firm, unpeeled apples
4 Tbl. butter
4 Tbl. sugar
1-1/2 tsp. ground cinnamon

• Core apples and cut in thirds. Heat butter in skillet. Add apples and brown over medium heat on each side. Cook until fork tender. Mix sugar and cinnamon and spread on large plate. Place cooked apples onto sugar mixture and coat both sides heavily. Transfer to buttered shallow baking dish. Bake apples at 375 degrees for 10 minutes. Yield 6 servings

Ray Powers
State Senator
Colorado Springs, CO

Ken Betchel, Wellington, Co.

Cucumber Canapes

1 small cucumber
4 oz. cream cheese
1/4 tsp. paprika
1 tsp. horseradish
1 Tbl. mayonnaise
1/2 baguette, thinly sliced and toasted
Salt and pepper

• Cut cucumber in half, lengthwise. Set one half aside. Peel other half, seed and grate flesh into bowl. Add cheese, paprika, horseradish and mayonnaise to grated cucumber. Season well with salt and pepper.
• Seed remaining cucumber and slice thinly without peeling.
• Spread cucumber/cheese mixture over toasted rounds of bread and top with slices of cucumber, avocado and alfalfa sprouts.

Elnora McCloughan
Dir. of Berthoud Area Community Center &
Employee of Fire Protection District

Bryon Butzin, Colorado Springs, Co.

Jeff's Meat Balls

Sauce
2 (8 oz.) cans tomato sauce
2 tsp. pepper
2 tsp. dry mustard
1 Tbl. chili powder
1 Tbl. sugar
A little water
Worcestershire Sauce
Tabasco Sauce
Meat Balls
2 lbs. hamburger
scant 1/2 cup chopped parsley
2 tsp. salt
1/4 tsp. pepper
2 eggs
2 cups bread crumbs
8 Tbl. water
4 Tbl. parmesan cheese

• Combine dry ingredients and add to tomato sauce. Add 3 squirts Worcestershire sauce and 2 squirts Tabasco sauce. Heat.

• Mix together. Form meat balls. Brown and drain. Add to heated sauce and cook 10 minutes. Serve in chafing dish. Okay to freeze.

State Senator
Jeff Wells
Colorado Springs, CO

Bacon Water Chestnuts

1 package (8 oz.) OSCAR MAYER bacon, cut in half crosswise
1 can (8 oz.) whole water chestnuts, drained
1/2 cup MIRACLE WHIP or MIRACLE WHIP LIGHT Dressing
1/2 cup firmly packed brown sugar
1/4 cup chili sauce

Prep time: 20 minutes
Cooking time: 45 minutes

• Heat oven to 350°F.
• Cook bacon in large skillet on medium heat until almost crisp; drain. Wrap bacon around water chestnuts; secure with toothpicks. Place in baking dish.
• Mix remaining ingredients; pour over water chestnuts.
• Bake 45 minutes. Makes about 24.

KRAFT Creative Kitchens

Lauren Alexander, Ft. Collins, Co.

APPETIZERS

Spicy Crab Cakes With Lime Sauce

1/2 cup KRAFT Real Mayonnaise
1 Tbl. lime juice
1/4 to 1/2 tsp. ground red pepper
2 cans (6 oz. each) crabmeat, drained, flaked
1 cup dry bread crumbs, divided
1 jar (2 oz.) diced pimientos, drained
2 Tbl. chopped green onions
2 Tbl. PARKAY Spread Sticks
COOL LIME SAUCE

COOL LIME SAUCE
1/2 cup KRAFT Real Mayonnaise
1/4 cup sour cream
1 Tbl. lime juice
2 tsp. grated lime peel

Prep time: 20 minutes
Cooking time: 6 minutes
• Mix mayonnaise, juice and pepper.
• Add crabmeat, 1/2 cup of the bread crumbs, pimientos and onions.
• Shape into 8 (1/2 inch thick) patties; coat in remaining 1/2 cup bread crumbs.
• Cook patties in spread in large nonstick skillet on medium heat 3 minutes on each side or until browned and thoroughly heated.
• Serve immediately with Cool Lime Sauce. Makes 4 servings.
COOL LIME SAUCE INSTRUCTIONS
• Mix all ingredients. Serve with Spicy Crab Cakes. Makes 3/4 cup.

KRAFT Creative Kitchens

Sugared Bacon Strips

1/2 to 1 lb. bacon, depending on desired sweetness. Have at room temperature for best results.
Approx. 1 cup brown sugar

• Roll (or pat or shake) raw bacon in brown sugar and place strips on any flat pan with sides. Bake in a slow oven (275 to 300°F) for about 25 to 30 minutes, until dark brown. You may turn over once with a pincher or tongs. When bacon appears well done, remove with tongs and DRAIN ON BROWN PAPER very thoroughly (grocery bags are very good for this). As it cools, it will get hard and can then be broken into smaller pieces or served whole. This tedious chore can be done earlier in the day. Store in aluminum foil, then reheat to serve.

Arnold and Winnie Palmer - Pro Golfer

Amy Whitt, Colo. Springs, Co.

Fresh Veggie Spread

8 oz. non-fat cream cheese, softened
1/3 cup fat-free mayonnaise
1 tsp. chopped onion
1 tsp. green pepper
1/3 cup chopped broccoli
1/3 cup chopped carrot
1/4 to 1/2 tsp. Worcestershire Sauce (optional)

• Mix together cream cheese and mayonnaise. Add onion, green pepper, broccoli, carrots and Worcestershire sauce. Refrigerate. Serve with crackers or bagels. Serves 32.

• **Nutrient Analysis**. One serving provides: 8.4 calories, 1 g protein, 5 g carbohydrates, 1 g dietary fiber, 0 fat, 1 mg cholesterol, 7 mg potassium, and 64 mg sodium. Calories from carbohydrates, 82%; fat, 0%; protein, 18%.

Barbara Witte
Wheat Foods Council
Englewood, Colorado

Party Sandwich Filling

1 (8-oz.) package cream cheese, softened
3/4 cup chopped green pepper
1/4 cup chopped onion
3 Tbl. chopped pimento
3 hard cooked eggs, sieved or chopped

• Mix thoroughly and spread on toast or crackers. Makes 2-1/3 cups filling.

Dolores Vaccaro
Colorado State Fair, First Prize Winner

11

Genny Williamson, Colo. Springs, Co.

Stegosaurus Vertebrae Party Roll

2 (8 oz.) packages cream cheese, softened
1 package Hidden Valley Ranch milk recipe -
    Original Ranch Salad Dressing
2 green onions, minced
4 (12 inch) flour tortillas
1/2 cup diced red pepper (or pimento)
1/2 cup diced celery
1 can (small) chopped black olives, drained

• Mix first 3 ingredients, spread on tortillas. Sprinkle on remaining ingredients. Roll and wrap fairly tight. Chill at least 2 hours. Cut into 3/4 inch slices. Arrange on platter like a "backbone".

This is a party roll for the King and Queen... Mmmm good. Try it, you will like it.

State Senator
Tilman "Tillie" Bishop
Grand Junction, CO

Cheese Ring

1 (16 oz.) package extra sharp cheddar cheese,
    shredded
1 (16 oz.) package medium cheddar cheese,
    shredded
1 small onion, grated
1 cup mayonnaise
1 teaspoon red pepper
1 cup chopped pecans
Parsley sprigs
Strawberry preserves (optional)

• Combine first 5 ingredients and mix well. Sprinkle about 1/4 cup pecans in an oiled 7-cup ring mold and press cheese mixture into mold. Chill until firm.
• Unmold on platter and pat remaining pecans onto cheese ring. Garnish with parsley sprigs. Serve on crackers with strawberry preserves on top if desired.
• Yield: 1 cheese ring.

Celeste Schoenmakers
Colorado State Fair Winner

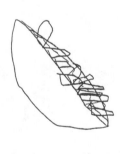

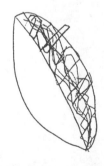

Cassy Glass, Wellington, Co.

APPETIZERS

Apricot Brie in Puff Pastry

1 (4-1/2 oz.) wheel of Brie cheese
1 sheet frozen Puff Pastry (in the grocery freezer case)
2 Tbl. apricot jelly or orange marmalade

• Unwrap puff pastry and allow to thaw 20 minutes. Slice top and bottom rind off the brie cheese. Spread both sides of brie with jelly. Place brie in center of puff pastry sheet and fold sheet so that it envelops brie completely. Bake in a 400°F oven for 15 to 20 minutes until puff pastry is golden. Serve with crackers.

Marty Meitus
Food Editor, Rocky Mountain News

Tom McChesney, Wellington, Co.

Dried Beef Spread

8 oz. non-fat cream cheese, softened
1 cup low-fat sour cream
2 Tbl. minced onion
1 Tbl. chopped green pepper
1 jar (2-1/2 oz.) dried beef, chopped

• Mix cream cheese and sour cream; add onion, green pepper and dried beef. Bake at 350 degrees for 15 minutes. Cool completely; refrigerate. Serve with crackers or bagels. Serves 20.

• **Nutrient Analysis.** One serving provides: 33 calories, 3 g protein, 7 g carbohydrates, .2 g dietary fiber, 1.5 g fat, 8 mg cholesterol, 13 mg calcium, 33.5 mg potassium, and 196 mg sodium. Calories from carbohydrates, 52%; fats, 26%; protein, 22%.

Barbara Witte
Wheat Foods Council
Englewood, Colorado

Jennifer Macias, Wellington, Co.

Sombrero Dip

1 lb. lean lamb (ground)
1/2 cup finely chopped onion
1/4 cup catsup
1/4 cup taco sauce
1-1/2 tsp. chili powder
1/2 tsp. salt
16 oz. can refried beans

TOPPINGS
1/2 cup sliced olives, black or green
1 cup chopped onions
1 cup shredded cheese

• Cook lamb and onion over medium heat until no pink remains in the lamb. Very important to DRAIN WELL. Mix remaining ingredients into the meat. Place in crock-pot or fondue dish and heat until hot and bubbly. Sprinkle topping ingredients over the mixture and serve with corn chips.

John M. Olson
Executive Director
American Sheep Industry Association
Englewood, Colorado

Witches Brew (Dip)

1 large onion, chopped
1 green pepper, chopped
2 Tbl. butter
2 Tbl. ketchup
1/2 tsp. Worcestershire Sauce
1 can cream of mushroom soup
1 package chipped beef, chopped
1/4 lb. shredded cheddar cheese

• Sauté onion and green pepper in butter. Add ketchup, worcestershire sauce, soup and beef. Add cheese and heat until melted. Serve warm with Nacho Chips.

Mark Koebrich
Channel 9
Good Afternoon Colorado

Dustin Durnwald, Wellington, Co.

Velveeta Salsa Dip

1 lb. VELVEETA Pasteurized Process Cheese
    Spread, cubed
1 jar (8 oz.) salsa
2 Tbl. chopped cilantro (optional)

Prep time: 5 minutes
Microwave cooking time: 5 minutes

• Microwave VELVEETA Pasteurized Processed
Cheese Spread and salsa in 1-1/2 quart
microwavable bowl on HIGH 5 minutes or until
smooth, stirring after 3 minutes. Stir in cilantro.
• Serve hot with tortilla chips, broiled green, red or
yellow pepper wedges or breadsticks. Makes 3
cups (24 servings).

KRAFT Creative Kitchens

Cottage Cheese Dip

4 parts cottage cheese
1 part sour cream
Lawry's Garlic salt
Worcestershire sauce
3 to 5 green onions

• Mix together cottage cheese and sour cream (4
to 1 ratio). Add Lawry's Garlic salt to taste. Add
Worcestershire sauce to taste, but not so much as
to discolor mixture. Add chopped green onion and
tops (3,4,5 or whatever!). This tastes better if it
sits in refrigerator for a few hours. Good with
veggies, chips, or whatever!

Sue Gano
Godfather's Pizza

Maurissa Moore, Wellington, Co.

15

Fiesta Favorite Dip

2 cans Jalapeno Bean Dip (found in aisle with
    potato chips at grocery store)
3 avocados
Lemon juice
Chili powder
Salt and pepper
16 oz. carton sour cream
1/2 cup real mayonnaise
1 package Lawry's Taco Seasoning mix
1-1/2 bunches chopped green onions
3 chopped, seeded tomatoes (squeeze out
    juice and seeds)
2 small cans chopped or minced black olives
1 package Longhorn Cheddar Cheese,
    shredded
Taco Chips - use Red Seal Chips

• Use a glass, lucite, or other flat platter. The
following are "piled" on in layers:

• Jalapeno Bean Dip.
• Avocados mixed with lemon juice, chili powder,
salt and pepper to taste.
• Sour cream, mayonnaise and taco seasoning
mix, mixed together. This layer should seal in
avocado so it won't turn brown.
• Sprinkle on green onions.
• Tomatoes.
• Olives.
• Cheese.

• Serve with Taco Chips. Make in the morning
(not a day ahead). Serves lots, but it goes fast!

Barry and Arlene Hirschfeld
Hirschfeld Press, Denver, CO

Chili Cheese Fondue

1 (4 oz.) can green chili peppers
1 onion
1 cup drained tomatoes
1/2 lb. Velveeta cheese
1 stick margarine
1/8 tsp. garlic powder
Salt and pepper to taste

• Melt margarine and cook onions. Combine all
ingredients in saucepan and cook until cheese
melts.

Dolores Vaccaro
First Prize - Colorado State Fair

Andrea Gutierrez, Wellington, Co.

Cheese Fondue a la Vaudoise

10.5 oz. gruyere cheese
10.5 oz. emmenfal cheese
7 oz. raclette cheese
3.5 oz. fribourg vacherin cheese
1 clove garlic
1-7/8 cup dry white wine
3 Tbl. corn starch
2 Tbl. kirsch
Freshly ground white pepper
Nutmeg to taste
White bread whole, cubed or French bread

• Grate or shred the cheese. Peel the garlic. Cut in half. Rub the inside of a fondue dish with garlic. Pour the wine into the dish. Place dish on hot stove. Add the cheese and stir until it has melted. Blend the cornstarch with the kirsch. Stir into cheese. Bring back to boil and stir continuously. Season with pepper and nutmeg. Transfer dish to burner and let simmer. Cut the bread into cubes. Impale a piece of bread on the fondue fork and dip into cheese. Serve with a dry white wine or black tea. Top the meal with a small glass of kirsch.

Hans T. Wyppler
Chef de Cuisine - Black Bear Inn
Lyons, Colorado

Watermelon Fire And Ice Salsa

3 cups seeded and chopped watermelon
1/2 cup green peppers
2 Tbl. lime juice
1 Tbl. chopped cilantro
1 Tbl. chopped green onion
1 to 2 Tbl. (2 to 3 medium) jalapeno peppers, chopped
1/2 tsp. garlic salt

• Combine all ingredients; mix well. Cover and refrigerate at least 1 hour. Makes 3 cups.
• Serving Tips: Serve on sliced oranges or cheese-filled manicotti or with corn or potato chips. Or, top 1 cup dairy sour cream with 1 cup salsa and serve with chips.

Nancy Rundel
National Watermelon Promotion Board
Pierce, Colorado

Jeremy Fassler, Wellington, Co.

17

Robert Morris, Wellington, Co.

The Beloved Hot Onion Dip

3-4 cups packaged chopped onions (measure
    while frozen)
3 (8-oz.) packages cream cheese, softened
2 cups parmesan cheese, grated
1/2 cup mayonnaise

• Thaw onions and drain well on paper towels.
Combine all ingredients and stir well. It will be thick.
Place in a shallow 2-quart souffle dish. Bake at
425° for 15 minutes, or until golden brown.

Wendy Lucero Shayes, Olympian
Danny Schayes, Ex-Nugget

Dan and Wendy's Favorite Garbage Mix

5-6 cups Corn Chex
5-6 cups Rice Chex
5-6 cups Crispix
5-6 cups Cheerios
5-6 cups pretzels (thin stix)
1 lb. Spanish peanuts
1 lb. pecans
2-1/2 sticks margarine
2/3 cup oil
5 tsp. garlic salt
Few shakes Tabasco sauce
5 tsp. Worcestershire sauce
4 tsp. salt

• Mix cereal, nuts and pretzels in a large baking
pan.
• Bring margarine, oil, garlic salt, Tabasco,
worcestershire and salt to a full boil. Stir and
spoon over cereal mixture. Stir mixture
thoroughly.
• Bake 300° for 1 hour, stirring well every 15
minutes.
• Cool. Freezes well.

Wendy Lucero Schayes, Olympian
Danny Schayes, Ex-Nugget

Paul Cox, Wellington, Co.

APPETIZERS

"My home town, Steamboat Springs, is famous for the light, fluffy snow known as 'champagne powder.' But wherever you ski in sunny, snowy Colorado, always remember: Keep the pointed ends in front! That's my never-fail ski tip for future Olympic ski stars of any age or ability."

Happy Skiing.

Billy Kidd
Olympic Medalist, and
former World Champion

Billy Kidd's Apres Ski Dip
(Hot Artichoke Dip)

1 (8-1/2 oz.) can artichokes (packed in water), drained
1 (7-1/2 oz.) can chopped green chilies
1 cup grated parmesan cheese
1 cup mayonnaise

• Preheat oven to 350°F.
• Break artichokes apart into small pieces. Combine all ingredients, and place in an ovenproof serving dish. Bake for 30 minutes. Let stand for 10 to 15 minutes before serving with tortillas or crackers.

Billy Kidd
Olympic Medalist, and
former World Champion

Gary Baker, Mancos, Co.

19

 APPETIZERS

Mushroom Phyllo Tarts

3-oz. package cream cheese, softened
1/4 cup dry bread crumbs
1 Tbl. dill weed
1/2 tsp. salt
3/4 cup dairy sour cream
1 to 2 Tbl. lemon juice
4.5-oz. jar Green Giant sliced Mushrooms,
    drained
1 garlic clove, minced
1/2 cup butter or margarine
8 (17 x 12-inch) frozen phyllo (fillo) pastry
    sheets, thawed
4.5-oz. jar Green Giant Whole Mushrooms,
    drained

Tip
• To make ahead: prepare, cover and refrigerate up to 4 hours before baking. Bake as directed above.

• Heat oven to 350°F. In small bowl, combine cream cheese, bread crumbs, dill weed, salt, sour cream and lemon juice; blend well. Stir in sliced mushrooms. Set aside. In small skillet over medium heat, cook garlic in butter until tender. Lightly coat 16 muffin cups with garlic butter; set aside.
• Brush large cookie sheet with garlic butter. On work surface, unroll phyllo sheets; cover with plastic wrap or towel. Brush one phyllo sheet lightly with garlic butter; place buttered side up on buttered cookie sheet. Brush second phyllo sheet lightly with garlic butter; place buttered side up on top of first sheet. Repeat with remaining phyllo sheets. With sharp knife, cut through all layers of phyllo sheets to make sixteen 3 x 4 x 1/4-inch rectangles. Place one rectangle in each buttered muffin cup. Spoon heaping tablespoonful cream cheese mixture into each cup. Top each with whole mushrooms, pushing stems into cream cheese mixture. Drizzle with remaining garlic butter. Bake at 350°F. for 18 to 20 minutes or until light golden brown.
• 16 appetizers.

Pillsbury Company

Brad Jewell, Wellington, Co.

20

 DRINKS

Cassy McDonald, Wellington, Co.

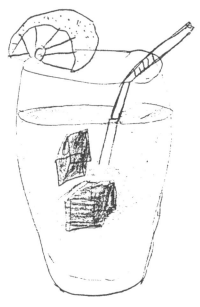

John Sosna, Wellington, Co.

Tori Bishop, Wellington, Co.

21

 DRINKS

Raspberry Smoothie

16 oz. apple juice
1 whole bananna
1/2 pint raspberries

• Put all ingredients in blender. Mix until fully blended.

Mark Simpson
University of Colorado
Golf Coach

Rhubarb Punch

3 quarts water
3 quarts cut rhubarb
2-1/2 cups sugar
1 (6oz.) package strawberry Jello
7-Up or Lemon-Lime Soda

• Boil together water, rhubarb, and sugar until soft, then strain. Add enough water to make 5 quarts. Bring juice to a boil and add jello. Freeze if desired. Add 7-Up when serving.

Ruth Gjelsness
Cook featured in Successful Farming Magazine

Instant Russian Tea

1-1/2 cup instant orange drink crystals
1 cup tea mix (presweetened with lemon)
1 tsp. ground cinnamon
1/2 tsp. ground cloves

• Mix together. Store in container.
• To serve stir in 1 teaspoon mix to 3/4 cup boiling water.

Nan Zimmerman
One of Eyestone's VIP's of the Year

Cassy McDonald, Wellington, Co.

 DRINKS

Orange Whirl

2 oranges
1 (8oz.) container banana or strawberry yogurt

• In an electric blender, combine 2 oranges, peeled and cut into bite-sized pieces and 1 container of yogurt. Blend until smooth. Makes 2 servings.
• For a Spiced Orange Shake: Combine 2 oranges, peeled and cut into bite-sized pieces, 1 cup vanilla ice cream, and 1/8 tsp. pumpkin pie spice. Blend until smooth for 2 more servings.
• *Healthful snacking is in order for growing young bodies, whether after school or after any outdoor activity. GO BRONCOS!

Kitty and Jim Fassel
Bronco Offensive Coordinator

Vanessa Nielsen, Wellington, Co.

Smoothie

1 cup orange juice
1-1/2 cups ice cubes
1 scoop of vanilla ice cream or frozen yogurt
1/2 cup fresh fruit (your choice)
2 Tbl. honey
1/2 banana

• Place all ingredients, in any order, into a blender. Blend on medium speed.

D.J. McCadams
Voted #1 Breakfast in Colorado
by "Snow Country" Magazine
Vail, CO

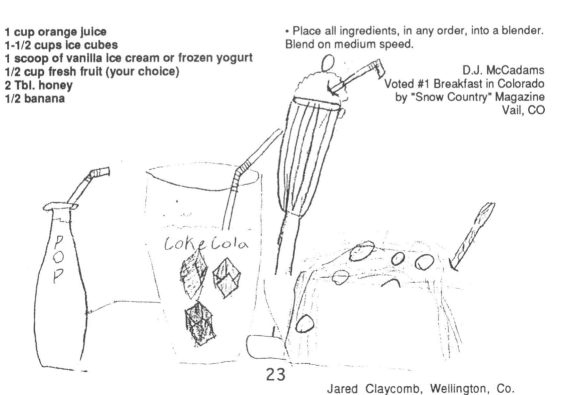

23

Jared Claycomb, Wellington, Co.

 **DRINKS**

Nurse Nancy's Russian Tea

1/2 cup sugar
1 cup water
9 cloves
2 inch cinnamon stick

2 cups (strong) brewed tea
6 oz. (3/4 cup) defrosted orange juice
        concentrate
2 oz. (1/4 cup) lemon juice

Pineapple juice

• Bring to a boil. Simmer 10 minutes. Turn burner off. Let steep 10 minutes. May remove spices.

• Add to spiced infusion. May continue to simmer and sip on all afternoon, or refrigerate and serve later.

• To serve: Add 1/4 cup pineapple juice to 3/4 cup tea. Microwave to warm.

Nancy Lancaster Battle
Friend of Education
Rocky Mount, NC

Homemade Holiday Eggnog

6 eggs
1/2 cup sugar
1/4 tsp. salt
3 cups milk
1 tsp. vanilla extract
1/2 tsp. ground nutmeg
1 cup whipping cream

• Serving size: 1/2 cup
• Calories: per serving 152
• Protein 5g, fat 10g, carbohydrate 10g, Calcium 84mg, riboflavin (B_2) .21 mg

• Yield: approximately 1-1/2 quarts
• In large saucepan, beat together eggs, sugar and salt. Stir in milk. Cook over low heat, stirring constantly, until mixture is thick enough to coat a metal spoon, about 15 minutes (thermometer should register 160°F). Remove from heat. Stir in vanilla and nutmeg. Cover and refrigerate until thoroughly chilled, several hours or overnight. Just before serving, beat whipping cream until soft peaks form. With wire whisk, gently fold whipped cream into custard mixture. Serve, if desired, with additional nutmeg.

American Dairy Association
Thornton, CO

24

Nathan Griffin, Wellington, Co.

BRUNCH - BREAD

Christina Lucardie, Wellington, Co.

"Cool Rise" Brioche - A Bread For Brunch

6-7 cups all-purpose flour
2 packages dry active yeast
1/2 cup sugar
1/2 tsp. salt
1/2 cup softened butter
1-1/3 cup hot tap water
4 eggs, at room temperature

1 egg yolk
1 Tbl. milk

• Combine 2 cups flour, the undissolved yeast, sugar and salt in a large bowl. Stir in softened butter.
• Add hot tap water all at once, beat with electric mixer 2 minutes.
• Add eggs and 2 cups flour - beat at high speed till thick and elastic.
• With wooden spoon, stir in enough of the remaining flour to make a soft dough that pulls away from the sides of the bowl.
• On floured surface, knead 5 minutes. Cover dough with plastic wrap and let it rest 20 minutes.
• Pull off a "fistful" of dough and shape into a ball. Shape the rest into a smooth round and set in well-greased shallow round pan. Poke a hole on top and rest smaller ball of dough in it.
• Cover loosely with plastic wrap.
• Refrigerate 2-24 hours.
• Preheat oven to 350 degrees, while brioche warms to room temperature.
• Bake 1 hour - halfway through (35 min.) brush bread with egg yolk/milk mixture.

Cynthia Hessin
Reporter/Anchor
KMGH-TV "Colorado's 7"

Brittany Lockwood, Wellington, Co.

Banana Date Bread

1/2 cup butter or margarine, softened
1 cup sugar
2 eggs
1 tsp. vanilla
1 cup mashed banana (3 medium)
2 cups sifted all-purpose flour
1 tsp. baking soda
1 tsp. baking powder
1/4 tsp. salt
1/2 cup 7-Up
1/2 cup chopped dates
1/2 cup chopped pecans

• Cream butter and sugar in a medium mixing bowl until light and fluffy. Add eggs and vanilla; beat well. Blend in bananas. Combine flour, soda, baking powder and salt; add to creamed mixture alternately with 7-Up. Fold in dates and pecans. Grease a 9x5x3-inch loaf pan; line with waxed paper. Spoon batter into prepared pan. Bake at 350°F for 1 hour and 15 minutes or until done. Cool in pan 10 minutes. Remove from pan; cool completely on a wire rack. Wrap tightly to store.
• Makes 1 loaf.

Dr. Pepper/Seven Up Companies, Inc.

Dick & Dottie Lamm's Very Simple, Sweet, & Sinful Banana Nut Bread

1/2 cup butter
1 cup sugar
2 eggs (beaten)
2 cups flour
1/2 tsp. salt
1 tsp. baking soda
2 ripe bananas, mashed
1/4 cup chopped walnuts (optional)

• Preheat oven to 350°F. Cream softened butter and sugar together. Add beaten eggs, mix well. Add flour, salt, soda, and mashed bananas. Pour into greased bread pan. Bake for 45 to 50 minutes. Cool before slicing. Store in plastic bag in ice box.

Dick Lamm - former Governor of Colorado
Dottie Lamm - former First Lady of Colorado

Mari Burgos, Wellington, Co.

27

Everlasting Bran Muffins

1 cup boiling water
1 cup bran (All Bran)
1/2 cup solid shortening
1-1/2 cup sugar
2 eggs
2-1/2 cups flour
2-1/2 tsp. baking soda
1/2 tsp. salt
2 cups buttermilk
2 cups bran
1-1/2 cups raisins

• Pour boiling water over 1 cup bran, set aside. Beat together shortening and sugar in large bowl. Beat eggs in, one at a time, then add flour, soda, salt and buttermilk, beat well. Add bran and water mixture; blend. Add 2 cups bran and raisins, blend well. Fill greased muffin tins 2/3 full - do not use paper liners. Bake in 400°F oven for 20 minutes. Batter may be kept in refrigerator and used as needed - will keep uncooked for up to 6 weeks.

Grace Casey
Wife of State Senator Lloyd A. Casey
Northglenn, CO

Morning Glory Muffins

1-1/4 cups granulated sugar
1/2 cup vegetable oil
3 eggs
2 tsp. vanilla
2 cups flour
2 tsp. baking powder
1/4 tsp. salt
1 tsp. cinnamon
2 cups grated carrots
1/2 cup raisins
1/2 cup coconut
1/2 cup diced raw apple
nuts optional

• Combine sugar, oil, eggs and vanilla in a large bowl. Set aside. In another bowl, sift together flour, baking powder, salt, cinnamon. Add to liquid ingredients and stir until just moistened. Gently fold in carrots, raisins, coconut and raw apple. Spoon into greased muffin tins to about 2/3 full. Bake in a 350 degree oven for 20-25 minutes.

Armetta Keeney
1992 Best Cook in the Country

Heather Marshall, Wellington, Co.

Pear-Yogurt Muffins

2 cups sifted flour
1/2 cup sugar
1-1/2 tsp. baking powder
1 tsp. baking soda
1/2 tsp. salt
1 cup yogurt
1 egg, slightly beaten
1/4 cup oil
1 (16-oz.) can pears, drained, diced

• Sift dry ingredients into bowl. Blend yogurt, egg, and oil in small bowl. Add to flour mixture with pears, stirring until just moistened. Fill greased muffin cups 2/3 full. Bake at 400°F for 20 to 25 minutes or until golden brown.
• Makes 12 servings.

Dolores Vaccaro
State Fair Winner
1993 Homemaker of the Year

Best Ever Cinnamon Rolls

2-1/2 cups lukewarm water
2 packages yeast (quick-rise is best)
1 box yellow cake mix
1 cup all-purpose flour
3 eggs
1/3 cup oil
1 tsp. salt
5-1/4 cups flour
Soft margarine
Sugar
Cinnamon

• Dissolve yeast in water for about 3 minutes. Add cake mix, 1 cup flour, eggs, oil and salt. Beat with beater until bubbles appear. Slowly add 5-1/4 cups flour. Stir with spoon, making a soft dough. Knead on board for about 5 minutes. Let rise until double. Roll out to about 1/4 inch thick. Spread with margarine and sprinkle with sugar and cinnamon. Roll up as jelly roll and stretch and cut into pieces Place cinnamon rolls on a greased 13 x 15 inch pan. Allow to rise until double. Bake in 350°F oven for 20 to 30 minutes. Ice with powdered sugar icing while hot.

Darlene Miller
Friend of Education
From Battle Mt. NV

Amy Westover, Wellington, Co.

Cinnamon Rolls

1/2 cup water
1/2 cup milk
1/3 cup butter or margarine

4 to 4-1/2 cups all-purpose flour, divided
1 tsp. salt
1/4 cup firmly packed brown sugar
1 package rapid-rise yeast

2 large eggs

1 cup firmly packed brown sugar
1/3 cup butter or margarine, softened
2 tsp. ground cinnamon

2 cups sifted powdered sugar
3 to 4 Tbl. milk
1/4 tsp. vanilla extract

Genesis Dionne, Wellington, Co.

• Combine water, 1/2 cup milk, and 1/3 cup butter in a saucepan over medium heat; cook until butter melts, stirring occasionally. Let mixture cool to 125°F to 130°F.
•Combine 3 cups flour and next 3 ingredients in a large mixing bowl. Gradually add milk mixture to flour mixture, beating at low speed with an electric mixer. Add eggs, and beat 2 minutes at medium speed.
• Gradually add 1 additional cup flour, beating 2 minutes. Gradually stir in enough remaining flour to make a soft dough.
• Turn dough out onto a well-floured surface, and knead 5 minutes or until smooth, elastic, and no longer sticky. Cover and let rest 10 minutes. Divide dough in half, and roll each half into a 12-inch square. Combine 1 cup brown sugar, 1/3 cup butter, and cinnamon. Spread evenly over both squares of dough. Roll dough, jellyroll fashion, pinch seams to seal. Cut each roll into 1-inch slices. Place rolls, cut side down, in two lightly greased 8-inch square pans.
• Cover and let rise in a warm place (85°F), free from drafts, 45 minutes or until doubled in bulk. Bake at 375°F for 15 to 20 minutes or until golden brown. Combine powdered sugar, milk, and vanilla; drizzle over warm rolls. Yield: 2 dozen.

Kaye M. Adams
Test Kitchens Director and Recipe Editor
SOUTHERN LIVING Magazine

James Smole, Wellington, Co.

Patty Turner's "Stop Light" Corn Bread

2 cups Bisquick mix
6 Tbl. white corn meal
2/3 cup sugar

1 cup milk
2 eggs, slightly beaten
1 cup butter, melted

• Blend Bisquick mix, corn meal and sugar. Add milk, eggs and melted butter to mix. Bake at 350°F for 35 minutes in 9x9-inch greased pan.
• Named "Stop Light" corn bread because many times it has been taken right out of the oven and driven to a pot luck picnic or party. Only if all the lights are green along the way will the cornbread remain intact. If there are red lights along the way, people begin to munch. Once, the corn bread arrived at a party with the whole center missing!

Patty and Fred Turner
Senior Chairman
McDonald's Restaurants

Hush Puppies

1-3/4 cups yellow corn meal
1/2 cup flour
2 tsp. salt
1 Tbl. baking powder
1/3 tsp. garlic powder
1-1/2 Tbl. sugar
1/2 to 3/4 cups grated onion
Sweet milk as needed to bring mixture to proper consistency.

• Mix dry ingredients. Add boiling water to make a stiff mush. Add onions, then add required milk. Drop by teaspoons full and fry in fish grease until brown.

Rex L. Utsler
President
Grease Monkey International, Inc.

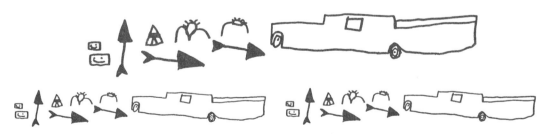

Ryan Stockweather, Wellington, Co.

Cream Biscuits

1-1/2 cups unsifted flour
4 tsps. baking powder
3/4 tsp. salt
1 cup whipping cream

• Measure flour, baking powder, and salt into bowl. Blend in whipping cream with fork to form stiff dough. Knead. Roll dough to 1/2-inch thickness. Cut with 2-inch cutter. Bake on ungreased baking sheet in hot oven at 425°F for 12 to 15 minutes.
• Makes 14 to 16 biscuits.

Celeste Schoenmaker
State Fair Winner

Popovers
(One Of Lady Bird's Specialties!)

1 cup sifted flour
1 cup milk
2 Tbl. shortening, melted
2 eggs, beaten
1/4 tsp. salt

• Mix and sift flour and salt. Combine eggs, milk and shortening; gradually add to flour mixture, beating about 1 minute or until batter is smooth. Fill greased sizzling hot muffin pans or popover tins 3/4 full and bake in very hot oven (450°F) about 20 minutes. Reduce heat to moderate (350°F) and continue baking for 15 to 20 minutes.

Lady Bird Johnson
Submitted by Steve Ruddick
Colorado State Senator

Bruce Hall, Wellington, Co.

BRUNCH - BREAD

Homemade Dinner Rolls

3-1/2 cups warm water
2 packages dry yeast
1/4 cup sugar
3 Tbl. shortening
5 to 7 cups flour
1 Tbl. salt

• Dissolve yeast in warm water; add sugar, salt, and shortening. Beat in about 3 or 4 cups flour, then knead in the rest until the dough is soft but not sticky. Put in greased bowl; cover with shortening; cover with towel. Let rise for one hour, punch down and let rise for one more hour, punch down again and shape rolls. Let the rolls rise for one more hour. Bake 15 to 20 minutes at 425 °F.
• Makes 30 large rolls or 45 small rolls.

Dolores Vaccaro
State Fair Winner
1993 Homemaker of the Year

Homemade Italian Bread

3-1/2 cups warm water
2 packages dry yeast
1/4 cup sugar
1 Tbl. salt
3 Tbl. shortening
5 to 7 cups flour

• Dissolve yeast in warm water; add sugar and shortening and beat. Add salt and gradually beat in flour (about 3 or 4 cups). Then knead in the rest of flour (just until it is soft but not sticky). Let rise. Punch down and then cut into fourths and shape bread loaves; cover and let rise one more hour.
• Bake 20 to 25 minutes in hot oven, 425°F.
• Makes 4 loaves

Dolores Vaccaro
Colorado State Fair Winner
1993 Homemaker of the Year

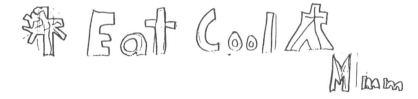

Amy Sarno, Wellington, Co.

33

Cheese Bread

2 packages dry yeast
1/4 cup warm water (105° to 115°F)
1 cup milk, scalded
1/2 cup butter or margarine
1/2 cup sugar
3/4 tsp. salt
3 eggs, beaten
5-1/2 to 6 cups all-purpose flour
2 cups (8 oz.) shredded cheddar cheese

(The sharper the cheddar, the more "cheesy"
    the bread will taste.)

• Dissolve yeast in warm water in a small bowl. Combine milk, butter, sugar, and salt in a large bowl; stir until butter melts. Cool to lukewarm (105° to 115°F). Stir in eggs and yeast mixture.
• Gradually add 2 cups flour, beating at medium speed of electric mixer until smooth. Stir in cheese and enough remaining flour to form a stiff dough.
• Turn dough out onto a lightly floured surface and knead 5 to 10 minutes until smooth and elastic. Place dough in a greased bowl. Turning to grease top. Cover and let rise in a warm place (85°F), free from drafts, 1 hour or until doubled in bulk. Punch dough down.
• Divide dough in half and shape each half into a loaf. Place each loaf in a greased 9x5x3-inch loaf pan. Cover and let rise in a warm place, free from drafts, 1 hour or until doubled in bulk.
• Bake at 350°F for 45 minutes or until loaves sound hollow when tapped. Remove loaves from pans and cool on wire racks.
• Makes 2 loaves.

Dolores Vaccaro
State Fair Winner
1993 Homemaker of the Year

Mike Lowell, Wellington, Co.

Nathan Hawley, Wellington, Co.

Cheese Bubble Loaf

1 recipe "No Knead" Roll Dough
   (see recipe below)
40 (1/2-inch) cheddar cheese cubes
1 Tbl. butter, melted
Parmesan cheese

• Divide half of dough in 20 portions. Shape each portion into ball around cheese cube. Place in 2 layers in well-greased 9x5-inch pan. Repeat with remaining dough. Brush tops with butter. Sprinkle with Parmesan cheese. Cover; let rise until light and doubled in size, 45 to 60 minutes. Bake at 350°F for 35 to 40 minutes. Remove from pans immediately.
• Makes 2 loaves.

"No Knead" Roll Dough
2 packages active dry yeast
1 cup warm water
1/3 cup sugar
2 eggs
3 cups flour
1 Tbl. salt
1/4 cup butter, melted
1 cup warm milk

• Place ingredients in mixing bowl in order listed. Beat at medium low speed for 3 minutes. Cover; let rest 15 minutes. Toss on well-floured surface until no longer sticky.

Dolores Vaccaro
State Fair Winner
1993 Homemaker of the Year

Jessica Carson, Wellington, Co.

35

Mashed Potato Waffles with Rosemary-Garlic Oil

For the Waffles
2 russet potatoes (total weight about 1-1/4 lbs.)
1/4 cup extra-virgin olive oil
1 small onion, peeled and finely chopped
2/3 cup fresh milk
Freshly ground black pepper to taste
2 large eggs
1 cup all-purpose flour
2 tsp. double-acting baking powder

• To make the waffles:
• Peel, wash and cut the potatoes into uniform small pieces. Put in a large pot with cold water to cover, salt well, and bring to a boil. Then lower the heat and cook till the potatoes can be pierced easily with a fork. Drain, reserving about 1/2 cup of the potato water. Transfer potatoes to a large mixing bowl.
• While the potatoes cook, heat olive oil and chopped onion in a small skillet over low heat till onion softens. Pour oil and onion over drained potatoes. Add milk to still-warm skillet, to take the chill off and then pour milk over potatoes.

• Using a potato masher or fork, mash potatoes with oil and milk. Add 1/4 cup potato water and continue to mash till mixture is smooth and creamy. If mixture seems stiff, add more potato water. It should be a little runnier than mashed potatoes you'd serve as a side dish. Season with salt and pepper to taste.
• Preheat waffle iron (a Belgian waffle iron works best) and finish batter by beating eggs into potatoes. Whisk together flour and baking powder and fold into potato mixture with a rubber spatula. Lightly butter or spray waffle iron grids. Brush or spray again only if subsequent waffles stick. Scoop batter by half-cup measure into hot iron (or follow manufacturer's directions), smoothing batter evenly almost to the edge of grids. Close iron and bake till brown and crisp. Serve drizzled with some of the Rosemary-Garlic oil.

Kevin Young
Chef at the Best Restaurant in
the North Denver Area, Gussie's

Adam Korby, Wellington, Co.

36

Rosemary Garlic Oil

3 large, plump garlic cloves
1/2 cup virgin olive oil
1(4-inch) sprig fresh rosemary or
   1 tsp. dried
1/2 tsp. salt, or to taste

Tom McChesney, Wellington, Co.

• To make the rosemary-garlic oil:
• Peel and cut the garlic into very thin slices. Pour the oil into a small heavy skillet or saucepan, add the sliced garlic and rosemary, crushing the herb between your fingers as you add it, and warm over low heat. When the aroma rises and the garlic just starts to take on color (it should not brown), about 5-7 minutes, remove from the heat. Add the salt to taste and strain the oil into a small pitcher. The oil can be made up to 2 weeks ahead, cooled to room temperature, and stored in the refrigerator in a tightly sealed container.

Kevin Young
Chef at the Best Restaurant in
the North Denver Area, Gussie's

"Silver Dollar-Size" Cinnamon Roll

1 cake yeast
1/2 cup warm water

2 cups milk

4 oz. margarine
4 heaping tsp. sugar
1 heaping tsp. salt

6 cups flour, divided
2 eggs

Currants
Cinnamon
Sugar

• Dissolve yeast in warm water. Scald milk and add sugar, salt and margarine. Cool to lukewarm. Add three cups flour to this mixture and beat by hand until smooth. Into this mixture beat the unbeaten eggs and yeast. Stir in remaining three cups flour and let rise till double in bulk. Roll the dough into a thin long narrow strip. Spread with melted margarine and sprinkle with a few currants, sugar and cinnamon, then roll lengthwise. Cut into 1 inch pieces. Let rise. Bake at 400°F until done. Spread powdered sugar icing while hot.
• Makes four dozen cinnamon rolls.
• Famous for over 30 years.

Historic El Rancho Restaurant
El Rancho, CO

Kennan Blehm, Wellington, Co.

Whole Wheat Waffles

2 eggs (separated)
1/2 cup oil
1-1/4 cup milk
1 cup whole wheat flour
3/4 cup white flour
1 Tbl. sugar
1 Tbl. baking powder

• Combine egg yolks, oil, milk, flour, sugar and baking powder, beat together well. In separate bowl, beat egg whites on high speed until stiff, then fold into flour mixture. Pour into greased waffle iron and bake
• Enjoy with cinnamon syrup.

Tim Foster
State Representative
Grand Junction, CO

Cinnamon Syrup

2 cups sugar
1 cup Karo Syrup
1/2 cup water
2 tsp. cinnamon
1 cup evaporated milk

• In a saucepan combine sugar, Karo syrup, water and cinnamon. On medium-high heat bring ingredients to a boil stirring constantly. Boil 3 minutes. Remove from heat and stir in 1 cup evaporated milk.
• This goes great with Whole Wheat Waffles.

Tim Foster
State Representative
Grand Junction, CO

Blanca Burgos, Wellington, Co.

Slovenian Doughnut (Krofee)

4 egg yolks
1 whole egg
2 Tbl. dry yeast or 1 cake yeast
1/3 cup water
1 tsp. plus 1/2 cup granulated sugar
1 cup milk
2 Tbl. margarine
1 tsp. salt
4 cups flour
1 tsp. lemon extract
1 tsp. vanilla

• Beat the 4 egg yolks and one whole egg. Set aside. Dissolve yeast, water, and 1 teaspoon sugar together. Set aside. Heat milk, margarine, 1/2 cup sugar, and salt. Set aside to cool. After cooled, add 2 cups flour and yeast mixture. Then add beaten eggs, lemon extract, and vanilla. Add 2 cups flour or enough to make soft dough but not sticky. Cover and let rise until double.
• Pat out dough until it is 1/2-inch thick and cut doughnuts with glass dipped in flour. Let rise until double again. Fry in deep fat and drain on paper towel. Do not reroll dough if possible (it comes apart while cooking). Fry doughnuts 4 minutes for smaller ones and 6 minutes for larger.
• Makes approx. 4 dozen.

This recipe was 1st prize winner in a Flav-o-rite contest.

Dolores Vaccaro
State Fair Winner
1993 Homemaker of the Year

Allison Hain, Wellington, Co.

Amy Westover, Wellington, Co.

My message to Colorado's children:

"Always do the right thing, give much and God will bless you with more."

Dennis Smith

D.S. #49 - Quick Fun Donuts

1 can of 10 Hungry Jack Flaky Biscuits
1/2 cup oil
1/4 cup granulated sugar
1 Tbl. cinnamon
1 twist-top bottle cap

• Use the bottle cap to cut a hole into each biscuit, so that when finished you will have 10 donuts and holes. Pour oil in large skillet, heat on Medium to High. Drop donuts into hot oil. After a few minutes flip donuts over. Once both sides are done, take them out and let them drain on a paper towel. Then repeat the procedure with the donut holes. Mix the sugar and cinnamon together in a bowl. Dip the donuts into the sugar, then eat.

Dennis Smith #49
Professional Football Player
Denver Broncos

Cristina Burgos, Wellington, Co.

Haley Perry, Wellington, Co.

Spice Zucchini Bread

2 cups sifted flour
2 tsp. baking powder
1 tsp. cinnamon
1 tsp. salt
1/4 tsp. baking soda
1/4 tsp. ground cloves and nutmeg
2/3 cup shortening
1 cup sugar
2 eggs
1 cup shredded zucchini

• Sift dry ingredients together. Mix shortening and sugar. Beat in eggs. Add half of the dry ingredients and mix. Add half of the shredded zucchini, then the rest of the flour mixture. Stir and continue to add the rest of the zucchini. (You can also add nuts or raisins if you like). If mixture appears dry, add a little water. Spoon into greased and floured loaf pans and bake at 350°F for 1 hour.
• Makes 2 loaves.
• Great for all that left over zucchini from the garden!

Beverly Weaver
KWGN-TV News Anchor
Channel 2

Graham Quick Bread

1/2 cup brown sugar
1/2 cup dark molasses
2-1/2 cups buttermilk
1 egg
Salt to taste
1 cup ground raisins
2 tsp. baking soda
1 tsp. baking powder
2 cups all-purpose flour
4-1/2 cups graham or whole wheat flour

• Mix sugar and molasses and egg with the milk, add dry ingredients gradually. Bake in two 8-1/2 x 3-5/8 x 2-5/8 inch loaf pans at 350°F for 1 hour.

Rusti Ruth
Friend of Education
from Redding, CA

41   Matthew Jarrett, Wellington, Co

Out-of-Sight Poppy Seed Bread

2-1/4 cups sugar
3/4 cup vegetable oil
3 eggs
1-1/2 tsp. vanilla
1-1/2 tsp. butter flavoring
2 Tbl. poppy seeds
3 cups all-purpose flour
1-1/2 tsp. salt
1-1/2 tsp. baking powder
1 cup Land-O-Lakes Lite Sour Cream
1/2 cup milk

Glaze
1/4 cup orange juice
1/2 tsp. vanilla
1/2 tsp. butter flavoring
1/2 tsp. almond flavoring
3/4 cup powdered sugar

• Combine sugar, sour cream, and oil in large bowl. Beat until blended. Add eggs, one at a time, beating well after each egg. Add flavorings; mix well. Set aside. In another bowl, combine flour, salt and baking powder. Add to creamed mixture, alternately with milk till blended. Stir in poppy seeds. Grease and flour two 8-1/2 x 4-1/2 inch loaf pans, pour batter into pans. Bake at 350°F for 45 minutes. Remove from oven, let cool for 10 minutes. Combine glaze ingredients, brush onto bread while slightly warm.
• Makes 2 loaves.

Theresa Schoenmakers
1st Prize, Land-O-Lakes
Lite Sour Cream Contest

Cheese Cloud Breakfast Casserole

8 slices bread, crusts removed, buttered on
    one side
1/2 lb. sharp cheddar cheese, grated
1 lb. hot sausage, browned and crumbled
1 lb. mild sausage, browned and crumbled
7 eggs
1 tsp. dry mustard
2-3/4 cups milk
1 tsp. salt

• Cut bread into 1-1/2 inch squares. Place half in buttered 13x9-inch casserole dish. Layer half of cheese on top of bread. Layer half of each kind of sausage on top of cheese. Repeat layers of bread, cheese and sausage. Beat eggs with milk, mustard, and salt. Pour over mixture. Cover and chill overnight. Bake at 350°F for 45 minutes. Let stand a few minutes before serving.

Sherry Sellers
Morning News Anchor, KUSA
Channel 9

Scott Peterson, Wellington, Co.

SOUP

Tony McDonald, Wellington, Co.

43   Julie Ann Ramirez, Wellington, Co.

Buffalo/Sausage Red Chile

1 lb. chopped buffalo
1 lb. breakfast style pork sausage

1 cup water
1/2 cup onion (diced 1/4 inch)
1/2 cup celery (diced 1/4 inch)
1 green pepper (diced 1/4 inch)
1/4 cup Red chili
2 Tbl. cumin
1 Tbl. salt
1 Tbl. white pepper
1 Tbl. sugar
3 Tbl. granulated garlic
1 can green chili strips (4 oz.)

1 can kidney beans (15 oz.)
1 can pinto beans (15 oz.)
1 can diced tomatoes (28 oz.)
2 Tbl. vinegar
1 Tbl. Worcestershire
2 tsp. beef base
1 tsp. chicken base

• Combine first group of ingredients in sauce pan and cook until meats are browned. Use potato masher to break up clumps of meat. Drain grease.

• Add second grouping of ingredients and simmer for 15 minutes.

• Add third grouping of ingredients and bring to a boil. Probably will need 1 to 2 cups of water to bring to desired consistency.
• Simmer 30 minutes.

George Carlberg, Executive Chef
Buckhorn Exchange
Denver, CO

Cassie Coppenger, Mancos, Co.

44   *Heurick Hall, Wellington, Co.*

Chili Con Carne

3 lb. ground beef
6 1/2 oz. chopped onion (1 medium onion)
1/2 clove garlic or 1 Tbl. pureed garlic
1 lb. or 16 oz. can of diced tomatoes
3/4 tsp. cumin
2 (1 lb.) cans chili beans
chili powder (to taste)
salt and pepper (to taste)

• Brown ground beef, drain thoroughly. Add onion, garlic and cumin. Sauté until onion becomes clear. Add tomato products, beans and seasonings.
• Simmer for 1/2 to 1 hour. May need to add water to desired thickness.

Dr. Albert C. Yates, President
Colorado State University

Dave's Old Fashioned Chili

2 lbs. fresh ground beef
1 qt. tomato juice
1 (29-oz.) can tomato puree
1 (15-oz.) can dark red kidney beans, drained
1 (15-oz.) can small red beans, drained
1 medium onion (1 1/2 cups) chopped
1/2 cup celery, diced
1/4 cup chili powder
2 tsp. cumin
1 1/2 tsp. garlic powder
1 tsp. salt
1/2 tsp. each: black pepper, oregano, sugar
1/8 tsp. cayenne pepper

• In frying pan, brown ground beef, drain. Add remaining ingredients and drained ground beef into 6 quart pot. Cover and simmer 1 to 1-1/2 hours; stirring every 15 minutes.
• Yield: 16 (8-ounce) servings.

• (Dave likes to add fresh, chopped onions on top of his chili serving.)

Dave Thomas
Founder of
"Wendy's Old Fashioned Hamburgers"

Brett Johnson, Wellington, Co.

45

 SOUPS

KBPI's Rock & Roll Rattlesnake Watermelon Chili

4 lbs. cubed rattlesnake meat (or a percentage of cubed top round)
2 (12 oz.) cans tomato paste
1 (16 oz.) can tomato sauce
4 large yellow onions, chopped
1 to 4 cans dark red kidney beans
3 Tbl. lemon juice
4 tsp. sugar
4 Jalapenos, seeded, washed and diced
2 tsp. salt
1/8 tsp. turmeric
1/4 tsp. curry powder
1/4 tsp. cayenne pepper
2 dashes Tabasco
5 Tbl. chili powder
3/4 tsp. dry mustard
1 tsp. ginger, powdered
watermelon cubes (just a few for effect)

• Brown meat in a large skillet, drain. Place in a large kettle with black pepper, cayenne, tomato sauce, tomato paste, salt and enough water and beer to thin consistency considerably. Simmer 2 hours, stir occasionally. Skim the fat. Add mustard, chili powder, turmeric, curry powder and beans. Simmer 1 hour, stir occasionally. Cook diced onions and jalapenos in fat until onions are clear. Add to pot. Add ginger, garlic, sugar, lemon juice and watermelon.
• Cover and simmer 1/2 to 1 hour. You may also add considerably more garlic powder and a few more tablespoons of chili powder, according to your taste.
• Invite all your friends over, pour the fire extinguisher of your choice (cold domestic beer always works best for us). Turn up your favorite rock and roll radio station and devour as much KBPI Rock and Roll Rattlesnake Watermelon Chili as you dare!

Pete MacKay
Rock and Roll D. J.
105.9 KBPI "Rocks the Rockies"

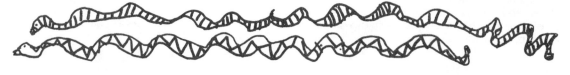

Terace Follett, Wellington, Co.

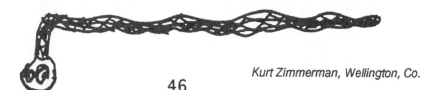

Kurt Zimmerman, Wellington, Co.

SOUPS

Broccoli & Tomato Soup

2 heads broccoli
1 large red onion(diced)
5 medium ripe tomatoes(diced)
1 Tbl. fresh minced garlic
1 Tbl. fresh chopped basil
1 gallon chicken stock
1 cup sherry
1 tsp. white pepper
1/2 cup corn starch
2 Tbl. whole butter

• Sauté chopped broccoli, onion, tomatoes, garlic, and basil in butter until broccoli is tender. Add Sherry and let simmer 2 minutes. Add chicken stock and white pepper. Bring to a boil. Dissolve corn starch in COLD water and add to the soup - turn down heat and let simmer 5 minutes until soup is thickened.

Scott R. Carter
Executive Chef of the Buckingham Broker
Golden, CO

The Castaway's Tomato Supreme Soup
(Recipe requested by Gourmet Magazine)

1-1/3 cup sliced onion
3 Tbl. unsalted butter
2 cup beef broth
1/8 tsp. salt
1/2 tsp. freshly ground black pepper
1/2 bay leaf
Pinch thyme
1/2 tsp. basil
1 Tbl. granulated sugar
2 tsp. Worcestershire sauce
1/4 cup brandy
4 cup canned whole tomatoes-crushed
1/2 cup heavy cream
1 cup milk

• Sauté onions in butter until soft. Add beef broth, salt, pepper, bay leaf, thyme, basil, sugar, Worcestershire sauce, brandy and tomatoes. Simmer for one hour. Remove bay leaf. Add cream and milk and adjust seasoning. Serve hot.

Judy Van Dyke
The Castaways
Manitou Springs, CO

Christina Lucardie, Wellington, Co.

Crock Pot

Tomato Soup en Croute

5 lbs. tomatoes, cut in fourths
32 oz. can of tomato juice
2 onions, diced
2 leeks, diced
3 carrots, diced
1 celery, diced
3 oz. olive oil
Basil (chopped)
3 Bay leaves
3 garlic cloves
1/2 tsp. sugar
Salt and pepper
Puff Pastry - cut into circles to fit oven-proof
    crocks

• Sauté onions in hot oil, but do not brown, then add diced leek, carrots and celery and "sweat" for 10 minutes, stirring occasionally. Vegetables should still be translucent.
• Add tomatoes and tomato juice. Increase heat and bring to a boil. Add bay leaves, pressed garlic cloves, salt and pepper and sugar. Boil gently for 45 minutes.
• Pass through soup strainer at low speed or through a sieve by hand. Check for thickness and if necessary, bind with 1 oz. olive oil mixed with 2 oz. flour. Add to soup and let boil for 5 minutes. Sprinkle with chopped basil.
• Pour soup into 6 oven-proof crocks to not more than 1 inch from the top (do not overfill). Brush the top of the crock on the outside edge with egg wash and cover with a circle of puff pastry. Secure pastry to the crock and brush pastry with egg wash and bake at 425° for 20 minutes or until the pastry is a golden brown.

Liz and Luc Meyers
The Left Bank Restaurant
Vail, CO

Chase Wearne, Wellington, Co.

Mickey Delaney, Wellington, Co.

48

Potato, Bean, Bacon Soup

1/4 lb. Hickory cured bacon, diced
2 tsp. fat (reserved)
1 Tbl. unsalted butter
1/2 small onion diced
1/2 carrot diced
1 rib celery, diced
4 cups chicken broth
2 med. - large leeks, 1/2" circles
2 med. - large potatoes 1" cubes
1 red pepper, diced
1 (10 1/2 oz.) can white beans drained

• Cover bacon with water: bring to boil and simmer 5 minutes. Drain and press on paper towel.
• Wipe out pot and fry bacon 4 minutes to crisp. Remove and drain on paper towels. Save 2 tsp. fat. Add butter; then onions, carrots, and celery. Sauté until light brown. Add stock, bacon, salt and pepper to taste. Simmer 5 minutes. Skim foam. Add leeks and potatoes. Simmer 5 minutes more. Add red pepper. Continue to simmer until potatoes are cooked and tender. Add beans and heat through. Turn off heat and let sit 30 minutes.

Tom Flanagon
President - Key Bank of Colorado

Super Simple Soup

2 cups coarsely chopped carrots
1 1/2 cups chopped potatoes
1 cup chopped onion
1 1/2 cups water
1 (10 oz.) package frozen peas (2 cups)
1 (1 lb.) jumbo frankfurters cut diagonally into
    slices
1 cup milk
1 can cream of celery soup
2 cups cheese or 8 oz. Cheez Whiz

• Cook vegetables in the water until slightly tender. Add franks and peas. Cook 5 minutes more. Stir in milk, soup and cheese. Heat through until cheese is melted.
Makes 5-6 servings

Ruth Gjelsness
Great Cook featured in
Successful Farming Magazine
and Friend of Education from Reynolds, ND

Vanessa Nielsen, Wellington, Co.

SOUPS

Buckhorn Exchange Bean Soup

1 lb. Great northern beans
1/2 cup diced onion
3 oz. diced ham
2 Tbl. chicken base
1 tsp. Aromat
1 tsp. liquid smoke
1 tsp. granulated garlic
1 tsp. white pepper
1/2 gal. water

2 Tbl. cornstarch
1/2 cup water

• Place first grouping of ingredients in a large pot, cover and place in 200 ° oven for 8 hours.
• When beans are tender, remove from oven, place on stovetop and bring to boil. Add starch and water to thicken and let simmer for 15 minutes

*Aromat is hard to find. Try the gourmet section at King Soopers

George Carlberg, Executive Chef
Buckhorn Exchange
Denver, CO

Curried Butternut Squash Soup

2 1/2 lbs. squash, peeled and chunked thin
1 cup chopped onion
2 Tbl. vegetable oil
4 garlic cloves, finely chopped
1 Tbl. curry powder
1 tsp. cumin
pinch cayenne
3 cans (14 1/2 oz.) chicken broth
1 lb. tart apples, peeled, cored and chopped

• In heavy saucepan, cook onion in oil until golden. Add garlic, curry powder, cumin, cayenne and cook 30 seconds. Add squash, broth, 3 cups of water and apples. Bring to boil and simmer, covered, until squash is tender. Puree' and season with salt and pepper. May add dollop of sour cream to each serving.

Tom Flanagan
President , Key Bank Of Colorado

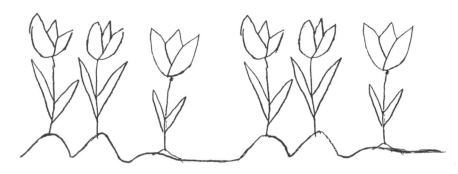

50   *Amy Westover, Wellington, Co.*

SOUPS

Minestrone

2 Tbl. oil or bacon fat
1/4 lb. ham or salami, chopped
1 large onion, chopped
1 medium carrot, chopped
1 stalk celery, chopped
1 large tomato, chopped or 1 cup canned
    tomatoes, slightly mashed
1 can undrained red kidney beans or
    garbanzos (chick peas)
2 quarts meat broth (may use bouillon cubes)
1 large potato, diced
1Tbl. dried basil
1 small clove garlic, minced, or 1/4 tsp. garlic
    powder
salt, as needed
1/4 small head cabbage, shredded and
    chopped
1 to 2 cups cut green beans
1/2 cup elbow macaroni
 Grated Parmesan Cheese

• Heat fat in skillet and fry ham and onion until it is soft but not brown. Transfer contents of skillet to a large saucepan or kettle. Add carrots, celery, tomato, kidney beans, (or garbanzos) and meat broth. Simmer covered for 30 minutes or more. Skim off some of the fat if desired. Add potato, basil, garlic, and salt. Simmer uncovered for 15 minutes. Add cabbage, green beans, and macaroni. Simmer until soup has thickened and all ingredients are cooked. Sprinkle generously with grated Parmesan Cheese.

Celeste Schoenmakers
Colorado State Fair Winner
Pueblo, CO

Homemade Vegetable Soup

"Have a strong belief in God, Family and Country"

"Fum" McGraw

2 meaty beef soup bones
1/2 lb. stew meat or sirlion (cut in pieces)
2 onions cut up

1 large can stewed tomatoes
1 can tomatoes and green chilies
1 tsp. sugar
5 medium carrots (sliced)
5 medium potaotes (cut up)
If desired add cabbage and celery pieces
    (chopped)
1 Tbl. Worchestershire sauce
1 tsp. Tabasco
Salt and pepper to taste

• Cover meat and oinons with water in large pot and boil 3-4 hours. Add salt and pepper.

• Add remaining ingredients. Keep adding water to desired consistency. If you want you can add Beef Bouillon.

• Serve in large soup bowl with hot bread and butter for a delicious, nutritious meal.

10-12 Servings.

"Fum" McGraw
Colorado Football Great
Fort Collins, CO

51

SOUPS

Chicken Wild Rice Soup

6 Tbl. butter
1 Tbl. minced onion
1/2 cup flour
2 1/2 cups chicken broth
2 cups cooked wild rice
2 cups cooked chicken
1/2 cup finely grated carrots
3 Tbl. silvered almonds
1 can (12 oz.) evaporated skimmed milk
minced parsley or chives

• Melt butter in saucepan. Sauté onion until tender. Blend in flour. Gradually add broth. Cook, stirring constantly until mixture comes to a boil; boil one minute. Stir in rice, chicken, carrots and almonds; simmer about five minutes. Blend in evaporated milk and chives or parsley. Heat to serving temperature.

Gary and Johanne Wayne
Colorado **Rockies'** Pitcher and Wife
Lakewood, CO

Miles Gracey, Wellington, Co.

Campaign Beef Stew
(With a Weld County flavor)

2 lbs. Monfort stewing meat (prime round)
1 lb. small potatoes
1 bunch small carrots
3/4 lb. small onions
2 fresh tomatoes
1 bunch bouquet garniture
2 1/2 pints beef stock (Monfort, of course)
Salt and pepper

• Stew meat until tender. Add vegetables and bouquet garniture (thyme, bay leaves, garlic, etc., in cloth bag). When vegetables are done, strain off 1 cup of stock from stew and thicken slightly with beef roux. Pour back into stew and let simmer for one-half hour.

• 6 Servings

Tom Norton, President
Colorado State Senate
Greeley, CO

Gideon Dione, Wellington, Co.

Buffalo Red Eye Stew

2 lb. buffalo stew meat (preferably sirloin)
1/2 yellow onion (diced 1 inch)
1/4 lb. butter
4 potatoes (peeled and cut in 1 inch cubes)
1/4 tsp. white pepper
1/4 tsp. leaf thyme
1/4 tsp. whole Rosemary
1/4 tsp. basil
1/2 tsp. salt
1 1/2 tsp. granulated garlic
1/2 cup Bourbon
1/2 cup strong coffee
1 can diced tomatoes (28 oz.)
1 Tbl. Worcestershire
1 cup flour
2 cups water

• Place potato cubes in sauce pan, cover with water and bring to a boil. Reduce heat to simmer and continue to cook until potatoes are about half done.
• While potatoes are simmering, in a large sauce pan melt the butter over medium heat. Add stew meat, onions, and dry spices. Allow to simmer while potatoes are cooking.
• When potatoes are about half done, add flour to pan with buffalo and mix in well, allow to cook for 5 minutes.
• Add the can of tomatoes and stir into buffalo mixture and let simmer for 5 minutes.
• Add the balance of ingredients (drain potatoes first). Gently stir together. Return to a boil. Reduce heat and allow to simmer for 1/2 hour (or until buffalo is tender, depending on cut).

George Carlberg, Executive Chef
Buckhorn Exchange
Denver, CO

Ray Thomas, Mancos, Co.

53

Seafood Pasta Chowder

6 oz. Miniature Pasta Bow Ties or Shells,
   precooked
3 oz. butter or margarine
8 oz. fresh mushrooms, sliced, 1/8"
2 (1 oz.) packets Knorr Newburg Sauce Mix
3 cups milk
1-1/2 cups water
1/4 cup dry white wine
1/4 cup green onions, sliced, 1/8"
3 oz. crab meat, frozen or canned
Parsley for garnish

• Cook pasta according to directions. Drain and rinse lightly with cold water to prevent sticking together and set aside.
• Sort crab meat to remove any shell pieces remaining.
• Melt butter or margarine in 3 qt. non-aluminum heavy saucepan.
• Add mushrooms and sauté 3 minutes. Add sauce mix and stir well. Add milk, water and wine. Stir well with a wire whip over moderate heat until mixture comes to a boil. Reduce the heat and simmer 5-8 minutes stirring constantly. Add green onions, precooked pasta and crab meat and stir to combine. Sprinkle with parsley. Serve immediately. Buono Appetito!
Serves 6

The Olive Garden Restaurant
Brad Kirby
Aurora, CO

Addam Zimmerman, Wellington, Co.

SALADS

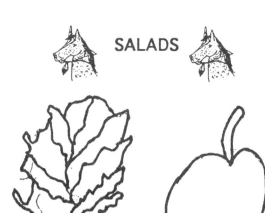

Derek Jekel, Wellington, Co.

Light Lemon Fluff Fruit Salad

8 oz. light Cool Whip
3.4 oz. package instant lemon Jello pudding
2 cups skim milk
3 cups miniature marshmallows
6 sliced bananas
3 cups seedless grapes, red or green
1/2 cup orange juice

• Prepare instant Jello pudding as directed, using skim milk, chill until firm; blend Cool Whip into firm pudding until smooth. Slice bananas into orange juice and drain. Fold bananas, marshmallows and grapes into pudding and Cool Whip mixture. Chill until served.

Cheryl L. Poage
Fire and Injury Prevention Educator
Parker Fire District

Lemonade "Salad"

3/4 cup pink lemonade
1 cup whipped cream
1 can sweetened condensed milk
2 drops red food coloring

Crust

35 Ritz crackers (crushed)
2 Tbl. powdered sugar
1/4 cup butter (melted)

• Mix together the lemonade, whipping cream, sweet milk and food coloring.
• Mix together all the "crust" ingredients and press half of the mixture into a pie pan. Pour lemonade mixture into pan then sprinkle with remaining "crust" mixture. Refrigerate 24 hours before serving.

Tim Foster
Colorado State Representative
Grand Junction, CO

Cassy McDonald, Wellington, Co.

Cranberry Gelatin Mold

1 large orange, seeded and quartered
4 cups fresh cranberries
2 cups sugar
1 envelope unflavored gelatin
1/4 cup cold water
2 (3 oz.) packages lemon-flavored gelatin
3 cups boiling water
Lettuce leaves
Garnishes: Orange Slices, Fresh Cranberries, Lettuce Leaves

Variations
If you like less sweetness decrease sugar to 1 cup.
May add: pinch of salt and 1/8 tsp. cinnamon

Try adding banana slices or leaving orange in chunks for a change.

• Position knife blade in food processor bowl; add orange. Process 30 seconds or until chopped. Add cranberries, and process 1 minute. Combine cranberry mixture and sugar in a bowl; let stand 15 minutes or until sugar dissolves.
• Sprinkle unflavored gelatin over cold water in a bowl; stir and let stand 1 minute. Add lemon-flavored gelatin and boiling water; stir 2 minutes or until gelatin dissolves. Chill until the consistency of unbeaten egg white.
• Stir cranberry mixture into gelatin mixture. Pour into a lightly oiled 12 cup Bundt pan or mold. Cover and chill until firm. Unmold onto a lettuce-lined plate, and garnish, if desired.

Makes 20 servings.

Judy Feagin
Test Kitchen Home Economist
Southern Living Magazine

Cran-Raspberry Salad

1 cup cooked barley
(about 1/4 cup uncooked medium barley)
1 cup cream (whipped)
1 (12 oz.) Cran-Raspberry Sauce
1 tsp. vanilla (optional)

• Cook barley until tender; drain and chill. Whip cream; add sauce and vanilla. Combine with cooked barley. Chill
Makes 6 servings

Ruth Gjelsness
Great Cook featured in
Successful Farming Magazine
and Friend of Education from Reynolds, ND

Heurick Hall, Wellington, Co.

 SALADS

"Ram" Pasta Fruit Salad

8 oz. medium pasta shells
8 oz. plain lowfat yogurt
1/2 cup orange juice concentrate
15 oz. mandarin oranges, drained
1 cup seedless red grapes, cut in half
1 cup seedless green grapes
1 apple, cored and chopped
3-4 ribs celery, sliced
1/2 cup walnut halves

• Cook shells and drain. Blend yogurt and orange juice in small bowl. In large bowl combine shells and remaining ingredients. Add yogurt mixture, toss to coat. Cover and refrigerate 2 hours.

Lisa Parker
Assistant Coach
Colorado State Women's Basketball

Oriental Spicy Slaw

1/4 cup sugar
1/2 cup rice or cider vinegar
1/2 cup vegetable oil
2 tsp. salt
2 tsp. pepper

2 lbs. green cabbage, finely shredded
1-1/3 cups chopped green onions

3 packages chicken flavored oriental noodles
    (raw, not prepared) and the seasoning
    packets
1/4 cup dark oriental sesame oil
1-1/2 tsp. hot chili oil

1 cup toasted Slivered Almonds
1/4 cup toasted Sesame Seeds

• Mix first 5 ingredients and pour over next 2 ingredients. Refrigerate overnight. Four hours before serving, sprinkle next 3 ingredients over refrigerated mixture. Mix together, cover and refrigerate. Just before serving, toss in next 2 ingredients.

Dona Kelley
President
Colorado Association for the
Education of Young Children

Mackenzie Krakel, Wellington, Co.

Grandma Jo's Frog Eye Salad

1 cup sugar
3 egg yolks
2 Tbl. flour
2 cups pineapple juice, (drained from canned
    pineapple)
1 Tbl. lemon juice
1 box (16 oz.) Acini de Pepe or Spezziello
    Macaroni
1 can (20 oz.) pineapple tidbits or crushed
    pineapple, drained
2 cans (11 oz.) mandarin oranges, drained
3/4 cup chopped maraschino cherries, drained
    (optional)
1 package miniature marshmallows
1 large container (9 oz.) whipped topping,
    thawed

• Combine sugar, yolks, flour, pineapple juice, and lemon juice. Cook over low heat until thick. Cook macaroni according to package directions (don't over cook), drain and combine with cooked mixture. Refrigerate at least 8 hours or overnight. Add fruit, marshmallows and topping. Refrigerate before serving.

Makes 24 - 1/2 cup servings.

Everyone loves this salad. You'll understand the name when you see the round macaroni in the salad.

Darlene Miller
Friend of Education
Battle Mt., NV

Amanda Smith, Wellington, Co.

Taboule

1 cup bulgar wheat
1 lb. fresh tomatoes
1 cup fresh parsley, chopped
4 Tbl. fresh mint, chopped
2 cups green onions, chopped
1/3 cup olive oil
4 Tbl. lemon juice
1 tsp. salt
1/2 tsp. pepper

• Cover wheat with boiling water and let stand for 1/2 hour. Drain. Express water with hands. Chop onions very fine. Salt and pepper them. Let stand 5 minutes. Chop and mix all the fresh vegetables with lemon juice, salt, pepper, olive oil and mint. Blend with chilled bulgar.

Kathy Brunner, Administrator
Child & Adult Care Food Program
Colorado Department of Health

Terrie Jo Howsden, Wellington, Co.

59

Zesty Pasta Salad

10 oz. rotini pasta
1-1/2 cups broccoli, cut into florets
1 can (15 oz.) kidney beans, drained and
    rinsed
1 large red or green bell pepper, chopped
1/3 cup onion, chopped
4 oz. part skim mozzarella cheese, cubed or
    grated
1 can (2 oz.) olives, chopped
8 oz. lean, cooked roast beef, cut in julienne
    strips
2 cups low-calorie Italian Dressing

• Cook pasta according to package directions.
Drain and rinse with cold water. Pour boiling water
over broccoli, drain and immediately rinse with cold
water. Combine additional ingredients and chill
before serving.

Makes 6 main dish servings.

Nutrient Analysis. One serving provides
395 calories, 10 g fat, 4 g fiber, 4 mg iron, 612 mg
sodium. Calories from carbohydrates, 51%; fat,
23%; and protien, 26%

Barbara Witte
Colorado Wheat Foods Council
Englewood, CO

Marshmallow Pineapple Salad

1 package lemon Jello
2 cups boiling water
1/2 lb. (32) marshmallows (miniature)
1 package (3 oz.) cream cheese
16 oz. can crushed pineapple, well drained
1/2 pint whipped cream
1 cup chopped nuts (optional)

• Mix Jello with boiling water. Cut marshmallows
into pieces and add while Jello is hot. Add cream
cheese. Fold in pineapple when mixture begins to
jell. Fold in whipped cream last. Return to
refrigerator to set. Chopped nuts may be added if
desired. Add after folding in whipped cream.

Norma Anderson
Colorado State Representative
District 30
Lakewood, CO

Blanca Burgos, Wellington, Co.

Andrew Laviolette, Wellington, Co.

Grilled Zucchini Salad with Gazpacho Dressing

1 green zucchini, sliced and grilled
1 yellow zucchini or other squash, sliced and grilled
2 fresh plum tomatoes
2 green onions (use scallions)
1 oz. lettuce/field greens
1/2 oz. pine nuts
1 sprig fresh cilantro
4 oz. Gazpacho Dressing, recipe follows:

• Spread dressing on plate. Sprinkle greens on top. Fan yellow and green squash alternating colors over dressing, on top of lettuce mix. Cross scallions on top and center over squashes. Slice plum tomatoes and fan on each side of squashes. Sprinkle pine nuts on top. Garnish with cilantro.

Makes 1 Serving. Double ingredients for 2 servings, etc.

Gazpacho Dressing

4 oz. fresh plum tomatoes
4 oz. red onions
4 oz. red bell peppers
4 oz. cucumbers
4 oz. yellow zucchini squash
1 Tbl. fresh oregano, or 1/2 tsp. crushed dry oregano
1 cup V-8 Juice
1/4 cup olive oil
Salt & pepper to taste

• Dice first 5 ingredients fine. Add chopped oregano to mix. Mix olive oil and V-8 Juice, add to mix. Season with salt and pepper.

Makes 3 cups

Stephen S. Kleinman
Executive Chef
Cherry Creek Inn, Denver, CO

Amanda Smith, Wellington, Co.

Nicole Bodkins, Wellington, Co.

 SALADS

Cy Young Salad

1 large head Romaine lettuce
3 oz. pkg. shredded parmesan cheese
1/4 cup Creamy Parmesan Salad Dressing
4 Tbl. Zesty Italian Salad Dressing

Wash lettuce leaves with water and drain. Tear lettuce into bite size pieces, removing the stems (throw stems away). Put lettuce in a large mixing bowl. Pour the shredded Parmesan cheese and both of the salad dressings over the lettuce.

**Secret ingredient - mix with hands, making sure all lettuce is covered. This is a game winning salad!

David Nied, Pitcher
Expansion Drafts #1 Pick for the
Colorado **Rockies**

Addam Zimmerman, Wellington, Co

 SALADS

Mike Berardi's Caesar Salad

For Dressing
1 whole egg
1 clove garlic
2 anchovy fillets
1-1/2 tsp. Dijon Mustard
3/4 tsp. lemon juice
3/4 tsp. black pepper
2 Tbl. grated Romano Cheese
1 tsp. red wine vinegar
2 drops Balsamic vinegar
3/4 cup olive oil

For Salad
Hearts of 2 heads Romaine Lettuce, washed & dried
2 Tbl. grated Romano Cheese
Croutons

Dressing
• Combine all ingredients except olive oil in blender cup. Blend until pureed. While blending slowly, add olive oil gradually until dressing is emulsified. (It should take 2-3 minutes to incorporate all the olive oil - add it slowly or it may separate.)
• May wish to use pasteurized eggs (egg beaters)
Salad
• Toss Romaine leaves with dressing until lightly and evenly coated. Lay out on plate and garnish with grated Romano and croutons.

Ed Bigg, General Manager
Mike Berardi's Italian Restaurant
Denver, CO

Copper Penny Salad

1 lb. carrots, sliced and cooked until done, but still firm
1/2 cup bell pepper, chopped
1 cup celery, chopped
1 large onion, chopped
1 can water chestnuts

1 can tomato soup (undiluted)
3/4 to 1 cup sugar
3/4 cup vinegar
1 tsp. mustard
1 tsp. Worcestershire Sauce

• Mix first 5 ingredients in a bowl and set aside. Combine remaining ingredients, pour over veggies and let set in refrigerator 24 hours before serving.

Option: Can substitute one small head cauliflower, cut up and cooked for 1 lb. carrots or add it to the total recipe.

Vi June
Colorado State Representative
Westminister, CO

Amsbry Ball, Wellington, Co.

Five Bean and One Pea Salad

1 can green beans
1 can kidney beans
1 can wax beans
1 can garbanzo beans
1 can lima beans
1 can peas
1 jar pimiento, chopped
1 onion, thinly sliced

Dressing
1/2 cup salad oil
1/2 cup wine vinegar
1/2 cup sugar
1 tsp. tarragon
1 tsp. salt
1/2 tsp. pepper

• Open and drain beans, peas and pimiento. Combine in a large bowl with onion. Place all dressing ingredients in blender or shaker. Blend well. Drizzle dressing over salad. Refrigerate in a tightly closed container for at least 12 hours.

Patricia A. Nolan, M.D., M.P.H.
Executive Director
Colorado Department of Health

Paul Cox, Wellington, Co.

Avocado Salad

2 chopped avocados (save shells)
4 hard boiled eggs (chopped)
4 green onions (diced)
1 Tbl. bacon bits
1 tsp. lemon juice
4 Tbl. mayonnaise
Salt and pepper to taste

• Mix mayonnaise with lemon juice and bacon bits. Add to diced onions, eggs, avocado. Put mixture in 4 shells. Chill

Rusti Ruth
Friend of Education
from Redding, CA

Scott Lesser, Wellington, Co.

Poppy Seed Dressing

2 cups vegetable oil
1-1/2 cups sugar
2/3 cup vinegar
3 Tbl. onion juice
2 tsp. salt
2 tsp. prepared mustard
2 tsp. poppy seeds

• Combine first 6 ingredients; stir until smooth. Stir in poppy seeds. Cover and chill.

Makes 3-1/2 cups.

• Especially good over spinach, scallions, red lettuce, mandarin oranges, and walnuts mixed together in whatever proportions you desire!

Nancy Richards
Radio News Director
Majic 100.3 - KMJI-FM

Western Chef Salad

1 lb. hamburger
1 (15 oz.) can kidney.beans
1 onion, chopped
2 tomatoes, chopped
1 head lettuce, chopped
1 cup shredded cheese
1 cup French salad dressing
1 large avocado, chopped
1 (6 oz.) bag Dorito Chips
Hot Sauce to taste

• Brown hamburger, drain. Drain beans. Toss all ingredients except chips. Break chips in pieces in bag, then add just before serving.

Makes 6 Main dish Servings.

Robert Shoemaker
State Representative, District #44
Canyon City, CO

T.J. Martinez, Mancos, Co.

65

HM Lemon Chicken Salad
(HM - Low in Fat & Cholesterol)

2 (8 oz.) pieces boneless, skinned chicken
  breast
1/4 cup lemon juice
1 tsp. garlic powder
1 tsp. salt
1 tsp. black pepper
4 oz. medium seashells, cooked and drained
4 oz. spinach rotini, cooked and drained
3-4 stalks celery, sliced fine
1 small red onion, diced
1 small can water chestnuts, sliced
1 small red pepper or pimento, diced small
1 medium green pepper, diced
1 pkg. Good Seasons Salad Dressing, omit
  vinegar, add lemon juice

• Lay chicken out on baking tray. Pour lemon juice and spices 3 through 5 over chicken and bake for 20 minutes in a 350°F oven. Cool and dice. Mix remaining ingredients with chicken.

Robert Riley, Manager
The Denver Salad Company
Englewood, CO

Message from company president, Edward Morton: "Our children's education is very important and we are pleased to be included in this cookbook."

Chris Evert's Healthy Chicken Salad

4 cups chicken, cooked and cut into bite sized
  pieces.
1 cup pineapple chunks
1 cup celery, chopped
1/2 cup scallions, chopped
1/4 cup dry-roasted unsalted peanuts
1/2 tsp. salt
2 Tbl. Chutney
2 Tbl. lemon juice
1/2 grated lemon rind
1/2 tsp. curry
2/3 cup mayonnaise

• Mix all ingredients together. If possible, use fresh pineapple and low-fat, low-cholesterol mayonnaise.

Enjoy.

Chris Evert
Pro Tennis Star

Tom McChesney, Wellington, Co.

66

BEEF - BUFFALO

Ray Thomas, Mancos, Co.

Derrick Gonzales, Mancos, Co.

Colorado is one of the top Beef Cattle Feeding States in the Nation.
C.S.U. - Dept. of Agriculture

"Enjoy your friends at school, but remember the best friends you'll ever have are Mom and Dad."
Bob Palmer
KCNC TV
Channel 4

Corned Beef with Mustard and Onion Sauce

3 -4 lb. corned beef

Sauce
1/2 onion (chopped)
4 Tbl. butter
2/3 cup dijon mustard
1/2 cup brown sugar
1/2 cup vinegar
3 tsp. horseradish sauce

• Simmer corned beef 4-5 hours or until tender. Rinse off spices. Baste with sauce and grill or broil.

Sauce
• Cook onion in butter and add remaining ingredients. Simmer slowly for twenty minutes.

Suggestion
• Boil new red-skin potatoes. Baste with sauce and grill with meat until skins have a mustardy crust.

Bob Palmer
KCNC TV
Channel 4

Mike McChesney, Wellington, Co.

Reuben Loaf

2-1/4 cup flour
1 package.quick rise yeast
1 Tbl. sugar
1 Tbl. butter
1 tsp. salt
1 cup very warm water
1/4 cup Thousand Island Dressing
12 oz. sliced corn beef
4 oz. sliced swiss cheese
1 (8 oz.) can sauerkraut, drained

• Mix first 6 ingredients together to make a ball. Knead on flowered board for 4 minutes. Divide the dough in half and divide the filling ingredients. Roll each part to about 6" x 12". Spread dressing down the center and follow with a layer of corned beef (folded), a layer of swiss cheese cut in 4 strips, and layer of sauerkraut. Fold end up over top and then the sides. Let rise for 15 minutes in warm place. Brush with beaten egg white and bake at 400° for 25 minutes.

Armetta Keeney
1992 - Best Cook in the Country

Mexican Lasagna

1-1/2 lbs. ground beef
1-1/2 tsp. ground cumin
1 Tbl. chili powder
1/4 tsp. garlic powder
1/4 tsp. red pepper
1 tsp. salt, or to tast
1 tsp. pepper, or to taste
1 can (16 oz.) tomatoes, chopped
10 to 12 corn tortillas
2 cups small curd cottage cheese, drained
1 cup grated Monterey Jack cheese with peppers
1 egg
1/2 cup grated cheddar cheese
2 cups shredded lettuce
1/2 cup chopped tomatoes
3 green onions, chopped
1/4 cup sliced black olives

• Brown ground beef; drain thoroughly. Add cumin, chili powder, garlic powder, red pepper, salt, pepper and tomatoes; heat through. Cover bottom and sides of 13 x 9 x 2 inch baking dish with tortillas. Pour beef mixture over tortillas; place a layer of tortillas over meat mixture and set aside. Combine cottage cheese, Monterey Jack cheese and egg; pour over tortillas. Bake at 350° for 30 minutes. Remove from oven, sprinkle with rows of cheddar cheese, lettuce, tomatoes, green onions and olives diagionally across center of casserole.
• Yield: 6-8 servings.

Elnora McCloughan
Director Berthoud Community Center
and Fire District Employee

Kristin Ratzlaff, Wellington, Co.

BEEF - BUFFALO

Chuck Wagon Pepper Steak

1 (3 lb.) top round steak cut 2 inches thick
2 tsp. unseasoned meat tenderizer
2 Tbl. minced onion
2 tsp. thyme
1 tsp. marjoram
1 bay leaf, crushed
1 cup wine vinegar
1/2 cup oil
3 Tbl. lemon juice
Coarsely ground black pepper to taste

• Sprinkle steak evenly on both sides with meat tenderizer.
• Combine onion, thyme, marjoram, bay leaf, vinegar, oil and lemon juice in small bowl; mix well.
• Pierce steak with fork. Place in shallow baking dish. Pour marinade over steak.
• Marinate for 1 to 3 hours, turning steak every half hour.
•Remove steak from marinade; drain. Sprinkle both sides generously with pepper; pound pepper into steak.
• Grill 6 inches above hot coals for 20 minutes per side.
• Slice 1/4 inch thick
• Yield: 4 servings.

Congressman Wayne Allard
Fourth Congressional District of Colorado

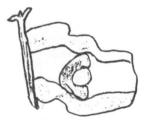

Nicole Bodkins, Wellington, Co.

70

BEEF - BUFFALO

Faux Thai/Bow Tie Flank Steak

1-1/2 lb. flank steak, lightly seasoned with salt
    and pepper
1/4 cup sesame tahini paste
1/4 cup frozen orange juice concentrate (no
    sugar added)
1 Tbl. olive oil
2 Tbl. soy sauce
1/2 tsp. crushed red pepper
1 large clove minced garlic
8 oz. bow tie pasta, cooked and hot
1 Tbl. chopped scallions
8-10 cherry tomatoes, quartered (optional)
1/4 cup coarsely chopped cilantro leaves
    (optional)
1 Tbl. toasted sesame seeds (optional)

• In a small sauce pan, combine tahini, orange juice concentrate, olive oil, soy sauce, crushed red pepper and garlic. Warm slightly over low heat until mixture is easily spreadable, approximately 1-2 minutes. Brush approximately 2 tablespoons of mixture on both sides of flank steak, reserve remaining mixture. Grill steak 5-7 minutes per side (if broiling, cook 2-3 inches from heat for 10 to 12 minutes). Toss remaining mixture with hot pasta and scallions. Slice steak thinly across grain and serve with pasta arranged around steak. Garnish with tomatoes and cilantro and sprinkle toasted sesame seed over all, if desired. Serve hot.
• Makes 4-6 servings

Tonya Sarina
Winner, 1993 Colorado State Beef Cook-off.
Director of Marketing, Pak Mail

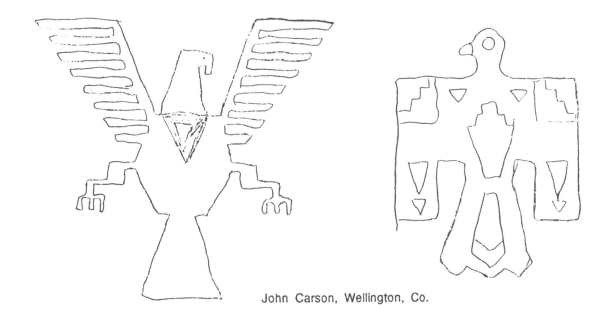

John Carson, Wellington, Co.

71

Sauerbraten

6 lb. lean beef (Fresh top or bottom round or
    chuck roast)
1 quart St. Mary's Gourmet Vinegar or other
    good quality Vinegar
1 quart water
Carrots
Onions
Parsley
1 bay leaf
Several cloves
Peppercorns
18 oz. tomato paste
Red wine

• Boil one quart of vinegar with an equal amount of water together with rough-cut carrots, parsley, onions, bay leaf, cloves and peppercorns for 15 minutes. Let cool and pour over meat which has been placed in crockery pot. Place in refrigerator for 72 hours.

• When preparing the meat, first dry the roast, then place in roasting pan with enough fat to brown meat on all sides in 450° oven. Add marinated vegetables with 1/2 the strained liquid and reduce temperature to 400°. When liquid turns golden brown after 1 hour, baste roast with broth and dust with flour. Cover and continue roasting another hour. Add remainder of marinade together with 18 ounces tomato paste. Cover and roast for 2 1/2 to 3 hours or until tender. Skim off all fat and strain liquid after roast has been removed to plate.

• Make gravy by thickening with 2 tablespoons flour and 8 ounces (1 cup) red wine.
Slice roast into 2 generous slices per person. Place on serving tray and totally cover with sauce. To complement this dinner, mashed potatoes, potato dumplings, spaetzle, potato pancakes, or buttered noodles may be served along with vegetables of choice.
Serves 6

Black Forest Inn
Black Hawk, Colorado

Shelly Stachurski, Wellington, Co.

Easy Thai Red Curry Beef (Kaeng Phed Nuer)

3 (13.5 fluid oz.) cans Coconut milk (Chaokoh is
   a good brand)*
1 (4 oz.) can of Thai red curry paste (red label
   with woman's face on it)*
2 lbs. stewing beef cut into 1/2 inch cubes
1/2 lb. fresh young tender bamboo shoots*,
   sliced into match stick sized pieces or a
   half pound can of bamboo shoots.
10 Fresh double wild lime leaves (Kefir)*
2-4 Red Birds Eye Chile-Peppers*, sliced in half
2 Tbl. fish sauce (Nam Pla/Nuoc Mam)*
1/2 tsp. salt
1/4 cup fresh basil leaves*

• Refrigerate the coconut milk a few hours before using. Take off enough of the thickened "cream" to make about one cup. Simmer this in a large saucepan, stirring until it comes to a boil. Then cook over low heat until the cream thickens and the oil starts to show in little bubbles. Add the can of curry paste and fry for 5 minutes or so, stirring constantly. When done, the curry paste will smell fragrant and the oil will separate from the mass. Add the beef and stir well. Then add remaining ingredients except the basil leaves, stirring well while bringing to a boil. Lower the heat and simmer until the beef is tender and the gravy seems to be cooking away, add a little more coconut milk or water. The gravy should be rich and red and there should be a lot of it. Thai curries are not thick like Indian ones. Just before removing from the fire, add the basil leaves and stir well.

• Serve with steamed rice. Jasmine rice* from Thailand is wonderful and authentic. A simple green salad with a light tart dressing accompanies well and beer is the drink with which to wash it all down. Singha, imported from Thailand, is available at liquor stores in the Asian area of South Federal Blvd.

• *All these items are available at pacific Ocean Grocers, 375 S. Federal Blvd. (Phone 935-2470) and at the many other Asian Produce shops on South Federal Blvd., south of Alameda.

Martin Fredmann
Artistic Director of Colorado Ballet

BEEF - BUFFALO

Ground Beef/Pork Casserole

1 can celery soup
1 lb. ground beef or pork, browned
1/2 cup sour cream
1/2 cup cracker crumbs
4 cups sliced raw potatoes
1/2 cup onions.
Sliced or shredded Cheddar cheese.

• Mix first 4 ingredients and set aside.
• Put the potatoes and onions into a greased casserole . Cover with sliced or shredded Cheddar Cheese. Top with meat mixture and seal the sides. Cover with lid. Bake 350° for 1 to 1 1/2 hours.
Note: A lid is necessary as the juices from the meat go down into the potatoes.

Armetta Keeney
1992 Best Cook in the Country

Quick and Easy Chili Cornpone Casserole

2 cans Chili (or equal amounts of homemade)
1 package corn muffin mix
Dash of salt
1 Tbl. Worcestershire Sauce

• Heat Chili in glass casserole dish 20 minutes at 350°. Mix corn muffin mix according to package directions. Add dash of salt and Worcestershire Sauce to batter. Remove Chili from oven, cover with batter. Bake according to package directions. May need an extra 5 minutes baking time to make sure center is done.
• Serve hot.

Nancy Richards
Majic 100.3 KMJI News Director

Tracie Alexander, Ft. Collins, Co.

Tom McChesney, Wellington, Co.

74

BEEF - BUFFALO

Message to Colorado Students,

"Invest in your future - - stay in school."

Senator Hank Brown

Hank Brown's Meatballs

1 lb. hamburger
1 large diced onion
2 Tbl. flour
Salt and pepper
1 can (16 oz.) tomatoes (strain pulp of
  tomatoes through a strainer)

• Mix first four ingredients with a fork and fingers. Roll into balls, a little larger than golf balls. Brown over slow heat, turning often.
• Add tomatoes. Simmer at least 1 full hour.
• Serve over mashed potatoes.

Hank Brown
United States Senator

Kennan Blehm, Wellington, Co.

Carol's Fire House Enchiladas

Topping
2 cans cream of chicken soup
1 large sour cream (16 oz.)
1 (7 oz.) can chopped green chilies

Base
2 lbs. of ground beef
1 (7 oz.) can chopped green chilies
1 medium size onion

1 dozen flour tortillas
Colby cheese to melt on top

Topping Instructions
• Mix together in sauce pan and heat on stove. Be careful not to burn, only warm it.

Base Instructions
• Mix together in fry pan and cook until meat is done. Drain off any excess grease.
• Place 3 or 4 large spoonfuls of topping mixture in baking pan. Microwave (45 seconds) 4 flour tortillas at a time. Place 2 or 3 spoonfuls of ground beef on a tortilla, roll it and place rolled tortilla in baking pan. Repeat with remaining tortillas.
• Once all tortilla rolls are in baking pan, pour rest of the topping over the tortilla rolls. Bake at 350° covered for 30 minutes. The last 10 minutes, bake uncovered and place cheese over topping.

Carol E. Small
Fire Marshal
Evergreen Fire Protection District

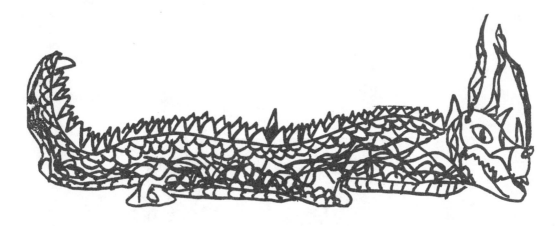

Adam Yee, Wellington, Co.

 BEEF - BUFFALO

To the Children of Colorado:

Jean and I hope that you enjoy this marvelous book of recipes. Eyestone Elementary has worked hard and has had a lot of fun in putting it together. It has lots of delicious dishes between the covers! And you will see that they got a number of very big names to contribute! We hope that you enjoy eating the favorite dishes of all these stars!

We know that you will make the most of your years in school and will work hard at both your studies and your activities. In the past two years, I have had the privilege of visiting many schools in Colorado---high schools, middle schools and grade schools, and I have been impressed by the high standards of behavior and courtesy as well as the dedication of your teachers that I found in every one of them. The future of the United States is in good hands, in my opinion!

I can tell you that I surely was glad of MY education during all that time in captivity in Lebanon. It was the basis of my survival, along with all the books that we were given to read. The books literally gave me "freedom in captivity" and furthered my education even while I was chained to the wall!!!

Colorado is a wonderful place in which to grow up and live. We appreciate it more than ever, with its sunshine, fresh air, beautiful mountains, and friendly people. Enjoy it, and may God richly bless you, one and all.

Tom and Jean Sutherland

Scottish Mince'n Tatties

1 lb. hamburger
4 carrots, sliced crosswise
1 onion, chopped
1 bouillon cube and 1 Tbl. of flour
3-4 potatoes
Salt and pepper to taste

• Fry hamburger and chopped onion together and remove excess fat. Sprinkle mixture with flour and mix well. Cover with water and add bouillon cube and sliced carrots. Reduce heat and simmer for 1/2 hour or more. Season with salt and pepper.
• Cook potatoes and mash with butter and salt. Meat mixture can be served on top of mashed potatoes or potatoes can go on top of meat and carrot mixture in a baking dish to make a shepherd pie for a pot luck dish.

Thomas M. Sutherland
Former Hostage in Lebanon

77

BBQ Beef

3 or 4 lbs. beef brisket (as fresh as possible)
1 (18 oz.) bottle smoked BBQ sauce (I use
    Kraft)
1/2 can beer

• Marinate beef in BBQ sauce/beer mixture for 3 days in refrigerator in baking bag. Cook at 250° for 5 to 6 hours. Shred beef mixed with sauce. Serve on bun. Can be frozen in convenient portions after beef is cooked and shredded.

Jeanne Faatz
State Representative
Denver, CO

Italian Style Tortillas

1 dozen flour tortillas or more if desired
Olive oil
1/2 lb. of ground round or ground sirloin,
    browned and fat drained
1 medium sweet onion, peeled and chopped
1 clove garlic peeled and chopped
1 large can spaghetti or pizza sauce
Mozzarella cheese
Parmesan cheese
Corn meal
Cookie sheets

• Sprinkle cookie sheets with corn meal. Preheat oven to 400°. Place as many tortillas on cookie sheets as will fit. Brush with olive oil.
• Mince onion and garlic together.
• Cover each tortilla with: 2 Tbl. browned chopped meat; 2 tsp. onion and garlic mixture; 2 Tbl. pizza or spaghetti sauce (any additionals that you wish , i.e. pepperoni, sausage, etc.)
• Sprinkle with Parmesan cheese.
• Sprinkle with shredded mozzarella cheese.
• Cook for approximately 10 minutes or until cheese melts and lightly browns.
Use pot holders at all times.
• Remove cookie sheet(s) from oven and remove pizzas with a spatula.

Georgi White
Marvel Entertainment Group, Inc.
Home of X-Men and Spiderman!
"Keep Reading" and Your Marvel-ous"

Tom McChesney, Wellington, Co.

BEEF - BUFFALO

Bill Kuster's Tournedos

Seems appropriate ... a weatherman cooking Tornados!

1 to 1 1/2 lbs. of beef flank steak
non-seasoned meat tenderizer
1/2 lb. bacon
1 tsp. garlic salt
1/2 tsp. freshly ground pepper
2 Tbl. snipped parsley
1 (3/4 oz.) envelope Hollandaise sauce mix
1/4 tsp. dried tarragon, crushed

Tom McChesney, Wellington, Co.

• Pound flank steak to even thickness, about 1/2 inch thick. Use meat tenderizer according to package directions. Meanwhile, cook bacon until almost done, but not crisp. Sprinkle flank steak with garlic salt and pepper. Score steak diagonally making diamond-shaped cuts. Place bacon strips lengthwise on flank steak. sprinkle with parsley. Roll up jelly roll fashion, starting at narrow end. Skewer with wooden picks at 1-inch intervals. Cut in 1-inch slices with serrated knife
• Grill over medium coals 15 minutes, turning once for rare. Meanwhile in saucepan prepare Hollandaise sauce mix according to package directions, adding the tarragon to the dry mix.
• Serve sauce with the steaks.
• Serves 4 (2 pinwheel steaks each).

Bill Kuster
Channel 9

Hamburger Roll Ups

1 lb. ground beef
1 onion (chopped fine)
4 crackers (crushed fine)
1 tsp. lemon pepper
1 tsp. garlic salt
2 (10 pack) rolls (refrigerated biscuits)

• Mix ground beef, onion, crackers and seasonings.
• Place small roll of hamburger mixture in each biscuit and seal tightly. Bake on cookie sheet at 375° for 30 minutes.

Rusti Ruth
Friend of Education

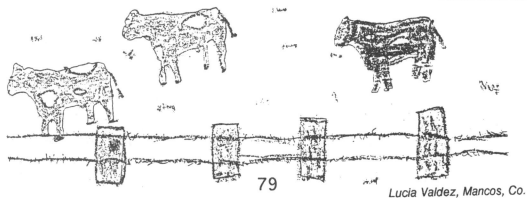

79

Lucia Valdez, Mancos, Co.

Prime Rib of Buffalo with Seven Seed Crust

6 to 7 lbs. buffalo prime rib
1 Tbl. anise seeds
1 Tbl. whole coriander
1 Tbl. fennel seeds
1 Tbl. mustard seeds
1 Tbl. celery seeds
1 Tbl. tellicherry peppercorns
1 Tbl. green peppercorns
1 tsp. sea salt

Olive Oil

1 cup beef stock
1 cup good Cabernet

• One day prior to cooking remove the roast from refrigerator. Trim all exterior fat to 1/8 inch and tie between the rib bones in order for roast to hold its shape.
• Rub the exterior of the rib with a small amount of olive oil until evenly coated.
• Place the seven seeds and the salt in a blender or spice grinder and process until the consistency of coarse corn meal.
• Evenly coat the roast with the spice blend and refrigerate for about 24 hours.
• Preheat the oven to 425°. Place the roast in a shallow pan and place in the oven for 20-30 minutes until the seeds are roasted to a deep brown. Reduce the oven temperature to 325° and continue to cook until reaching an internal temperature of 120°.
• Remove from the oven and let stand for 15 minutes. Remove the roast from the pan and place on a cutting board and cover with foil and a kitchen towel.
• Pour the pan drippings through a mesh strainer filled with lots of ice into a small sauce pan. (This removes the excess grease). Place the sauce pan on the stove and add the beef stock. Add the cabernet and bring to a boil, reduce to a simmer.
• Remove the rack of bones and slice into servings of desired thickness or number. Serve with Au Jus.

Buckhorn Exchange
George Carlberg
Exec. Chef
Denver, CO

Kristin Ratzlaff, Wellington, Co.

Ray Thomas, Mancos, Co.

BEEF COOK-OFF

Derrick Gonzales, Mancos, Co.

Steak with Mixed Peppercorn Sauce

4 beef tenderloin or boneless top loin steaks,
   cut 1 inch thick
2 medium zucchini or yellow squash
2 medium carrots
2 tsp. mixed peppercorns (black, white, green,
   pink) cracked
2 Tbl. butter or margarine
Salt (optional)

Peppercorn Sauce

2/3 cup dry white or red wine
1 tsp. chopped shallot or sliced white portion
   of green onion
1/2 cup seeded and coarsely chopped plum
   tomatoes
1 Tbl. mixed peppercorns (black, white, green,
   pink) cracked
1 Tbl. chopped fresh parsley

Total preparation and cooking time: 35 minutes.

• Remove stem ends from squash and carrots.
Using a vegetable peeler, cut outer portion of
squash and carrots lengthwise into long thin
strips. Reserve inner portion (seeded area of
squash; core area of carrots) for another use.
Place steamer basked in 1/2 inch water (water
should not touch bottom of basket). Place
vegetable strips in basket. Cover tightly and heat
to boiling; reduce heat. Steam 2 to 3 minutes or
until crisp-tender; keep warm.
• Meanwhile, press 2 teaspoons cracked
peppercorns into both sides of each beef steak.
Heat butter in medium non stick skillet over
medium heat until melted. Place steaks in skillet
and cook 9 to 11 minutes for rare to medium
doneness, turning once. Remove steaks to warm
platter and season with salt, if desired; keep
warm.
• In same skillet, add wine and shallot; cook and
stir until browned bits attached to skillet are
dissolved. Stir in tomato, 1 tablespoon cracked
peppercorns and parsley; heat through.
• To serve, spoon sauce over steaks; serve with
vegetables.
• Makes 4 servings (serving size: 1/4 of recipe).
Cook's tip
• To crack whole peppercorns, place on cutting
board; cover with plastic wrap. Coarsely crush
peppercorns with rolling pin or side of wide chef
knife.

Marilou Robinson
Portland, OR

"Recipe provided with permission from the
National Beef Cook-Off® sponsored by the
American National CattleWomen, Inc. in
cooperation with the Beef Industry Council and the
Beef Board."

Sarah Delozier, Wellington, Co.

Lemon Herb Roast

3 lb. beef round tip or eye round roast
Salt
Herb Seasoning:
1/2 cup finely chopped fresh parsley
1 Tbl. olive oil
4 or 5 cloves garlic, crushed
2 tsp. grated fresh lemon peel
1/4 tsp. pepper

Roasted Vegetables
1 Tbl. olive oil
1 lb. new red potatoes, cut in half
1/2 lb. carrots, cut diagonally into 1/2 inch
    thick slices
4 small onions, cut lengthwise in half
2 medium zucchini, cut into 3/4 inch thick
    slices.

Mike Lowell, Wellington, Co.

"Recipe provided with permission from the National Beef Cook-Off® sponsored by the American National CattleWomen, Inc. in cooperation with the Beef Industry Council and the Beef Board."

Total preparation and cooking time: 2 to 2 1/2 hours.

• Heat oven 325°. In large bowl, combine seasoning ingredients; remove half and reserve for beef roast. Add additional 1 tablespoon oil to remaining seasoning; mix. Add vegetables; toss to coat. Set aside.
• Press reserved seasoning mixture evenly into surface of beef roast. Place roast, fat side up, on rack in shallow roasting pan. Insert meat thermometer so bulb is centered in thickest part, not resting in fat. Arrange all vegetables except zucchini on rack around roast. Do not add water. Do not cover.
• Roast beef and vegetables in 325° oven until rare to medium doneness. Allow 1-1/2 to 1 3/4 hours for round tip roast (1 hour for eye round roast). Remove roast when meat thermometer registers 135° for rare, 155° for medium. Tent roast with foil; let stand 15 to 20 minutes. (Roast will continue to rise about 5° in temperature to 140° for rare, 160° for medium.)
• Meanwhile, increase oven temperature to 425°. Add zucchini to vegetables in pan; return to oven. Continue roasting vegetables 15 to 20 minutes or until tender.
• Trim fat from roast, if necessary. Carve roast into thin slices; season with salt, as desired. Serve with roasted vegetables.

• Makes 8 to 10 servings (serving size: 1/8 to 1/10 of recipe).

Janice Skousen
Logan UT

Tiffany Bishop, Wellington, Co.

90's Style Swiss Steak

1-1/2 lb. boneless beef round or chuck
    shoulder steaks, cut 1/2 inch thick
3 Tbl. all-purpose flour
1 tsp. salt
1/2 tsp. pepper
5 tsp. vegetable oil
3/4 cup finely chopped carrots
3/4 cup finely chopped onion
3/4 cup water
1/2 cup finely chopped celery
1/2 cup finely chopped green bell pepper
1/2 cup prepared medium picante sauce
1/4 cup ketchup
1 Tbl. white vinegar
2-1/2 cups uncooked farfalle (bow tie) pasta
Fresh parsley sprigs

"Recipe provided with permission from the
National Beef Cook-Off® sponsored by the
American National CattleWomen, Inc. in
cooperation with the Beef Industry Council and the
Beef Board."

Total preparation and cooking time: 1-3/4 hours.

• Trim fat from beef steak. Cut steak into 6
pieces; pound to 1/4 inch thickness. Combine
flour, salt, and pepper. Lightly coat both sides of
steaks with flour mixture. In Dutch oven, heat oil
over medium-high heat. Place steaks in pan (1/2
at a time) and brown on both sides. Pour off
drippings, if necessary.
• Stir in remaining ingredients except pasta and
parsley. Bring to a boil; reduce heat to low.
Cover tightly and simmer 1 1/2 hours or until beef
is tender. (If sauce becomes too thick, stir in a
few tablespoons additional water during last 5 to
10 minutes of cooking.)
• Meanwhile, cook pasta according to package
directions. Keep warm.
• To serve, spoon sauce over pasta; arrange
steaks over sauce. Garnish with parsley.
• Makes 6 servings (serving size: 1/6 of recipe).

Ann Dixon
North Vernon, IN

Bryce Hall, Wellington, Co.

84

Special Beef and Spinach Burritos

1 lb. lean ground beef
1 small onion, chopped
1 clove garlic, crushed
1/2 tsp. salt
1/2 tsp. chili powder
1/4 tsp. ground cumin
1/4 tsp. pepper
1 package (10 oz.) frozen chopped spinach,
    defrosted, well drained
2 jalapeno peppers, seeded, finely chopped
1-1/2 cups shredded Monterey Jack cheese
4 large (10 inches) or 8 medium (8 inches)
    flour tortillas, warmed
Lime slices (optional)
Jalapeno pepper slices (optional)
1 cup prepared chunky salsa

"Recipe provided with permission from the National Beef Cook-Off® sponsored by the American National CattleWomen, Inc. in cooperation with the Beef Industry Council and the Beef Board."

Total preparation and cooking time: 25 minutes.

• In large nonstick skillet, brown beef, onion and garlic over medium heat 8 to 10 minutes or until beef is no longer pink, stirring occasionally. Pour off drippings. Season with salt, chili powder, cumin and pepper.
• Stir in spinach and jalapeno peppers; heat through. Remove from heat; stir in cheese.
• To serve, spoon equal amount of beef mixture in center of each tortilla. Fold bottom edge up over filling. Fold right and left sides to center, overlapping edges. Garnish with lime and jalapeno slices, if desired; serve with salsa.
• Makes 4 servings (serving size: 1/4 of recipe).

Julie Dematteo
Clementon, NJ

Kirt Royball, Wellington, Co.

Barbecue Beef Focaccia-Style Pizza

1-1/2 lbs. lean ground beef
3/4 cup frozen corn, defrosted
3/4 cup prepared barbecue sauce
1/2 cup sliced green onions
1/2 tsp. salt (optional)
1 large (16 oz.) Italian bread shell or prepared
   pizza crust
1-1/2 cups (6 oz.) shredded Cheddar cheese
Pepperoncini peppers (optional)

"Recipe provided with permission from the
National Beef Cook-Off® sponsored by the
American National CattleWomen, Inc. in
cooperation with the Beef Industry Council and the
Beef Board."

Total preparation and cooking time: 35 minutes

• Heat oven 425°. In large nonstick skillet, brown
ground beef over medium heat 8 to 10 minutes or
until beef is no longer pink, stirring occasionally.
Pour off drippings. Stir in corn, barbecue sauce,
green onions and salt, if desired. Heat through.
• Place bread shell on large ungreased baking
sheet. Spread beef mixture evenly over bread
shell. Sprinkle with cheese. Bake in 425° oven
15 or 20 minutes or until cheese is melted.
• Cut pizza into 6 wedges; garnish with
pepperonicini peppers, if desired.
• Makes 6 servings (serving size: 1/6 of recipe).

Larry A. Lentz
Nicholasville, KY

Fantastic Stir-Fried Beef Fajitas

1 lb. beef top round or boneless chuck
   shoulder steaks, cut 1/2 inch thick
1 green *or* red bell pepper, cut lengthwise into
   thin strips
1 medium onion, cut lengthwise into thin strips
8 flour tortillas (8 inches), warmed
1 cup shredded Co-Jack cheese
1 cup prepared picante sauce
2 avocados, peeled, seeded, cut lengthwise
   into thin slices
Marinade:
2 Tbl. fresh orange juice
2 Tbl. white vinegar
1 tsp. finely chopped garlic or 1 large clove
   garlic, crushed
1/2 tsp. ground cumin
1/2 tsp. ground oregano
1/8 tsp. salt
1/8 tsp. pepper

"Recipe provided with permission from the National Beef Cook-Off® sponsored by the American National CattleWomen, Inc. in cooperation with the Beef Industry Council and the Beef Board."

• Combine marinade ingredients. Trim fat from beef steak. Cut steak lengthwise in half and then crosswise into 1/8-inch thick strips. Place beef and half of marinade in plastic bag, turning to coat. Close bag securely and marinate in refrigerator 6 to 8 hours or overnight, if desired, turning occasionally.
• Place bell pepper, onion and remaining marinade in separate plastic bag, turning to coat. Close bag securely and marinate in refrigerator while marinating beef.
• Heat large nonstick skillet over medium-high heat until hot. Remove vegetables from marinade. Add vegetables to skillet and stir-fry 3 minutes or until crisp-tender. Remove from skillet.
• Heat same skillet until hot. Remove beef from marinade; discard marinade. Add beef to skillet and stir-fry (1/2 at a time) 1 to 2 minutes or until outside surface is no longer pink. (Do not overcook.) Return vegetables to skillet; toss to combine.
• Serve beef and vegetable mixture in tortillas; serve with cheese, picante sauce and avocados.
• Makes 4 servings (serving size: 1/4 of recipe).

Dana Gregory
Lincoln, NE

Scott Smith, Wellington, Co.

87

Steak Oriental

4 boneless beef rib eye or top loin steaks, cut 3/4 inch thick or tenderloin steaks, cut 1 inch thick
3 Tbl. coarsely chopped peanuts
Orange slices (optional)

Marinade:
1/3 cup soy sauce
1/3 cup canned pineapple orange juice
3 Tbl. honey
3 Tbl. ketchup
3 Tbl. packed brown sugar
2 Tbl. peanut butter
1 Tbl. finely chopped fresh garlic or 3 large cloves, crushed
1-1/2 tsp. coarse-grain Dijon-style mustard
1/2 tsp. five-spice powder

"Recipe provided with permission from the National Beef Cook-Off® sponsored by the American National CattleWomen, Inc. in cooperation with the Beef Industry Council and the Beef Board."

Total preparation and cooking time: 30 minutes.
Marinating time: 30 minutes

• In small saucepan, combine marinade ingredients. Heat marinade over medium heat until sugar is dissolved and mixture is blended, stirring frequently. Remove from heat; cool slightly. Cover and refrigerate 1/4 cup marinade for brushing on steaks while broiling.
• Place beef steaks and remaining marinade in plastic bag, turning to coat. Close bag securely and marinate in refrigerator 30 minutes.
• Remove steaks from marinade; discard marinade. Place steaks on rack in broiler pan so surface of meat is 2 to 3 inches from heat. Broil rib eye and top loin steaks 8 to 12 minutes (tenderloin steaks 10 to 15 minutes) for rare to medium doneness, turning once. Brush cooked side with reserved marinade after turning.
• Sprinkle steaks with peanuts; garnish with orange slices, if desired.
• Makes 4 servings (serving size: 1/4 of recipe).
• Cook's Tip:
Five-spice powder can be found in the Oriental section of the supermarket.

Aleta Van Kampen
Spearfish, SD

Nathan Hawley, Wellington, Co.

Chili Salsa Beef

1-1/2 lbs. boneless beef chuck shoulder roast
1 Tbl. olive oil
1 cup prepared medium or hot chunky salsa
2 Tbl packed brown sugar
1 Tbl. reduced-sodium soy sauce
1 clove garlic, crushed
1/3 cup coarsely chopped fresh cilantro
1 Tbl. fresh lime juice
2 cups cooked rice
Cilantro sprigs (optional)
1 lime, cut crosswise into quarters (optional)

"Recipe provided with permission from the National Beef Cook-Off® sponsored by the American National CattleWomen, Inc. in cooperation with the Beef Industry Council and the Beef Board."

Total preparation and cooking time: 1-3/4 hours

• Trim fat from beef roast. Cut roast into 1-1/4 inch pieces. In Dutch oven, heat oil over medium heat until hot. Add beef and brown evenly, stirring occasionally. Pour off drippings, if necessary.
• Stir salsa, sugar, soy sauce and garlic into beef. Bring to a boil; reduce heat to low. Cover tightly and simmer 1 hour. Remove cover, continue cooking, uncovered, an additional 30 minutes or until beef is tender.
• Remove from heat; stir in chopped cilantro and lime juice. Spoon beef mixture over rice; garnish with cilantro sprigs and lime quarters, if desired.
• Makes 4 servings (serving size: 1/4 of recipe).

Robert Logan
Garnett, KS

Andrew Kisner, Wellington, Co.

89

Italian Bistro Steak Subs

1-1/2 lb. boneless beef top sirloin steak, cut 1 inch thick
6 hoagie or crusty Italian rolls (6 to 7 inches long), split lengthwise in half
12 romaine lettuce leaves
1/2 tsp. garlic salt
1/4 tsp. pepper
1/3 cup shredded fontinella or mozzarella cheese

Pepper Relish
1 jar (9-1/2 oz.) pepper salad
1/2 cup prepared mild chunky salsa
1/4 cup sliced ripe olives

Genesis Dionne, Wellington, Co.

"Recipe provided with permission from the National Beef Cook-Off® sponsored by the American National CattleWomen, Inc. in cooperation with the Beef Industry Council and the Beef Board."

Total preparation and cooking time: 30 minutes

• Drain pepper salad, reserving 2 teaspoons of oil mixture. Coarsely chop pepper salad. In small bowl, combine chopped pepper salad, salsa and olives; set aside.
• Brush reserved oil mixture over both sides of beef steak. Place steak on grid over medium coals. Grill 16 to 20 minutes for rare to medium doneness, turning once.
• Trim fat from steak. Carve steak crosswise into thin slices; season with garlic salt and pepper.
• Line bottom half of each roll with 2 lettuce leaves. Arrange steak slices over lettuce. Top each sandwich with 2 tablespoons pepper relish; Sprinkle with cheese. Close sandwiches. Pass remaining pepper relish. Makes 6 servings (serving size: 1 sandwich).
•Cook's Tips:
Test about 4 inches above coals for medium coals with a 4-second hand count.
• If pepper salad is not available, 3/4 cup chopped, roasted red peppers plus 1/4 cup seeded chopped mild cherry peppers may be substituted for 1 jar (9-1/2 ounces) pepper salad. Omit brushing steak with oil mixture.

Joyce Lee Sproul
Bath, MA

Heather Marshall, Wellington, Co.

30-Minute Beef and Black Bean Soup

1 lb. coarse or chili grind beef chuck
1 can (11 or 19 oz.) black bean soup
1 can (15 oz.) black beans, rinsed, drained
1-1/3 cups water
1 cup prepared medium or hot chunky salsa
1/4 cup thinly sliced green onions
1/4 cup dairy light sour cream
Fresh Cilantro sprigs
4 corn muffins, warmed

"Recipe provided with permission from the National Beef Cook-Off® sponsored by the American National CattleWomen, Inc. in cooperation with the Beef Industry Council and the Beef Board."

Total preparation and cooking time: 30 minutes

• In Dutch oven, brown beef chuck over medium heat 8 to 10 minutes or until beef is no longer pink, breaking up into 3/4-inch crumbles. Pour off drippings.
• Stir in black bean soup, black beans, water and salsa. Bring to a boil; reduce heat to low. Simmer, uncovered, 15 minutes.
• Stir in green onions; remove from heat. Garnish with sour cream and cilantro; serve with corn muffins.
• Makes 4 servings (serving size: Approx. 1-1/4 cups).

Terryl A. Propper
Nashville, TN

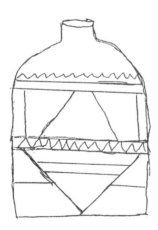

Krystal Hanson, Wellington, Co.

91

Beef Primavera

1 lb. boneless beef top sirloin steak, cut 1 inch thick
3 cups (8 oz.) uncooked rotini (spiral) pasta
2 small yellow squash, cut diagonally into 1/4 inch thick slices
2 med. carrots, cut diagonally into 1/8 inch thick slices
1 cup broccoli flowerets
2 Tbl. olive oil
3 cloves garlic, crushed
1/2 cup ready-to-serve beef broth
1/4 tsp. crushed red pepper
1/2 cup lightly packed fresh basil leaves, thinly sliced
1 cup cherry tomatoes, cut crosswise in half
1/4 tsp. salt (optional)
1/4 cup freshly grated Parmesan cheese
fresh basil sprigs (optional)

"Recipe provided with permission from the National Beef Cook-Off® sponsored by the American National CattleWomen, Inc. in cooperation with the Beef Industry Council and the Beef Board."

Total preparation and cooking time: 50 minutes.
Chilling time (optional): 30 minutes

• If desired, partially freeze beef steak to firm (approx. 30 minutes) for easier cutting.
• Meanwhile cook pasta according to package directions. About 6 to 8 minutes before pasta is done, stir in squash, carrots and broccoli. Cook pasta and vegetables just until tender. Drain; keep warm.
• Trim fat from steak. Cut steak lengthwise in half and then crosswise into 1/8-inch thick strips. Heat oil in large non stick skillet over medium-high heat until hot. Add beef and garlic (1/2 at a time) and stir-fry 1 to 2 minutes or until outside surface of beef is no longer pink. (Do not overcook.) Remove beef, with slotted spoon, to medium bowl; keep warm.
• Add beef broth and red pepper to skillet; cook and stir 1 minute or until browned bits attached to skillet are dissolved. Remove from heat; stir in basil. Spoon 1/4 cup of sauce over beef; toss to coat. Add reserved pasta mixture and tomatoes to remaining sauce in skillet; toss to coat. Season with salt, if desired.
• To serve, arrange pasta mixture on large platter; top with beef. Sprinkle with cheese; garnish with basil sprigs, if desired.
• Makes 4 servings (serving size; 1/4 of recipe).

Nancy Labrie
Rye, NH

Darcy Ely, Wellington, Co.

Calypso Steak

1-1/2 lb. boneless beef top sirloin or top round steak, cut 1 inch thick
Edible flowers (optional)
Marinade:
1/2 medium onion, cut into quarters
1/4 cup honey
1/4 cup fresh lime juice
1/4 cup soy sauce
10 to 20 quarter-size slices, peeled fresh ginger (cut from 1" wide by 1-1/2 to 3" long piece)
1 to 2 jalapeno peppers, stems removed, cut in half
3 cloves garlic, peeled
1/2 tsp. ground allspice
1/2 tsp. ground paprika
1/2 tsp. dried thyme leaves

"Recipe provided with permission from the National Beef Cook-Off® sponsored by the American National CattleWomen, Inc. in cooperation with the Beef Industry Council and the Beef Board."

Total preparation and cooking time: 35 minutes
Marinating time: 20 minutes to 2 hours

• Place marinade ingredients in blender or food processor fitted with steel blade; process until blended. Place beef steak and marinade in plastic bag, turning to coat. Close bag securely and marinate in refrigerator 20 minutes to 2 hours, turning once.
• Remove steak from marinade; reserve marinade. Place steak on rack in broiler pan so surface of meat is 3 to 4 inches from heat. Broil top sirloin 16 to 21 minutes (top round 15 to 18 minutes) for rare to medium doneness, turning once.
• Meanwhile, in small saucepan, bring reserved marinade to a rolling boil over high heat. Boil 2 minutes; strain and set aside for sauce.
• Trim fat from steak. Carve steak crosswise into thin slices; arrange on serving platter. Garnish with edible flowers, if desired; serve with sauce.
• Makes 6 servings (serving size: 1/6 of recipe).

Robin Bonifay Hill
Arlington, TX

Julie Ann Ramirez, Wellington, Co.

Margarita Beef with Orange Salsa
1992 Best of Beef and Outdoor Barbecue (Winner)

1-1/2 lb. well-trimmed boneless beef top round
  steak, cut 1 inch thick
2/3 cup frozen orange juice concentrate,
  thawed
1/2 cup tequila
1/3 cup fresh lime juice
2 Tbl. olive oil
2 Tbl. chopped fresh ginger
2 medium cloves garlic, crushed
1 tsp. each salt and dried oregano leaves
1/4 tsp. ground red pepper
Orange Salsa*
Cilantro sprigs
Lime wedges

*Orange Salsa
2 oranges, peeled and cut into 1/2-inch pieces
1 small red or white onion, chopped
1 jalapeno pepper, seeded and finely chopped
1/4 cup chopped fresh cilantro
2-3 Tbl. fresh lime juice
2 Tbl. Olive oil
1/2 tsp. each salt and dried oregano leaves

"Recipe provided with permission from the
National Beef Cook-Off® sponsored by the
American National CattleWomen, Inc. in
cooperation with the Beef Industry Council and the
Beef Board."

Preparation time: 30 minutes
Marinating time: 4 hours or overnight
Cooking time: 22-26 minutes

• Combine orange juice concentrate, tequila, lime
juice, oil, ginger, garlic , salt, oregano and red
pepper. Place steak in plastic bag; add marinade,
turning to coat. Close bag securely and marinate
in refrigerator 4 hours or overnight, as desired.
Prepare Orange Salsa. Remove steak from
marinade; discard marinade. Place steak on grid
over medium coals.** Grill 22-26 minutes for
medium rare (150°F) to medium (160°F)
doneness, turning once. Remove steak to carving
board; let stand 10 minutes. Carve steak
crosswise into thin slices; arrange on serving
platter. Garnish with cilantro and lime. Serve with
Orange Salsa.

5 to 6 servings

Orange Salsa Directions
Preparation time: 5 minutes
• Combine all ingredients in non-metallic bowl and
refrigerate at least one hour.

Yield: 1-1/2 cups

**Test about 4 inches above coals for medium
with 4-second hand count.

John W. Hurd
San Francisco, CA

Nicole Bodkins, Wellington, Co.

Tenderloin Steaks with Pepper Jelly Sauce

1992 Indoor and Most convenient Recipe (Winner)

4 well-trimmed beef tenderloin steaks* cut 1
    inch thick (approx. 4 ounces each)
3/4 tsp. each garlic salt and chili powder
1/2 tsp. coarse grind black pepper
1/4 tsp. each ground cumin and dried oregano
    leaves
1 Tbl. vegetable oil
1/2 cup ready-to-serve beef broth
1/4 cup balsamic or red wine vinegar
2 Tbl. jalapeno pepper jelly
Parsley sprigs
Red and green chili peppers

Preparation time: 15 minutes
Cooking time: 15 minutes

• Combine garlic salt, chili powder, pepper, cumin and oregano. Rub over both sides of steaks. Heat oil in heavy large skillet over medium-high heat 3 minutes. Add steaks. Cook 6 to 8 minutes for rare (140°F) to medium rare (150°F) doneness, turning once. Transfer steaks to serving platter; keep warm. Pour off drippings. Add broth, vinegar and jelly to skillet; cook 5 minutes or until slightly thickened, stirring occasionally. Spoon sauce over steaks; garnish with parsley and chili peppers.

• 4 servings

"Recipe provided with permission from the National Beef Cook-Off® sponsored by the American National CattleWomen, Inc. in cooperation with the Beef Industry Council and the Beef Board."

• *Beef top sirloin, cut 1 inch thick, may be substituted for the beef tenderloin. Cook over medium heat and increase cooking time to 12 to 15 minutes.

Frances C. Andrews
Wilson, NC

Brandon Stull, Wellington, Co.

Spicy Beef Barley Bean Soup
1992 Indoor (Honorable Mention)

1 lb. ground beef (90 percent lean)
2 Tbl. instant minced onion
1 Tbl. olive oil
5 cups ready-to-serve beef broth
2 cups prepared chunky salsa, medium or hot
1 cup julienned carrots (2 x 1/4-inch)
2/3 cup quick barley
1 Tbl. minced fresh basil
1/2 cup each cauliflowerets and fresh or frozen peas
1 can (15 or 16 ounces) red beans* rinsed and drained
Basil sprigs

"Recipe provided with permission from the National Beef Cook-Off® sponsored by the American National CattleWomen, Inc. in cooperation with the Beef Industry Council and the Beef Board."

Preparation time: 20 minutes
Cooking time: 25 minutes

• Brown ground beef with onion in oil in deep 12-inch skillet or Dutch oven, breaking into 3/4-inch pieces, until beef is no longer pink. Pour off drippings, if necessary. Add beef broth, salsa, carrots, barley and minced basil. bring to a boil; reduce heat to medium. Cook uncovered 10 minutes, stirring occasionally. Add cauliflowerets and peas; continue cooking until vegetables are crisp-tender, about 6 minutes. Add beans; heat through. Ladle into soup tureen; garnish with basil sprigs.
• 4 servings
• *One can (15 or 16 ounces) kidney beans or shelled beans may be substituted.
• Note: If thinner soup is desired, additional beef broth may be added.

Ann Holz
Temple, NH

Stephanie Pfaff, Wellington, Co.

Sweet 'N Sour Beef Chuck

1975 Best of Beef (Winner)

3-lb. beef chuck roast
Garlic powder
Coarse grind black pepper
2 Tbl. all-purpose flour
2 Tbl. vegetable oil
1/2 tsp. ground cinnamon
1/4 tsp. ground allspice
1 medium onion, halved
1-1/2 cups water
Sauce*
Hot cooked rice
Fresh mint leaves

*Sauce

1 cup cooking liquid from roast, fat skimmed
    off
2 cans (13-1/4 ounces each) pineapple chunks
    in heavy syrup
1/2 cup packed brown sugar
1/4 cup cornstarch
1/2 cup vinegar
1/4 cup soy sauce
1 can (2-1/2 ounces) sliced mushrooms,
    drained
1 can (8-1/2 ounces) water chestnuts, drained,
    sliced
1 large green bell pepper, cut into thin strips
1 cup thinly sliced red onion

"Recipe provided with permission from the
National Beef Cook-Off® sponsored by the
American National CattleWomen, Inc. in
cooperation with the Beef Industry Council and the
Beef Board."

Preparation time: 15 minutes
Cooking time: 2 hours 15 minutes to 3 hours 15
minutes.

• Sprinkle both sides of beef roast with garlic
powder and pepper, as desired. Rub both sides
with flour and brown in oil in large frying pan or
Dutch oven. Pour off drippings. Sprinkle beef
with cinnamon and allspice. Add onion and water.
Cover and simmer on top of range or cook in 350°
oven 2 to 3 hours or until beef is tender. Discard
onion. Remove roast and reserve 1 cup cooking
liquid. Cut beef into large bite-size pieces. Place
on a hot serving platter; keep warm. Prepare
sauce and spoon over beef. Serve with rice and
garnish with mint.

6 to 8 servings

Sauce Instructions

• Drain pineapple, reserve syrup. Combine sugar
and cornstarch in medium saucepan; add
pineapple syrup, vinegar, soy sauce, mushrooms,
water chestnuts and cooking liquid. Cook, stirring
constantly, until sauce thickens. Add pineapple,
green pepper and onion; continue cooking 2
minutes.

Betty Morrow
Oklahoma

Darcy Ely, Wellington, Co.

Apple-Glazed Beef Brisket

1984 Best of Beef (Winner)

4 to 5 pound boneless beef brisket
1 medium onion, quartered
2 large cloves garlic, halved
10 whole cloves
1 jar (10 ounces) apple jelly
1/3 cup dry white wine
3 Tbl. Dijon-style mustard
3 Tbl. minced green onions with tops
1-1/2 tsp. salt
3/4 tsp. cracked black peppercorns
3/4 tsp. curry powder
Parsley
Tomato roses

Preparation time: 10 minutes
Cooking time: approx. 3 hours 45 minutes

• Place brisket, onion, garlic and cloves in large Dutch oven. Add water to cover. Bring to a boil, reduce heat, cover and simmer 2-1/2 to 3 hours or until tender. Drain brisket, cover and refrigerate up to 24 hours. To prepare glaze, combine apple jelly, wine, mustard, green onions, salt, pepper and curry powder in small saucepan and heat until jelly melts, stirring occasionally. Place brisket in shallow roasting pan. Brush with glaze and heat in 325°F oven* 45 minutes, basting frequently with glaze. Place brisket on heated serving platter and garnish with parsley and tomato roses. Carve brisket into thin slices and serve with remaining glaze.

• 8 servings

• *Brisket may also be heated on charcoal grill 30 minutes; baste often with the glaze.

"Recipe provided with permission from the National Beef Cook-Off® sponsored by the American National CattleWomen, Inc. in cooperation with the Beef Industry Council and the Beef Board."

Vicki Wadlington
Tennessee

Natosha Kennedy, Wellington, Co.

Hot Hunan Hoagies
1986 Best of Beef (Winner)

2-lbs. beef top round steak, cut 1 inch thick
3 cloves garlic, minced
1/2 cup each dry sherry and dark soy sauce*
1/4 cup vegetable oil
1 Tbl. grated fresh ginger
Relish**
8 hoagie rolls

**Relish

2 tsp. vegetable oil
1 tsp. each dark sesame oil and white wine
　　vinegar
1/2 tsp. dark soy sauce*
1/4 tsp. sugar
1/8 tsp. hot pepper sauce
1/2 cup each sliced green onions, chopped
　　mushrooms, chopped green bell pepper
　　and chopped red bell pepper

"Recipe provided with permission from the
National Beef Cook-Off® sponsored by the
American National CattleWomen, Inc. in
cooperation with the Beef Industry Council and the
Beef Board."

Preparation time: 30 minutes
Marinating time: 4 to 8 hours
Cooking time: 15 to 18 minutes

• Place beef steak in plastic bag. Combine garlic,
sherry, soy sauce, oil and ginger; reserve 1/4 cup.
Pour remaining marinade over steak. Close bag
securely and marinate in refrigerator 4 to 8 hours,
turning at least once. Meanwhile prepare Relish.
Remove steak from marinade; discard marinade.
Place steak on rack in broiler pan so surface of
meat is 4 inches from heat. Broil 15 to 18
minutes, turning once and basting with reserved
marinade. Let stand 5 minutes. Meanwhile split
hoagie rolls and toast under broiler. Carve steak
diagonally across the grain into thin slices. Place
beef in hoagie rolls; top with Relish and serve.
• 8 servings
*Dark soy sauce is available in Oriental section of
the supermarket.

Relish Instructions
• Combine vegetable oil, sesame oil, vinegar, soy
sauce, sugar and hot pepper sauce. Add green
onions, mushrooms and bell peppers. Let stand
30 minutes.

• Yield: About 1-3/4 cups

Bette Phillips
New Jersey

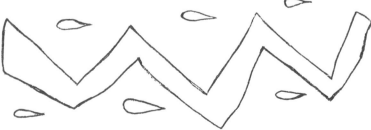

99　　　*Kylee Smylie, Wellington, Co.*

Tropical Grilled Flank Steak with Fresh Fruit Salsa

1987 Best of Beef (Winner)

1-1/2 lb. beef flank steak
1/4 cup fresh orange juice
2 Tbl. each chili sauce, soy sauce and
   vegetable oil
1 tsp. each sugar and grated orange peel
2 cloves garlic, minced
1/2 tsp. salt
1/8 tsp. hot pepper sauce
1 medium orange, thinly sliced
fresh Fruit Salsa*
Orange wedges
Fresh cilantro

*Fresh Fruit Salsa

1/2 cup each diced pineapple, mango, papaya
   and green apple
1/4 cup each diced red and green pepper
2 Tbl. rice vinegar or white wine vinegar
1 Tbl. minced fresh cilantro
4 tsp. sugar
1/4 tsp. crushed red pepper pods

"Recipe provided with permission from the National Beef Cook-Off® sponsored by the American National CattleWomen, Inc. in cooperation with the Beef Industry Council and the Beef Board."

Preparation time: 25 minutes
marinating time: 3 hours or overnight
cooking time: 10 to 14 minutes

• Combine orange juice, chili sauce, soy sauce, oil, sugar, orange peel, garlic, salt and hot pepper sauce. Place beef steak in plastic bag; add marinade, turning to coat. Place orange slices on top of steak. Close bag securely and marinate in refrigerator 3 hours (or overnight, if desired), turning occasionally. Pour off marinade and orange slices; discard. Place steak on grid over medium coals.** Grill 10 to 14 minutes, turning once. Meanwhile prepare Fresh Fruit Salsa. Carve steak into thin slices. Serve steak with salsa. Garnish with orange wedges and cilantro.
• 4 servings.

• Combine pineapple, mango, papaya, apple, red and green pepper, vinegar, cilantro, sugar and red pepper pods. (may be prepared one day in advance, if desired.)
• Yield: About 2-1/2 cups.

• **Test about 4 inches above coals for medium with 4-second hand count.

Debbie Vannie
Illinois

Nick Stanton, Wellington, Co.

Oriental Short Rib Barbecue
1988 Best of Beef (Winner)

4 lbs. beef rib short ribs, trimmed of excess fat
    and cut crosswise no more than 3/8 to 1/2-
    inch thick*
2/3 cup thinly sliced green onions
1/2 cup each soy sauce and water
1/4 cup dark sesame oil
2-1/2 Tbl. packed brown sugar
1-1/2 Tbl. toasted sesame seeds, crushed
1 Tbl. each minced garlic and grated fresh
    ginger
1/2 tsp. ground red pepper
1/8 tsp. freshly ground Szechuan
    peppercorns**
Fresh red chili peppers
Green onions
Radish roses

Preparation time: 15 minutes
Marinating time: 4 to 6 hours
Cooking time: 10 to 12 minutes

• Combine sliced green onions, soy sauce, water, sesame oil, brown sugar, sesame seeds, garlic, ginger, red pepper and Szechuan peppercorns; reserve 1/2 cup marinade. Place beef ribs and marinade in plastic bag, turning to coat. Close bag securely and marinate in refrigerator 4 to 6 hours, turning occasionally. Remove ribs from marinade. Place ribs on grid over medium coals*** and grill 5 to 6 minutes. Turn ribs over; brush with reserved marinade. Cover and continue cooking 5 to 6 minutes or until desired degree of doneness. Place ribs on platter; garnish with chili peppers, green onions and radish roses.
• 6 servings

• *Beef rib short ribs, cut 3/8 to 1/2-inch thick, may be special-ordered from your meat retailer. Each rib piece should contain 3 crosscut rib bones.
**Szechuan peppercorns are available in the Oriental section of the supermarket. Freshly ground black pepper may be substituted for the Szechuan peppercorns.
***Test about 4 inches above coals for medium with 4-second hand count.

"Recipe provided with permission from the National Beef Cook-Off® sponsored by the American National CattleWomen, Inc. in cooperation with the Beef Industry Council and the Beef Board."

John Michels
Minnesota

Ron Betts, Wellington, Co.

Mexican Carne

3-lb. boneless beef brisket
2 Tbl. vegetable oil
2 cups mild picante sauce
3/4 cup water
1/2 cup slivered almonds
2 Tbl. distilled white vinegar
1 tsp. garlic powder
1/2 tsp. salt
1/4 tsp. each ground cinnamon, dried oregano
    leaves and dried thyme leaves
1/8 tsp. each ground cloves and pepper
Mexican Rice*
Red and green pepper strips
Toasted slivered almonds
Fresh Oregano sprig.

Mexican Rice

2 Tbl. vegetable oil
1 cup long grain rice
4 green onions, chopped
2 to 2 1/4 cups water
1 tsp. salt
1/4 tsp. garlic powder
1/4 cup diced red bell pepper
2 Tbl. diced green bell pepper

"Recipe provided with permission from the National Beef Cook-Off® sponsored by the American National CattleWomen, Inc. in cooperation with the Beef Industry Council and the Beef Board."

Preparation time: 25 minutes
Cooking time: 3 hours

• Trim excess fat from boneless brisket; cut into 1-inch cubes. Brown beef in batches (1/3 at a time) in oil in Dutch oven over medium-high heat. Combine picante sauce, water, slivered almonds, vinegar, garlic powder, salt, cinnamon, dried oregano, thyme, cloves and pepper. Combine with beef in Dutch oven; bring to a boil. Reduce heat; simmer, covered 2 1/2 to 3 hours or until beef is tender, adding water if needed. Prepare Mexican Rice 35 minutes before serving. Serve beef with Mexican Rice. Garnish with bell pepper strips, toasted almonds and fresh oregano.
• 6 to 8 servings

Mexican Rice Instructions
Preparation time: 5 minutes
Cooking time: 35 minutes
• Heat oil in medium saucepan over medium-high heat until hot. Add rice and green onions. Cook 10 minutes or until rice is golden brown, stirring frequently. Stir in 2 cups water, salt and garlic powder; bring to a boil. Reduce heat; simmer, covered, 20 minutes. Add remaining water if rice is dry, Sprinkle red and green bell peppers on top of rice; do not stir. Simmer, covered, 5 minutes longer or until water is absorbed and rice is tender. Yield: 4 cups

Susan Bartel
Colorado

Sarah Smith, Wellington, Co.

Prairie Chili Verde

1 1/2 lbs. coarse ground beef (80 percent lean)*
1 Tbl. chili powder
Coarsely ground black pepper to taste
1 medium onion, chopped
1 green bell pepper, chopped
2 cloves garlic, minced
1 can (16 ounces) tomatoes, broken up
1 can (15 ounces) black or pinto beans, drained
1 can (7 ounces) diced mild green chilies**
1/2 cup single-strength beef broth
1 Tbl. each finely chopped fresh cilantro and fresh lemon juice
1 tsp. diced oregano leaves, preferably Mexican
Salt to taste
1.4 tsp. hot pepper sauce, if desired
Shredded Cheddar cheese

"Recipe provided with permission from the National Beef Cook-Off® sponsored by the American National CattleWomen, Inc. in cooperation with the Beef Industry Council and the Beef Board."

Preparation time; 20 minutes
Microwave cooking time: 19 minutes

• Combine coarse ground beef, chili powder and black pepper in 3-quart microwave-safe casserole; mix lightly. Add onion, green pepper and garlic; mix lightly. Microwave, uncovered, at high 5 to 7 minutes or until beef is only slightly pink, stirring occasionally. Pour off drippings. Add tomatoes, beans, chilies, beef broth, chopped cilantro, lemon juice, oregano and salt; mix well. Microwave, uncovered, at HIGH 14 minutes, stirring every 4 minutes. If hotter chili is desired, stir in pepper sauce. Garnish with cheese.
• 6 servings

*Coarse ground beef may be ordered and ground by your meat retailer.
**Three cans (4 ounces each) diced chilies may be substituted for one 7-ounce can plus one 4-ounce can.

Elaine Laue
Colorado

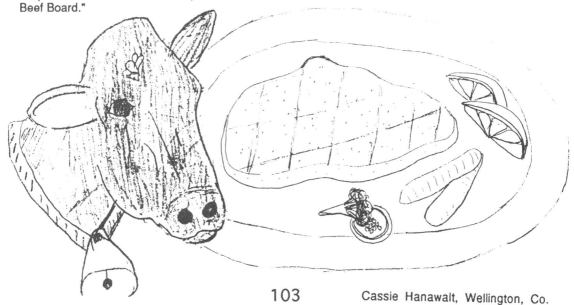

103   Cassie Hanawalt, Wellington, Co.

BEEF COOK-OFF

Pronto Spicy Beef and Black Bean Salsa
1993 Best of Beef (Winner)

1 beef tri-tip (bottom sirloin) roast or tip sirloin
    steak, cut 1-1/2 inches thick
1 can (15 ounces) black beans, rinsed, drained
1 medium tomato, chopped
1 small red onion, finely chopped
3 Tbl. coarsely chopped fresh cilantro
Fresh Cilantro sprigs (optional)

Seasoning
1 Tbl. chili powder
1 tsp. ground cumin
1 tsp. salt
1/2 tsp. ground red pepper

Total preparation and cooking time: 40 minutes

• Combine seasoning ingredients: reserve 2 teaspoons for salsa. Trim fat from beef roast. Press remaining seasoning mixture evenly into surface of roast.
• Place tri-tip on grid over medium coals(medium-low coals for top sirloin). Grill 30 to 35 minutes (top sirloin 22 to 30 minutes) for rare to medium doneness, turning occasionally. Let stand 10 minutes before carving.
• Meanwhile, in medium bowl, combine beans, tomato, onion, chopped cilantro and reserved seasoning mixture; mix until blended.
• Carve roast across the grain into slices. Arrange beef and bean salsa on serving platter; garnish with cilantro sprigs, if desired.
• Makes 6 servings (serving size: 1/6 of recipe).

Cook's Tip
• Test about 4 inches above coals for medium-low with a 4 to 5 second hand count.
• To broil tri-tip, place roast on rack in broiler pan so surface of meat is 4 to 5 inches from heat. Broil 25 to 30 minutes for rare to medium doneness, turning once.

Sylvia Harber
Boulder City, NV

Jolene Charvat, Wellington, Co.

 LAMB

Chance Tarr, Wellington, Co.

Colorado ranks as the number one state for lamb feeding in the nation, and number four for inventory of sheep and lambs, with an estimated 685,000 head.

C.S.U. Dept. of Agriculture

Travis Bredehoft, Wellington, Co.

LAMB

Rocky Mountain Grill

4 American lamb chops (about 1 lb.)
    loin, rib or shoulder chops
2 Tbl. each: water, oil, balsamic vinegar
1/2 tsp. lemon pepper
1/4 tsp. cayenne pepper
1-1/2 tsp. dry sage, crumbled
1 tsp. grated onion
1/2 tsp. coarse-grained mustard
    (Dijon)

• Mix all ingredients except the chops. Place in non-metal container. Marinate the chops covered in the refrigerator for 2 - 24 hours. Remove from marinade and broil or grill about 12 minutes, turning once. If in a hurry, mix the marinade and baste the chops with the mixture while cooking. Calories 133, Total Fat 8 g, Saturated Fat 2g, Cholesterol 44 mg, Sodium 148 mg.

John M. Olson
Executive Director of the American Sheep
Industry Association

Mexican Lamb Stew

1-1/2 lbs. boneless lamb, cut into 1/2 inch
    cubes
1 tsp. salt
1/4 tsp. chili powder
1/4 cup flour
1-1/2 tsp. black pepper
1/2 tsp. garlic powder
1 Tbl. oil
1 tsp. instant chicken bouillon
3 Tbl. picante sauce
1 green pepper, diced
2 tsp. chili powder
1 (4 oz.) can green chilies, drained
8 oz. tomato sauce
1/2 cup onion, chopped
12 oz. can corn, drained
15 oz. can pinto beans, drained

•Combine flour and seasonings in plastic bag. Add lamb cubes and coat thoroughly. Heat oil and brown lamb over medium heat.

•Add bouillon, picante, green pepper, chili powder, tomato sauce and onion to the meat mixture. Cook in slow cooker for 8 hours on low. Add the corn, pintos and green chilies the last hour of cooking. Top with grated cheese, sour cream and olives if desired. Can also be simmered on top of the stove.

John M. Olson
Exec. Dir. American Sheep Industry Assoc.
Englewood, CO

Heather Marshall, Wellington, Co.

30 Minute Szechwan Lamb Stir-Fry

1 lb. boneless American lamb shoulder, cut
    into 1/8" strips
2 Tbl. reduced sodium soy sauce
4 tsp. Oriental dark roasted sesame oil,
    divided
1-1/2 tsp. sugar
1 tsp. cornstarch
2 cloves garlic, crushed
1 Tbl. minced fresh ginger
1/4 tsp. crushed red pepper pods
1 small red bell pepper, cut 1 inch strips
1 pkg. frozen baby corn, defrosted
1/4 lb. snow pea pods, julienned

• Combine soy sauce, 2 teaspoons oil, sugar and cornstarch; stir into lamb strips. Heat remaining 2 teaspoons of oil in large skillet over medium high heat. Add garlic, ginger and crushed red pepper pods. Cook 30 seconds. Add bell pepper and corn; stir-fry 1-1/2 minutes. Add pea pods, stir-fry 30 seconds. Remove vegetables from skillet; reserve.
• Stir-fry lamb strips for 2-3 minutes. Add vegetables to lamb strips and stir-fry until lamb and vegetables are heated through.

Nancy Rundel, Grand Prize Winner
1993 Hi-Country Lamb Cook-off
Pierce, Colo.

Meghan Scott, Wellington, Co.

LAMB

Lamb Loin ala Dalton

Lamb loin, boned
1/2 cup olive oil
1 tsp. freshly grated orange peel
1 tsp. Dijon mustard
2 large garlic cloves, minced
1-1/2 tsp. minced fresh thyme
1 bay leaf, crumbled
1 Tbl. fresh parsley
1/2 tsp. ground pepper
1/2 tsp. salt

• Mix all ingredients in bowl. Place loin in ziplock bag with ingredients. Refrigerate overnight. Remove from refrigerator. Bring to room temperature before cooking. Cook on grill until done to medium to medium rare (approx. 5-7 mintues on each side).

The Dalton Gang
Jim Dalton Family, Eaton, CO
3rd Place Grand Prize Winner
1993 Hi-Country Lamb Cook-Off

Lamb-Pita Pocket Picnic

<u>Lamb Patties:</u>
1-1/2 lbs. lean ground lamb
2 Tbl. each: chopped fresh oregano, mint and chives
Salt and lemon pepper (use during cooking)
Pita pocket bread

<u>Cucumber Sauce:</u>
1 cucumber, seeded and peeled
1/2 cup sour cream
2 Tbl. plain yogurt or mayo
1 Tbl. fresh lemon juice
Dried dill weed
Salt and pepper to taste

• <u>Patties:</u> Mix fresh chopped herbs into ground lamb. Form patties 3/4 - 1" in thickness and 3-1/2 to 4 inches round. Grill over charcoal approx. 3-4 minutes each side. Do not overcook! Serve patties in pocket bread with thinly sliced tomato and feta cheese slices, topped with cucumber sauce.
• <u>Cucumber sauce:</u> Puree cucumber in blender or cuisinart until pulp. Add remaining ingredients. You can really use your imagination with garnish on these.

Mrs. Harold Harper
Wife of lamb feeder in Weld County
Shoulder - 2nd place 1993 Hi Country Lamb
Cook-off

Natosha Kennedy, Wellington, Co.

Marinated Lamb Florentine

1 butterflied boneless leg of lamb
1/2 lb. ground lamb

Marinade:
16 oz. Kikomann soy sauce
12 oz. beer
1/4 tsp. ginger
1/8 tsp. clove
1 tsp. garlic
15 leaves minced fresh mint
1 cup brown sugar

Ground Lamb:
Knead the following ingredients into the ground
    lamb:
1/2 tsp. garlic
1/8 tsp. clove
1/8 tsp. ginger
1/2 tsp. salt
1/2 tsp. pepper
10 leaves minced fresh mint
1/4 cup marinate

• Stir marinade well. Let stand overnight.

• Marinate boneless leg for three hours. After marinating lay leg out flat. Place ground lamb mixture in center of leg. Roll and tie. Grill approx. 2 hours and 15 minutes at indirect heat. Let roast breathe for 10 minutes. Slice and serve.

Tim Sebald & Gary Schrecongost
Monfort Corp. Lamb Sales - Greeley, CO
2nd Place Grand Prize Winner
1993 Hi-Country Lamb Cook-Off

Tiffany Bishop, Wellington, Co.

Bryce Hall, Wellington, Co.

Modern Moussaka

2 med. eggplants (7-8" not Japanese)
Oil
Garlic salt
2 large, chopped onions
2 onions
2 Tbl. margarine or oil
1 lb. ground lamb
6 oz. tomato paste
1-1/2 cups red wine
1/2 cup fresh parsley - chopped
1/4 tsp. cinnamon
6 Tbl. butter
6 Tbl. flour
4 cups milk
4 beaten eggs
2 cups cottage cheese
1/8 tsp. nutmeg
1 cup bread crumbs
1 cup grated Parmesan cheese

• Peel and slice eggplants thinly (1/3 " to 1/2"). "Sweat" slices - see pg. 140. Rinse and pat dry. Lay slices on oiled jelly roll pan. Brush with oil, sprinkle with garlic salt and broil both sides for 2-3 minutes until lightly browned.
• Sauté onions in oil until transparent.
• Microwave lamb until all pink is gone - stirring each minute; or brown in a skillet. Be sure to drain off ALL grease and blot the cooked meat with paper towels. Add cooked lamb to onions.
• Stir in tomato paste, wine, parsley and cinnamon. Cook over medium heat, stirring frequently until liquid is absorbed. Set aside.
• Make white sauce with butter, flour and milk. When thick and smooth, remove from heat. Cool slightly. Stir in eggs, cottage cheese and nutmeg.
• Grease 11x16 pan. Sprinkle with bread crumbs and Parmesan cheese. Alternate layers of eggplant and meat sauce, sprinkling between each layer with bread crumbs and Parmesan cheese. Pour white sauce over entire pan (may have to shake out some air bubbles).
• Bake 1 hour at 375°, or until top is golden. Cool 20-30 minutes before serving. May refrigerate and reheat the next day. After the flavors blend it will be even better!

Nan Zimmerman
One of Eyestone's VIP's of the Year

Nathan Hawley, Wellington, Co.

 CHICKEN / POULTRY

Stephanie Pfaff, Wellington, Co.

The annual impact of the turkey industry on the Colorado economy is estimated to be $100 million.

C.S.U. - Dept. of Agriculture

Chicken In Sour Cream

1 cut-up frying chicken
1 can mushrooms
1 can cream of mushroom soup
1/2 cup sherry
1 cup sour cream

• Arrange chicken in shallow pan; cover with mushrooms. Combine sherry, mushroom soup and sour cream. Stir until blended. Pour over chicken. Bake at 350° for 1-1/2 hours.
• I like to add fresh tarragon for a "punch". Great with baked potatoes.

Representative Maryanne "Moe" Keller
Colorado State Representative
Wheatridge, Colo.

Haley Perry, Wellington, Co.

Chicken - Artichoke Casserole

1 can chicken broth
4 large whole chicken breasts
1 can (14 oz) drained artichoke hearts
1/4 - 1/2 lb. sliced mushrooms
6 Tbl. butter
1/4 cup flour
1/4 tsp. salt
1/8 tsp. pepper
3/4 cup half and half
2 Tbl. sherry
1/2 tsp. dried rosemary
1/2 cup grated parmesan cheese

• Cook chicken in chicken broth. Remove skin and debone chicken.
• In shallow casserole, arrange artichoke hearts, mushrooms and chicken (large pieces or slices).
• In pan over medium heat melt butter, stir in flour, salt and pepper until blended. Gradually add 3/4 cup chicken broth, 3/4 cup half & half. Cook until mixture boils. Stir in parmesan cheese, sherry and rosemary. Then pour over chicken in casserole.
• Bake uncovered 325° for 30-40 minutes.
Serves 6-8.

Byron R. White
Retired Associate Justice US Supreme Court

Blanca Burgos, Wellington, Co.

 CHICKEN - POULTRY

100% Parmesan Chicken Breast

6 boneless skinless chicken breast halves
(about 2 lbs.)
2 Tbl. Parkay Spread Sticks, melted
1/2 cup (2 oz.) Kraft 100% Grated Parmesan
Cheese
1/4 cup dry bread crumbs
1 tsp. each dried oregano leaves and parsley
flakes
1/4 tsp. each paprika, salt and black pepper

• Heat oven to 400° F. Spray 15 x 10 x 1-inch baking pan with no stick cooking spray.
• Dip chicken in melted Parkay Spread; coat with combined remaining ingredients. Place in prepared pan.
• Bake 20 to 25 minutes or until tender.
• Makes 6 servings.
• Spicy: Substitute 1/8 to 1/4 tsp. ground red pepper for black pepper.

KRAFT Creative Kitchens

Swiss and Chicken Casserole

4 cups chopped cooked chicken
2 cups croutons
2 cups sliced celery
1 pkg. (8 oz.) Kraft Natural Aged Swiss Cheese
Slices, cut into thin strips
1 cup Miracle Whip Salad Dressing
1/2 cup milk
1/4 cup chopped onion
1 tsp. salt
Dash pepper
1/4 cup chopped walnuts, toasted

• Heat oven to 350° F.
• Mix all ingredients except walnuts.
• Spoon into 2-quart casserole; sprinkle with walnuts.
• Bake 40 minutes or until thoroughly heated. Makes 6 servings.

MICROWAVE: • Substitute 12 x 8-inch microwavable baking dish for 2-quart casserole. • Mix all ingredients except walnuts. • Spoon into baking dish; sprinkle with walnuts. • Microwave on HIGH 15 minutes or until thoroughly heated, turning dish every 5 minutes.

KRAFT Creative Kitchens

Brittany Barella, Wellington, Co.

Chicken Diane

4 chicken breast halves, 8 oz. each, skinned and boned
2 Tbl. butter
1/4 cup green onions, thinly sliced
2 oz. mushrooms, thinly sliced
1-1/2 Tbl. flour
1/8 tsp. thyme
1/4 cup chicken broth
1/4 cup milk
1/4 cup dry white wine
Salt and freshly ground black pepper to taste
4 oz. crabmeat
2-2/3 Tbl. parsley, minced
2-2/3 Tbl. bread crumbs
3/4 cup Swiss cheese

• Pound chicken breasts between wax paper until 1/4 inch thick. Set aside.
• Melt butter in sauté pan over medium heat. Add onion and mushrooms and cook 5 minutes. Stir in flour and thyme and cook 1 minute. Slowly add chicken broth, milk and wine. Cook, stirring constantly, until sauce thickens. Remove from heat and season with salt and freshly ground black pepper.
• In a small bowl, mix together 1/4 cup sauce, crab, parsley and bread crumbs. Place 1/4 of filling on each chicken breast. Roll chicken breast around filling. Place, seam side down, in a greased baking dish.
• Pour remaining sauce over rolled chicken breasts. Sprinkle with cheese. Cover and cook in a 400° oven for 30 minutes or until done.

Dione Fabeck
The Castaways Restaurant
Manitou Springs, Colorado

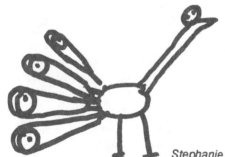

Stephanie Pfaff, Wellington, Co.

Tiffany Bishop, Wellington, Co.

Spiced Roast Chicken

1 (3-1/2 lb.) chicken
1 Tbl. margarine
2/3 cup marsala (white wine)

Mushroom Stuffing:
2 Tbl. olive oil
1 onion, finely chopped
1 tsp. garam marsala (at Alfalfa's)
4 oz. button, brown or chestnut mushrooms, chopped
1 cup coarsely grated parsnips
1 cup coarsely grated carrots
1/4 cup minced walnuts
2 tsp. chopped fresh thyme
1 cup fresh white bread crumbs
1 egg, beaten
Salt and pepper to taste

To Garnish:
Thyme and watercress sprigs

• Preheat oven to 375° F (109° C)
• Prepare Stuffing: In a large saucepan, heat olive oil; add onion and sauté 2 minutes or until softened. Stir in garam marsala and cook 1 minute. Add mushrooms, parsnips and carrots; cook, stirring 5 minutes. Remove from heat; stir in remaining stuffing ingredients.
• Stuff and truss chicken. Place breast down, in a roasting pan; add 1/4 cup water. Roast 45 minutes; turn chicken breast up and dot with margarine. Roast about 45 minutes or until a meat thermometer inserted in thickest part of thigh (not touching bone) registers 185°F (85 C°). Transfer to platter; keep warm.
• Pour off and discard fat from roasting pan; add marsala to remaining cooking juices, stirring to scrape up any browned bits. Boil over high heat 1 minute to reduce slightly; adjust seasoning.
• Remove skin and carve chicken. Garnish with thyme and watercress springs. Serve with stuffing, flavored meat juices and seasonal vegetables.
• Makes 4 servings.

Tipper Gore
Wife of Vice-President Al Gore

Adam Scripture, Wellington, Co.

Blanca Burgos, Wellington, Co.

115

CHICKEN - POULTRY

The Bowlen Family Chicken Recipe

6 whole skinned chicken breasts with bone in
   and not split
4 egg yolks slightly beaten in dipping bowl
1-1/2 cups fresh white bread crumbs blended in
   Cuisinart
1-1/2 cups grated parmesan cheese
1/2 cup soft margarine
3 Tbl. butter for frying pan
3 Tbl. oil for frying pan
Salt, pepper and ginger for seasoning

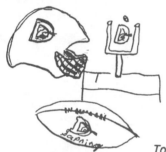

• Mix bread crumbs and parmesan cheese in a large bowl. Heat butter and oil in a large electric skillet. Set skillet to 350°. Use enough butter and oil to keep from sticking to the pan. Season chicken with salt, pepper and ginger. Smooth the softened margarine over chicken breasts and dip in egg yolk. Coat and pat bread crumbs and parmesan cheese mixture over entire chicken breasts. Brown all sides of chicken. Turn frequently to avoid burning. After browning, place chicken breasts side up, turn heat down to very low, cover and cook slowly for approximately 45-50 minutes. Do not overcook.
• This dish is perfectly complimented when served with Fettucine Alfredo!

Pat Bowlen
President and Chief Executive Office
Denver **Broncos** Football Club

Tom McChesney, Wellington, Co.

Barbecue Chicken Pizza

1 Tbl. oil
4 boneless skinless chicken breast halves
   (about 1-1/4 lbs.), cut into thin strips
1/2 cup Kraft Thick N' Spicy Mesquite Smoke
   Barbecue Sauce
1 lg. (1 lb.) Boboli Italian Bread Shell
1 green pepper, cut into strips
1 cup red onion rings
1 pkg. (8 oz.) Kraft Natural Shredded Sharp
   Cheddar Cheese

• Heat oven to 350° F.
• Heat oil in large skillet on medium-high heat; add chicken. Cook until chicken is lightly browned. Reduce heat to low; stir in barbecue sauce. Cook 5 minutes.
• Place bread shell on cookie sheet. Top with chicken mixture, green pepper, onion and cheese.
• Bake 12 to 15 minutes or until cheese is melted. Makes 4 servings.

KRAFT Creative Kitchens

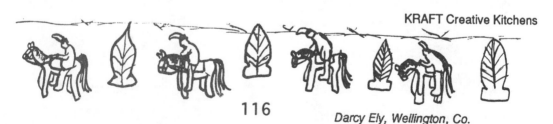

116

Darcy Ely, Wellington, Co.

CHICKEN - POULTRY

Keith's "Over-The-Counter" Chicken

1 lb. boneless, skinless chicken breasts, sliced
    into strips
1 medium to large onion, sliced and separated
    into rings
2 cloves minced garlic
1/2 Tbl. chili powder
1/2 Tbl. seasoned pepper
1 cup salsa
1/3 cup shredded low-fat Monterey Jack
    cheese
1 to 1-1/2 cups whole-grain, fast-cooking wild
    rice

• Sprinkle on seasoned pepper and chili powder while browning chicken in a small amount of oil using a 10-inch skillet on medium-high heat.
• After chicken browns slightly, add onions and garlic. Stir and cook two more minutes. Stir in salsa. Heat to very slow boil. Stir in rice, cover tightly, reduce heat and simmer 5 minutes.
• Remove from heat and let stand 5 minutes. Add cheese. Re-cover to let cheese melt.

Keith Weinman, Business Editor and Reporter
KCNC TV Channel 4/News Radio 85 KOA
Denver, CO

Honey Mustard Chicken

1 can (20 oz.) pineapple slices in juice
4 boneless, skinless chicken breast halves
Salt and pepper to taste
2 large cloves garlic, pressed
1 tsp. thyme, crumbled
2 tsp. vegetable oil
1 Tbl. cornstarch
1/4 cup honey
1/4 cup Dijon mustard

• Drain pineapple; reserve juice. Sprinkle chicken with salt and pepper to taste. Rub with garlic and thyme. Brown in hot oil in a non-stick skillet.
• Combine 2 Tbl. reserved pineapple juice with cornstarch. Set aside.
• Combine honey and mustard and stir into chicken skillet with remaining pineapple juice.
• Spoon sauce over chicken, cover and simmer 15 minutes. Stir cornstarch mixture into pan juices. Add pineapple and cook stirring until sauce boils and thicken.

Great! Serves 4.

Gary and Johanne Wayne
Colorado Rockies' Pitcher and Wife
Lakewood, CO

Kirt Royball, Wellington, Co.

117

Chicken and Rice "Salsa"

2 boneless chicken breasts
1 cup uncooked brown rice
1 Tbl. oil
1 cup salsa

Flour tortillas
2 cups frozen corn

• Cut chicken into cubes. Brown in frying pan with oil. While you are doing this, cook the cup of brown rice according to package directions. After the chicken is cooked add cup of salsa. Simmer while rice cooks. When rice is finished cooking add to chicken. Simmer for 5 minutes. Serve with cooked corn and flour tortillas. for a complete meal.

Sonia Danielsen
President Eastwood Printing
Denver, CO

Kathern O'Brien, Wellington, Co.

Chicken Enchiladas

4 cups cooked diced chicken (I use all white meat)
1/2 cup diced onions
2 cups cheddar cheese
3 cans cream of chicken soup
1 or 2 cans diced green chili peppers (mild or hot)
10 or 12 corn tortillas
1 cup sour cream

• Mix 1-1/2 cups cheddar cheese, onions, soup, chilies and sour cream. After mixing put some in an extra bowl to spread on top of tortillas before baking. Add chicken and mix well. Spoon filling into tortilla and roll up and place in a greased 9 x 13 pan. Place side-by-side. Top with extra sauce and extra cheese. Bake at 350° for 45 minutes.

Sue Gano
Godfather's Pizza

Eddie Rodrigues, Wellington, Co.

118

"Will's Fabulous" Green Chili Chicken Casserole

2 pkgs. chicken breasts (about 6 split chicken
　　breasts with bone)
3/4 lb. cheddar
3/4 lb. Monterey Jack
1 doz. corn tortillas
1 small can evaporated milk
1 can cream of celery soup
2 cans cream of chicken soup
1 small jar HOT Pace Picante sauce
1 can (approx. 4 inches by 4 inches) green chili
　　strips (not diced or chopped)

• Boil chicken until cooked. Hand-shred the meat from the bones *after* cooling. Grate the cheeses and mix together. Prepare the goop (mix together in bowl): evaporated milk, soups and 2/3 of small jar of picante.

• Preheat oven to 350°. Cut tortillas into long strips 1 to 1-3/8 inches wide. In large casserole dish (quantities will make 2nd smaller one to freeze) baste the bottom of pan with thin later of goop; <u>save half the goop for the top of the casserole.</u> Start layering, as with lasagna, 2-3 thin layers of: shredded chicken, tortilla strips, grated cheese, green chili strips and sprinklings of goop

• Top layer of dish is liberal layer of goop. Spike the entire dish in 7-10 places with knife to allow some goop to dribble into under layers. Cover with cover or aluminum foil. Bake for approx. 1 hour. For the last 10 minutes remove cover. Probe to see if center is hot. Cool for 10 minutes to allow casserole to set up. Freezes well; serve with Spanish rice and green salad.　　THAT'S IT!

Will Hobbs
Author of young adult novels:
<u>Bearstone</u>, <u>Beardance</u>, <u>Downriver</u>,
<u>The Big Wander</u> and <u>Changes in Latitude</u>
Colorado Blue Spruce winner -1992

Devani Dawson, Wellington, Co.

Scott Smith, Wellington, Co.

119

Old-Fashioned Chicken Pot Pie

1 (3-1/2 lb.) broiler-fryer
2 quarts water
1 tsp. salt
1/2 tsp. pepper
1 stalk celery, cut into 2-inch pieces
1 medium onion, quartered
1 bay leaf

1 (16 oz.) package frozen mixed vegetables
2 large potatoes, peeled and cubed

1/2 cup butter or margarine
1/2 cup all-purpose flour
1 cup milk
1-1/2 tsp. salt
1-1/4 tsp. pepper
1/4 tsp. dried thyme

2 hard-cooked eggs, sliced
1 (9-inch) refrigerated pie crust

• Combine first 7 ingredients in a large Dutch oven; bring to a boil. Cover, reduce heat, and simmer 1 hour or until chicken is tender. Remove chicken, reserving broth in Dutch oven; discard vegetables and bay leaf. Let chicken cool. Skin, bone, and cut into bite-size pieces. With a large spoon, skim fat (oily liquid) from surface of broth reserved in Dutch oven; bring broth to a boil. Add frozen vegetables and potatoes; return to a boil. Reduce heat, cover, and simmer 8 minutes or until tender. Remove vegetables from broth, and set aside. Measure 3 cups broth; set aside. Reserve remaining broth for other uses.
• Melt butter in Dutch oven over low heat; add flour, stirring until smooth. Cook 1 minute, stirring constantly. Gradually add 3 cups broth and milk; cook over medium heat, stirring constantly, until mixture is thickened and bubbly. Stir in 1-1/2 tsp. salt, 1-1/4 tsp. pepper and thyme. Add vegetables, chicken and hard-cooked eggs; stir gently. Spoon into a lightly greased 13 x 9 x 2-inch baking dish; set aside.
• Roll out pie crust on a lightly floured surface into a 15 x 11-inch rectangle (pie crust will be very thin). Place over chicken mixture; crimp edges, pressing against sides of baking dish. Cut slits in top for steam to escape; bake at 400° for 20 minutes or until golden brown. Yield: 6 to 8 servings.

Amanda McGregor, Wellington, Co.

Peggy T. Smith
Foods Assistant - Southern Living

Brittany Lockwood, Wellington, Co.

Lavender Pepper Duck Breast with Raspberry/Red Zinfandel Sauce

Raspberry/Red Zinfandel Sauce:
2 cups cold water
12 oz. Individually quick frozen raspberries
1-1/2 tsp. chicken base
2/3 cup sugar
2 cups Red Zinfandel
1/3 cup dark rum
2 Tbl. corn starch
1/2 cup cold water
2 Tbl. creme de cassis
6 each boneless duck breasts

Lavender Pepper Rub:
2 Tbl. Tellicherry black peppercorns
2 Tbl. sea salt
2 Tbl. fennel seeds
2 Tbl. lavender
1 Tbl. white pepper

• Combine raspberries and water in heavy sauce pan and bring to boil. Reduce heat, simmer for 5 minutes; add chicken base and sugar. Stir until sugar dissolves and continue to simmer. Add Zinfandel and rum and continue to simmer until reduced by 1/4. Combine cornstarch with 1/2 cup cold water and add to sauce. Bring sauce back to a boil, simmer for 5 minutes and remove from heat. Stir in creme de cassis. Force sauce through double mesh strainer.
• Lavender Pepper Rub:
Combine all ingredients in a blender and process until all seeds are reduced to a coarse grind. Skin duck breasts and rub with lavender mixture 1 hour prior to cooking. Grill duck breasts over hot fire until medium rare. Allow to stand for 5 minutes and slice.
• Serve each breast with 2 ounces of sauce.

Buckhorn Exchange
George Carlberg, Executive Chef
Denver, CO

Sara Foote, Wellington, Co.

Natosha Kennedy, Wellington, Co.

Shoyu Chinese Chicken Wings

6 Tbl. cooking oil
1-1/2 cup shoyu (soy sauce)
5 Tbl. brown sugar
1/2 cup water
3 - 4 pieces star anise
1/2 tsp. cinnamon
3 - 4 boxes (1 lb.) chicken wings

Chinese parsley
Onions

Heat pan. Add oil, shoyu (soy sauce), brown sugar, water, star anise and cinnamon. Bring to boill and add wings. Simmer for 20 minutes or until tender. Garnish with Chinese parsley and onions.

Rusti Ruth
Friend of Education
Redding, Calif.

Turkey and Stuffing Quiche

Mari Burgos, Wellington, Co.

2-1/2 - 3 cups leftover stuffing or 6-oz. pkg.
    chicken stuffing
1 cup chopped, cooked turkey
1 cup shredded Swiss cheese
4 eggs, beaten
1 (5-1/2 oz.) can evaporated milk
1/2 tsp. freshly ground black pepper

If using stuffing mix, prepare according to package directions. Press stuffing into greased 9-inch pie plate or quiche pan, forming a crust. Bake at 400° for 10 minutes. Remove from oven. In small bowl, combine turkey and Swiss cheese; set aside. In separate bowl, beat eggs, milk and pepper. Sprinkle turkey and cheese mixture over hot crust. Pour egg mixture over turkey. Lower oven temperature to 350° and bake quiche for 30-35 minutes or until knife inserted in center comes out clean. Let quiche stand 10 minutes before serving.
Yield: 6 servings

From Junior League of Denver's
Fantastic Cookbook: "Créme De Colorado"

Heather Marshall, Wellington, Co.

PORK

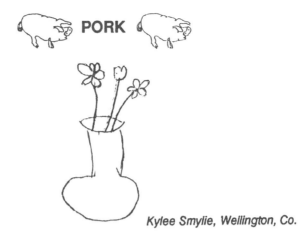

Kylee Smylie, Wellington, Co.

Colorado's pork industry produced more than 600,000 hogs in 1993.
C.S.U. Dept. of Agriculture

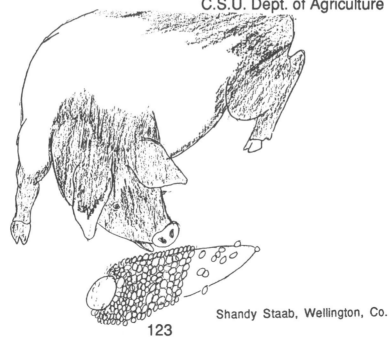

Shandy Staab, Wellington, Co.

 PORK

Biscuits and Sausage Gravy

3 cup self-rising soft wheat flour
1/4 tsp. baking soda
1 tsp. sugar
1/2 cup butter-flavored shortening
1-1/4 cup buttermilk
Butter or margarine, melted

Sausage Gravy
1/2 lb. ground pork sausage
1/4 cup butter or margarine
1/3 cup all-purpose flour
3-1/4 cup 1% low-fat or whole milk
1/2 tsp. salt
1/2 tsp. pepper
1/8 tsp. Italian seasoning

• Combine first 3 ingredients in a large bowl; cut in shortening with a pastry blender until mixture is crumbly. Add buttermilk, stirring just until dry ingredients are moistened. Turn dough out onto a lightly floured surface, and knead lightly 4 or 5 times.
• Roll dough to 3/4-inch thickness; cut with a 2-1/2-inch biscuit cutter. Place on a lightly greased baking sheet. Bake at 425° for 12 minutes or until golden. Brush tops with butter. Split biscuits open; serve with Sausage Gravy.
Yield: 12 to 14 servings.
Sausage Gravy:
• Brown sausage in a skillet, stirring until it crumbles. Drain, reserving 1 Tbl. drippings in skillet. Set sausage aside.
• Add butter to drippings; heat over low heat until butter melts. Add flour, stirring until smooth. Cook 1 minute, stirring constantly. Gradually add milk; cook over medium heat, stirring constantly, until thickened and bubbly. Stir in seasonings and sausage. Cook until thoroughly heated, stirring constantly.
Yield: 3-3/4 cups.

Diane Moats Hogan
Southern Living - Test Kitchen Home
Economist

Travis Bredehoft, Wellington, Co.

Creamy Ham-and-Chicken Medley

1 Tbl. butter or margarine
1/2 cup sliced fresh mushrooms
1/3 cup butter or margarine
1/3 cup all-purpose flour
2-1/2 to 3 cups milk, divided
1 cup whipping cream
1 cup freshly grated Parmesan cheese
1/2 tsp. salt
1/4 tsp. freshly ground black pepper
1/4 tsp. ground nutmeg
Dash of ground red pepper
2 cups chopped cooked chicken
2 cups chopped cooked ham
2 (10 oz.) pkg. commercial frozen puff pastry
    shells, baked
Paprika

• Melt 1 Tbl. butter in a large saucepan over medium heat; add mushrooms, and cook until tender, stirring constantly. Remove from saucepan; set aside.
• Melt 1/3 c. butter in saucepan over low heat; add flour, stirring until smooth. Cook 1 minute, stirring constantly. Gradually add 2-1/2 cups milk; cook over medium heat, stirring constantly, until thickened and bubbly. Stir in whipping cream and next 5 ingredients. Cook, stirring constantly, until cheese melts and mixture is smooth; stir in chicken and ham and mushrooms. Add enough of remaining 1/2 cup milk for a thinner consistency, if desired. To serve, spoon into shells, and sprinkle with paprika.
Yield: 12 servings.
Note: Creamy Ham-and-Chicken Medley may be served over hot, cooked angel hair pasta instead of pastry. Sprinkle with freshly grated Parmesan cheese, if desired.

Jane Cairns
Southern Living - Test Kitchen Home
Economist

Travis Bredehoft, Wellington, Co.

Aaron Valenciano, Wellington, Co.

 **PORK**

DAN ISSEL

"Stay away from drugs and stay in school. I know you hear this often but it is so very important. Each one of you are special in your own way and have a chance to do whatever and become whoever you want to be."

Dan Issel
Head Coach

Baked Pork Chops

4 potatoes
4 pork chops
1 can cream of celery soup
1 can green beans
1 large onion

• At the bottom of casserole dish, layer 4 sliced medium potatoes, add sliced onion, 1/3 can cream of celery soup, add green beans, 1/3 can cream of celery soup, salt and pepper, pork chops and remaining 1/3 can cream of celery soup. Cover. Bake at 325° for 1 hour and 45 minutes. Uncover. Bake an additional 15 minutes.

Dan Issel
Head Coach - Denver Nuggets

Sausage Jambalaya

2 Tbl. olive oil
1-1/2 cup chopped onion
1/2 cup chopped green onions
1/2 cup chopped bell pepper
1/4 cup chopped fresh parsley
1 cup tomato sauce
1 tsp. minced garlic
1/4 tsp. crushed dried mint
1 cup dry white wine
1-1/2 cup uncooked long grain rice
1 lb. Andouille or Cajun sausage (cooked)
Salt to taste
Louisiana hot sauce to taste

• In a large, high-walled skillet, heat the oil over medium-high heat and sauté the onions, green onions, bell pepper and parsley until the onions are clear. Stirring, add the tomato sauce, garlic, mint and wine. Then the rice, salt, hot sauce, smoked sausage and enough water to cover the rice by about 1 inch. Cook until most of the juice is gone. Reduce the heat to low, cover and simmer for 1 hour. Don't lift the lid until this has been cooking at least 45 minutes. This makes a red jambalaya. Yield: 4 to 6 servings.

Ceal Barry, Women's Basketball Coach
University of Colorado
From Justin Wilson's "Homegrown Louisiana
Cookin"

Pork Loin Roast with Brandied Fruit

4 - 5 lb. center cut pork loin roast (have your butcher prepare it by cutting a pocket along the bone)
1 part each: dried figs, raisins, dried apricots, prunes, dried sour cherries (or less of the cherries) - coarsely chopped
1 onion, chopped
1 apple, chopped
4 oz. apple cider
1/4 cup brandy
3 Tbl. maple syrup

• Sauté onion in a little oil. Add chopped apple and dried fruits and warm. Remove pan from fire and add brandy. Return to heat and CAUTIOUSLY flambé. Add maple syrup and heat through. Spoon this mixture into the pocket of the roast. Cook at 325° F for 20 - 25 min. per pound - until internal temperature of meat reaches 165° F.
• To insure that your roast will be tender and moist, try adding a little red wine and some broth to the roasting pan before putting it in the oven.

Paul Gingerich
Alfalfa's

127

Meghan Scott, Wellington, Co.

Kylee Smylie, Wellington, Co.

 PORK

BBQ Country Spareribs

4-6 lbs. country style ribs

Sauce
2 cups catsup
1 cup brown sugar
1/4 cup white wine vinegar
1 Tbl. chili powder
1 Tbl. lemon juice
2 tsp. salt
1/2 tsp. pepper
2 tsp. celery seed
1 onion (chopped)
1 cup water (or less for desired consistency)

• Place ribs in shallow baking pan. Bake at 400° for 30 minutes. Drain juices.
• Make sauce, bring to boil, and spread on ribs. Turn heat down to 300° and bake 1 hour or longer, basting every 20 minutes until done.
• Serves 6

Dennis Brimhall
CEO University Hospital
University of Colorado
Health Science Center

Schweinekotelette und Sauerkraut
(Pork Chops and Sauerkraut)

6 pork chops or country style ribs
1 medium onion (chopped)
1 lb. sauerkraut (may rinse and drain if milder
    product is desired)
2 lbs. potatoes (quartered)

• Brown chops slowly in "nonstick" skillet. Remove chops to plate. Pour off drippings. Sauté onions until clear
• in 13 x 9 inch baking dish combine onions, potatoes and sauerkraut. Tuck pork chops in.
• Cover with foil and bake at 350°F for 1 hour.

Variations: Return chops to frying pan with onions. Add 1/2 cup water. Cover and simmer 45 minutes. Make pork gravy with drippings. Simmer 10 more minutes while mashing potatoes and heating sauerkraut.

Nan Zimmerman
One of Eyestone's VIP's of the Year

Travis Bredehoft, Wellington, Co.

128

SEAFOOD - FISH

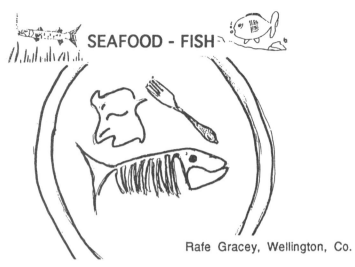

Rafe Gracey, Wellington, Co.

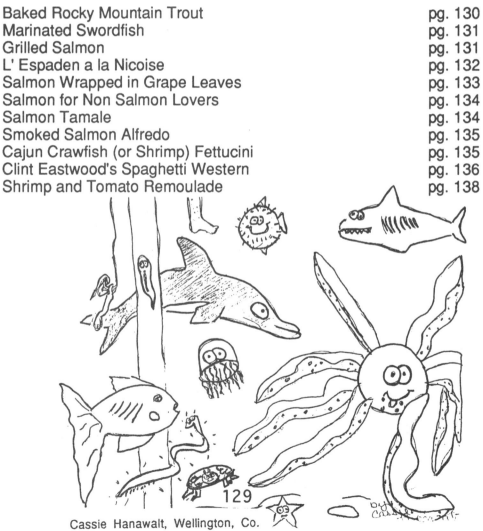

Cassie Hanawalt, Wellington, Co.

"Education is the road to opportunity and opportunity leads to success. So stay in school."

Congressman Dan Schaefer

Baked Rocky Mountain Rainbow Trout

6 fresh 1 to 1-1/2 lb. rainbow trout
6 small yellow onions, quartered
6 lemons, cut into wedges
12 strips of smoked bacon, uncooked
1 Tbl. butter-flavored salt

• Rub the cavity of each fish with butter-flavored salt. Stuff each fish with onion quarters and lemon wedges. On a section of foil, place a piece of uncooked bacon. Place fish on the bacon and top with a second piece of bacon and wrap tightly in the foil. Bake for 20-30 minutes at 350°. The fish can also be cooked on the grill over hot coals for 5-7 minutes a side. Serves 6.

Congressman Dan Schaefer
Colorado's 6th District

Aaron Scripture, Wellington, Co.

Marinated Swordfish

2 Tbl. soy sauce
2 Tbl. orange juice
1 Tbl. olive oil
1 Tbl. tomato paste
1 Tbl. chopped parsley
1 garlic clove minced
1/2 tsp. lemon juice
1/4 tsp. oregano
1/4 tsp. black pepper
4 (3/4") swordfish steaks

• Combine all ingredients well. Marinate fish for 1 hour, turning once. Grill over glowing coals, 4-5 minutes per side.

Tom Flanagan
President - Key Bank of Colorado

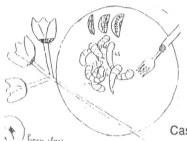

Casey Dennehy, Wellington, Co.

Grilled Salmon

Salmon fillet
Garlic spread
Grey Poupon
Onions - red
Red and yellow peppers

• Smother salmon with garlic spread and Grey Poupon.
• Cut onions and peppers into 1 inch squares.
• Wrap salmon with onions and peppers in foil.
• Grill until cooked.
• Optional - put garlic cloves, and red potatoes in with above.

Mark Simpson
University of Colorado Golf Coach

Chris Clark, Wellington, Co.

L'Espadon a la Nicoise (Swordfish a la Nicoise)

Tomato Concasse:
6 large ripe tomatoes
2 Tbl. olive oil
2 onions, finely chopped
2 cloves garlic, peeled and minced
1 bay leaf
1 branch fresh thyme or pinch of dried thyme

Swordfish: (Ingredients are for one serving.)
8 oz. fresh swordfish
1/2 oz. olive oil
2 oz. tomato concasse
1/2 shallot, chopped
1 oz. dry white wine
1 oz. vegetable stock
1 small garlic clove
Chervil
2 oz. butter (optional)

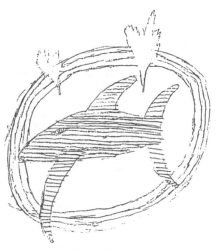

Erik Martin, Wellington, Co.

Tomato Concasse: Preheat oven to 400°
• Using a paring knife, cut out the stem and score a small "x" on the bottom of each tomato. Plunge the tomatoes in boiling water for 1 minute, then rinse under cold water. The skins will slip off easily. Cut the tomatoes in half widthwise and wring out the pulp and seeds by squeezing the tomato halves in the palm of your hand. Coarsely chop the tomatoes with a large knife.
• Heat the olive oil in an ovenproof frying pan and gently cook the onions over low heat for 2 to 3 minutes or until soft and translucent, but not browned. • Stir in the garlic, bay leaf, thyme and coarsely chopped tomatoes and place in preheated oven.
• Bake for 40 minutes or until all of the vegetable juices have evaporated. Do not let the tomato mixture brown. Alternatively, cook mixture in a heavy pot, covered, on top of the stove, stirring from time to time with a wooden spoon to prevent scorching.
Note: This will keep for 4 to 5 days in the refrigerator and can also be frozen.
• **Swordfish:** Oil the bottom of a saute pan and cover with tomato concasse. Add shallots and dry white wine and vegetable stock. Place swordfish on top and sprinkle with salt and fresh ground pepper.
• Bring to a boil on top of the stove, then cover with waxed paper and cook in a hot oven at 400° for 5 minutes, or until slightly under cooked.
• Take fish out and place on a warm plate. Put sauté pan back on stove top, add crushed garlic and bring to boil.
• If you wish to make the sauce richer, add 2 oz. butter and swirl around in the pan to melt it and to bind it to the sauce and thicken it. Lastly, add the chopped chervil and check the seasoning. Pour immediately over the swordfish and serve.
• This dish is also delicious with fillet of salmon, or any other fish that you may like.

Luc and Liz Meyer
The Left Bank Restaurant
Vail, Colorado

Josh Petty, Wellington, Co.

Salmon Wrapped in Grape Leaves

"I have always had a passion for food in little packages, neatly and tidily wrapped. So when I found this recipe from California, I couldn't wait to try it. Be assured it lives up to my expectations."

3/4 cup raisins
1/2 cup pine nuts
2-1/4 lbs. salmon fillets, 1/2" to 3/4" thick, cut into six pieces
1 (6 oz.) jar grape leaves (18), rinsed of brine, or 18 fresh grape leaves, blanched: both patted dry, stemmed
3 Tbl. lemon juice
1/4 tsp. salt
1/4 tsp. freshly ground pepper
3/4 cup olive oil
1 medium tomato, skinned, seeded, diced

One broiling pan, lightly greased

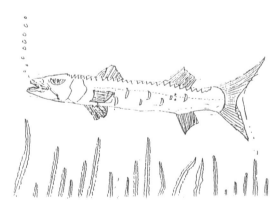

Kraig Kennicutt, Wellington, Co.

• Preheat oven to 350°.
• In small bowl, put raisins with hot water to cover and macerate 30 minutes.
• On baking sheet, spread pine nuts and bake 7 to 8 minutes until lightly toasted. Stir once.
• Meanwhile, trim salmon of any remaining skin or bones. Use a tweezer to extricate bones. Lay each fillet on 2 to 3 grape leaves to cover and wrap each individually. Roll each fillet to cover lengthwise, and then fold sides to make envelope. Set packages on prepared broiling pan. Cover pan tightly with plastic wrap and set aside.
• Preheat broiler or light charcoal grill.
• Drain raisins and squeeze out excess moisture. In food processor with metal blade, puree 1/4 cup raisins with lemon juice, salt and 1/8 tsp. pepper. Scrape down sides of bowl. With machine running, through feed tube, dribble 1/2 cup plus 2 Tbl. olive oil. Transfer to small bowl and stir in remaining 1/2 cup whole raisins. (Sauce may be prepared up to 3 hours ahead. Cover and keep at room temperature.)
• Remove plastic wrap from broiling pan and brush grape leaf packets with remaining 2 Tbl. olive oil and season with remaining 1/8 tsp. pepper. Broil or grill 4 inches from heat, 3 to 4 minutes on each side. Turn once. Broil or grill until grape leaves are brown around edges, with center of fillet moist, but opaque.
• Transfer to warmed dinner plates. Spoon sauce over each serving and sprinkle with toasted pine nuts and diced tomato.
Outstanding!

Katie Stapleton
Famous Denver Cook
Radio KOA "Cooking with Katie"

133

Salmon for Non-Salmon Lovers

Salmon fillet
Mayonnaise
Lemon pepper
Garlic salt

• Place salmon skin side down on broiler pan or foil. Cover with 1/4" of mayonnaise. Sprinkle generously with garlic salt and lemon pepper. Place under broiler until mayonnaise is dark brown and bubbling. Turn to bake and set at 325° for 15-20 minutes depending on thickness of fillet.
• Serve with rice or pasta and a veggie.

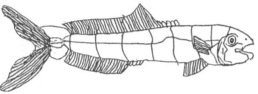

John E. Kelly
President & CEO Pak Mail
Centers of America, Inc.

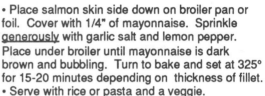

Paul Cox, Wellington, Co.

Salmon Tamale

7 oz. fillet of salmon
3 oz. rock shrimp (41-50 ct.) raw
1/4 oz. brook mint
1 tsp. garlic mayo
1/2 oz. pine nuts
4 corn husk
1 tsp. olive oil

• Sauté shrimp in olive oil for 1 minute, add pine nuts & mint. Sauté for 1 minute longer, set aside off heat. Lay corn husk down, place salmon on center (oil corn husk first) cover with shrimp mixture, top with garlic mayo. Place 2 corn husks on top and fold ends up, wrap with butcher's twine. Charbroil for apporximately 10-15 minutes and serve.
• Serves 1 person.

Henry's at the Strater
Steve Coakley
Executive Chef
Durango, Colorado

STRATER HOTEL
BARKER & CO.
PROPRIETORS
Durango,

M. STEVE COAKLEY
Executive Chef

P.O. DRAWER E • DURANGO, COLORADO 81302 • (303) 247-4431

Smoked Salmon Alfredo

3/4 cup unsalted butter, cut into pieces
1-1/2 cups heavy cream
1-3/4 cups grated parmesan cheese
Black pepper, to taste
4 oz. smoked salmon, boneless, in chunks
Fettucine noodles for 4 - 6 people

• In a medium saucepan, heat the butter and cream over medium heat, stirring occasionally, until the butter melts and the cream is hot.
• Gradually stir in 1-1/4 cups of parmesan cheese. As soon as the cheese has melted and thickened the sauce, add smoked salmon. Cook on low heat until salmon is heated all the way through. Cook fettucine noodles. Pour the sauce over the pasta and top with remaining parmesan cheese and pepper.
• Serves 4 - 6 people.

Ed Greene
Channel 4 Weathercaster

Tom McChesney, Wellington, Co.

Cajun Crawfish (or Shrimp) Fettucini

3 sticks butter
3 med. chopped onions
3 ribs chopped celery
2 chopped bell peppers
1/4 cup flour
3 lbs. crawfish or shrimp
2 pts. half & half cream
1 (16 oz.) Velveeta cheese - cubed
1 pkg. (16 oz.) fettucini noodles
1 can Rotel tomatoes
Salt & pepper to taste

• Sauté onions, bell pepper & celery in butter. When limp add Rotel tomatoes and flour. Mix well, cover and cook 5 minutes on low, stirring occasionally. Add shellfish, cook 20 minutes, stirring often. Add half & half, cheese, salt and pepper. Cook covered on low heat 20 minutes. Cook noodles and drain. Serve sauce over noodles.

Doug Kershaw, singer
"The Ragin' Cajun"

Paul Cox, Wellington, Co.

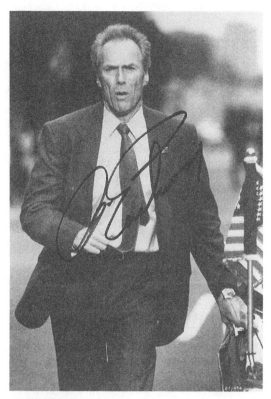

Clint Eastwood's Spaghetti Western

Ingredients:

3 Tbl. vegetable oil

3 medium-size shallots, chopped, about 1/2 cup

1 medium-size rib celery, finely chopped, about 1/2 cup

1 small red bell pepper, cored, seeded and thinly sliced, about 1/2 cup

1 small yellow or green bell pepper, cored, seeded and thinly sliced, about 1/2 cup

2 large cloves garlic, crushed

1 (16 oz.) can whole tomatoes

1/2 cup tomato puree

1/2 cup fish stock or bottled clam juice

1 bay leaf

1 tsp. anchovy paste

1/2 tsp. saffron threads or ground turmeric

Salt and freshly ground black pepper, to taste

12 large mussels in shells, scrubbed and "beards" removed

1 (10 oz.) pkg. frozen artichoke hearts, thawed and drained

4 fresh jumbo shrimp, peeled and deveined

4 large sea scallops, about 4 ounces, quartered

1/2 cup heavy cream

2 Tbl. Pernod liqueur, optional

Half (16 oz.) pkg. spaghetti

1 (6-1/2 oz.) can clams, drained and chopped

Cooking Directions on next page:

136

Clint Eastwood's Spaghetti Western

Cooking Directions:

• In deep 12-inch skillet over medium heat, heat oil; add shallots, celery, red and yellow peppers and garlic; cook about 10 minutes, stirring frequently until tender.
• Add tomatoes with their liquid, tomato puree, fish stock, bay leaf, anchovy paste, saffron, salt and pepper; bring to boil. Reduce heat to medium-low; simmer, covered, 10 minutes. Meanwhile, in 3-quart saucepan bring 1 inch water to boil. Add mussels in their shells; cook, covered, 4 minutes just until shells open. Drain. Using sharp knife, cut mussels away from shells; reserve 12 half shells, discarding remainder. Rinse mussels under cold running water. Set aside. Add artichoke hearts, shrimp and scallops to skillet; increase heat to medium-high. Cook about 5 minutes, stirring frequently until shrimp just turn pink.

Cooking Directions (cont):

• Meanwhile, in deep 4-quart saucepan over high heat, bring 2 quarts water to boil, 8 to 10 minutes. Stir cream and Pernod, if desired, into mixture in skillet; bring to boil. Reduce heat to low; simmer, covered, 10 minutes.
• Meanwhile, add spaghetti to boiling water cook 8 to 10 minutes until tender, stirring frequently. At end of cooking time, stir clams and mussels into mixture in skillet; cook about 1 minute until heated through.
• *To serve:* Drain spaghetti well; divide among 4 large, flat serving bowls. Remove shrimp, mussels and artichoke hearts from sauce; set aside, returning mussels to reserved shells. Spoon sauce over spaghetti; garnish each serving with one reserved shrimp, 3 mussels, 3 artichoke hearts and celery leaves, if desired. Makes 4 servings.

Clint Eastwood
Hog's Breath Inn
Carmel, Calif.

Austin Sutton, Wellington, Co.

Shrimp and Tomato Remoulade

8 small tomatoes, hollowed
3/4 lb. cooked shrimp, deveined and chopped
1/2 stalk celery, diced small
2 green onions, finely chopped
2 Tbl. chopped pimento
1 tsp. horseradish
1 Tbl. Dijon mustard
2 Tbl. chopped fresh parsley
3 Tbl. wine vinegar
1/4 cup olive oil
Juice of 1/2 lemon
Salt, pepper, paprika

• Season cavities of tomatoes with salt and pepper; set aside.
• Place shrimp, celery, green onion and pimento in bowl. Season with salt and pepper; set aside.
• Mix horseradish, mustard and parsley together in another bowl. Season with salt, pepper and paprika. Whisk in vinegar. Add oil in thin stream, mixing constantly with whisk.
• Pour dressing over shrimp mixture and mix well. Stir in lemon juice, and stuff tomatoes with mixture.
• Serves 6 to 8.

Elnora McCloughan
Director of Berthoud Community Center and
Employee of Fire District

138   Marcus Williams, Wellington, Co.

MAIN DISH

Nicole Bodkins, Wellington, Co.

Cory Hallam, Mancos, Co.

Message to Colorado's Kids:
"Don't go to too many horror flicks; visit your local library."

Tim Allen

Tim's Favorite Manly Vegetable Lasagna

Butter for greasing baking dish
1 large onion
2 Tbl. olive oil
2 minced garlic cloves
1-1/2 lbs. each cut carrots and leeks
1 lb. zucchini or sweated eggplant*
1 chopped green pepper
2 lbs. ricotta cheese
Salt and freshly ground black pepper
At least 30 ounces of your favorite tomato
    sauce
1/2 pound cooked Lasagna or 3/4 pound fresh
    Lasagna
1/2 pound thinly sliced Mozzarella Cheese
Grated Parmesan Cheese

*Sweated Eggplant
Peel eggplant (if desired) and slice thinly.
Sprinkle salt on every side. Place all slices in
colander and put a weight on them (e.g. pan
with water in it.) Wait 20 minutes. Eggplant
will be limp, with bitter juices "sweated" out.
Rinse salt off and dry slices before proceeding
with recipe.

• Preheat oven to 400°F. Grease a large, shallow oven proof dish.
• Sauté the onion in the olive oil in a large saucepan over low heat for about 10 minutes. Do not brown.
• Add the garlic and the vegetables. Cover and sauté for about 10 to 20 minutes until tender. Mix in the ricotta cheese, salt and pepper.
• Cover the bottom of the dish with a thin layer of tomato sauce. Next cover with a layer of lasagna, follow with a layer of the vegetable mixture. Next make a layer of mozzarella cheese slices, then of tomato sauce.
• Continue layering until ingredients are used up. Finish with a layer of sauce. Top with any remaining mozzarella cheese that you have grated; and with the Parmesan cheese.
• Bake for 1 hour. If towards the end the casserole is getting too brown, cover the dish.

Tim Allen
From "Home Improvement"
TV Comedy

Vegetarian Lasagna

1 (16 oz.) package lasagna noodles
3 Tbl. olive oil
1 medium yellow onion, minced
2 cloves garlic, minced
1 lb. mushrooms, sliced
1 lb. carrots, grated
6 oz. tomato paste
15 oz. tomato sauce
Salt and pepper
15 oz. ricotta cheese
16 oz. mozzarella cheese, shredded
1 egg
1 Tbl. parsley, chopped
1/4 teaspoon nutmeg
1 tsp. sugar
Salt and pepper
2 lbs. spinach, cooked and well drained
1/2 cup parmesan cheese, grated

• Preheat oven to 375°F.
• Cook lasagna noodles according to package.
• In a 12 inch skillet, heat two tablespoons of olive oil. Stir in onion and garlic. Sauté two minutes at moderate heat. Add mushrooms. Sauté mixture until moisture evaporates, about 15 minutes. Add carrots. Cook 3 minutes more. Stir in tomato paste, tomato sauce, and salt & pepper. Combine well, and remove from heat.
• In a large bowl mix ricotta, mozzarella, egg, parsley, nutmeg, sugar, and salt & pepper to taste.
• Grease 9 x 13 inch pan with tablespoon of olive oil. Line bottom of pan with 1/3 of lasagna noodles. Spread 1/2 of cheese mixture, 1/2 of cooked spinach, and 1/2 of tomato mixture over noodles (in that order). Repeat. Then top with remaining noodles. Sprinkle with Parmesan Cheese.
• Bake, covered with aluminum foil, for 30 minutes. Remove foil and bake for 15 minutes more. Let stand 7 to 10 minutes before cutting.

Dr. Judith E. N. Albino
President
University of Colorado

CHEF HORSE

Jenny Jones, Mancos, Co.

141

...I remind the children of Colorado that they are our future. Kids, listen to your parents and your teachers and treasure your education. Many children do not have the opportunity to go to school.

I had a very difficult childhood and I dropped out of high school before I graduated. I thought I knew everything. Luckily, I had teachers who supported me and encouraged me to go back and to get a college degree. Without those teachers, I wouldn't be where I am today.

I learned the hard way the value of an education. It took me years of hard work to earn my GED and receive a college degree. I urge the children of Colorado to take advantage of their opportunities now so that tomorrow they may become great.

As a U.S. Senator, I represent the state of Colorado in the Senate. As the only Native American in Congress, I represent all Native Americans. I am proud of my heritage and proud of Eyestone PTO for teaching children the value of all different kinds of heritage. Without all the different people that make up our country, we wouldn't have the diversity that we do....

Sincerely,
Ben Nighthorse Campbell

Chile Relleno Casserole

3 cans (7 oz.) WHOLE green chilies or fresh Poblano chiles, roasted and peeled. Remove seeds, stem and open flat.
4-6 corn tortillas, cut into wide strips
2 cups shredded jack cheese (can use jalapeno-jack)
2 cups shredded cheddar cheese
8 eggs
1/2 cup milk
1/2 tsp. each salt, pepper, ground cumin, garlic powder
1 small yellow onion, diced
Simple salsa from a jar
1-2 sprigs fresh cilantro
Paprika

• Begin by covering the bottom of a well-greased 9-inch square baking dish with chilies. Top with a layer of onion, cheeses, sprinkle lightly with salsa and finally a layer of tortilla strips. Repeat layers beginning with chilies, etc. Build to three layers.
• Beat together eggs, milk, salt, pepper, cumin, and garlic powder. Stir in minced cilantro and paprika for color. Pour mixture evenly over casserole. Bake uncovered at 350°F until puffy and set in the center when lightly touched (about 40 minutes). Let stand for about 10 minutes before serving.

• Serves 6 for dinner, 10 for buffet.

This recipe is ideal for buffet-style gatherings where you would like to serve rellenos for many, without the trouble of making each individual relleno.

Ben Nighthorse Campbell
United States Senator

142

Jamie Lindsay, Wellington, Co.

Almost Pizza

7 cups potatoes thinly sliced
1 lb. ground beef
1 (11 oz.) can condensed Nacho Cheese Soup
1 cup milk
1 (10-3/4 oz.) can tomato soup
1/2 cup onion, chopped
1 tsp. sugar
1/2 tsp. oregano
1 (3-1/2 oz.) package sliced pepperoni or any favorite pizza toppings
1 - 2 cups mozzarella cheese, shredded

• Place the sliced potatoes in a greased 13x9x2" pan. In a large skillet cook ground beef until brown. Drain off fat. Meanwhile combine cheese soup and milk in small saucepan. Cook and stir over medium heat until heated through. In a mixing bowl, stir together tomato soup, onion, sugar and oregano. Sprinkle ground beef over potatoes. Pour cheese mixture over all.
• Top with tomato soup mixture and sliced pepperoni. Spread the mozzarella cheese on top. Cover and bake about 1-1/2 hours until potatoes are tender.
Yields: 6 - 8 servings.

Ruth Gjelsness
Featured cook in "Successful Farming Magazine"
and Friend of Education from Reynolds, N.D.

Pizza Casserole

1 lb. hamburger
1 small onion, diced
1/2 green pepper, diced
1 small can mushrooms, drained
1 large can and 1 small can pizza sauce
1/2 lb. mozzarella cheese, shredded
1/2 lb. box rotini

• Brown hamburger and onion. Add green pepper and mushrooms. Cook rotini as directed. In a 9 inch square casserole, layer rotini, sauce, meat mixture and cheese, ending with cheese on top.
• Bake at 350° for 20-25 minutes.
• 6 servings

William G. "Bill" Kaufman
State Representative District 51
Loveland, CO

Samantha Norris, Wellington, Co.

Nacho Supreme

12 oz. bag salted tortilla chips
1 white onion
1 tomato (large)
6 oz. monterey jack cheese, grated
6 oz. sharp cheddar cheese, grated
3 oz. can jalapeno peppers, chopped
1 lb. cooked ground beef
Salt and white pepper
Garlic powder
Chili powder
Dried chili pepper pods
12 oz. can enchilada sauce
12 oz. can refried beans with chorizo

• Mix cheeses and jalapenos in saucepan. Heat and stir until melted and smooth. In separate pan combine enchilada sauce and beans. Heat and stir until melted and smooth. Mince onions and sauté in frying pan for 5 minutes. Add crumbled ground beef. Add salt, garlic powder, chili powder and crushed chili pepper pods, as desired for taste. Preheat oven to 350°F.
• Place tortilla chips in single layer on 18 inch pizza pan. Heat 10 minutes. Remove pizza pan with chips; add enchilada sauce, onion and beef. Add cheese-jalapeno sauce. Cut up tomato and put on top. Return to oven for 10 minutes. Put extra chips on another pan and heat these in oven to use for scoops. Remove pan of nachos and eat.

Steve Ruddick
State Senator
Aurora, CO

Crystal Harrington, Wellington, Co.

144

Amity White, Wellington, Co.

POTATO - PASTA - RICE

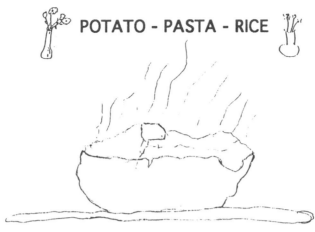

Seth Atkinson, Wellington, Co.

Colorado ranks third in the U.S. in potato production, with quality as high as our mountains.

C.S.U. - Dept. of Agriculture

Darcy Ely, Wellington, Co.

Potato Pancakes

2 baking potatoes
1/2 small onion
1 egg
1 Tbl. flour
1/2 tsp. baking powder
1/2 tsp. salt
Pepper to taste

• Peel potatoes. If using more than two, place in a bowl of cold water until ready to use. If the mixture sits out too long, the potatoes will turn brownish. They can still be used.
• Shred potatoes with the shredding disk of your food processor. Remove from bowl and place steel blade in processor. Add shredded potatoes and use on-off motion briefly, about four or five times.
• Remove potatoes to another bowl.
• Chop onion fine and add to potatoes.
• In a work bowl, process egg, flour, baking powder, salt and pepper. Add to potato, onion mixture and mix thoroughly.

<u>To cook</u>
• Heat 1/4 inch of vegetable oil in a large frying pan. When temperature reaches 375° drop potato mixture from a kitchen tablespoon, allowing excess liquid to drip back into the bowl. Flatten pancake with the back of the spoon. Brown one side, turn with spatula and brown the other side. Add oil as needed before frying each new batch. Each side should take 5 or 6 minutes. Drain on paper toweling. Can be frozen. Thaw and reheat in a single layer 400° for 12 to 15 minutes or until hot.
• Can be doubled or tripled.
• Serve with applesauce or sour cream.

Pat Miller
Gabby Gourmet

Goldie Morris, Wellington, Co.

Ashley Marquardt, Wellington, Co.

Potato Casserole

2 pkg. of frozen hash brown potatoes
1 tsp. salt
3/4 cup chopped onions
1 can cream of chicken soup
2 cups grated cheddar cheese
1/2 cup margarine (melted)
1/4 tsp. pepper
2 cups sour cream

Topping
2 cups crushed cornflakes
1/4 cup melted margarine

• Thaw potatoes - combine margarine, salt, pepper, onions, sour cream, soup and cheese. Blend with potatoes and pour in a 3 quart casserole.
Topping Instructions
•Melt margarine and mix with cornflakes Sprinkle topping over potato mixture
Bake 45 minutes at 350°. Cover lightly with foil the last 20 minutes.
•Serves 10 to 12 people
•Notes: Could be divided and frozen in serving amounts, then thawed and baked.
•When reheating sprinkle top with a little water.
•Submitted by two of Colorado's Celebrities as their favorite - so it is good!

Congressman Dan Schaefer
and State Rep. Don & Mickie Armstrong

Barley Hot Dish

1-1/2 lbs. ground beef
1 cup chopped celery
1 cup chopped onions
3 Tbl. oil
2-1/2 tsp. salt
Pepper to taste
4 cups whole tomatoes
1 can mushroom soup
2-1/2 cups water
3/4 cups pearl barley (not quick cooking)
1/2 cup chopped green pepper
2 cups frozen peas

• Sauté beef, celery and onion in oil. Add all other ingredients. Bring to a boil. Place in casserole and bake at 375° for 45 minutes. Stir and bake an additional 45 minutes.
Serves 10-12.

Ruth Gjelsness
Featured cook in "Successful Farming Magazine"
and Friend of Education from
Reynolds, ND

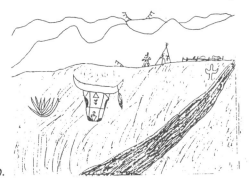

C.J. Altenburg, Wellington, Co.

POTATO - PASTA - RICE

Saratoga Chips

4 potatoes
Peanut oil
Dutch oven
Candy or deep fryer thermometer
Slotted spoon

• Pour peanut oil 3 inches deep in Dutch oven and place directly in coals, place additional coals around base (or heat on your range).
• Slice potatoes about 1/16 inch thick with a food slicer and place in cold water.
• Once oil has reached 340°-360°, take a handful of potatoes and shake the excess water from them. Gently disperse them evenly over the surface of the hot oil. **(Careful! Any water droplets on the potatoes will "pop" when they hit the hot oil.)** Stir occasionally with slotted spoon to prevent them from sticking together. Remove from oil when golden and crispy. Place them in towel lined bowl near the fire to keep warm until serving.

Kylee Smylie, Wellington, Co.

Buckhorn Exchange
George Carlberg, Exec. Chef

Those Potatoes

6 baked potatoes large
4 Tbl. butter

1 cup whole cream
1 Tbl. salt, pepper, garlic, dill weed
2 cups sour cream

1/2 cup real bacon bits
1/2 cup diced green onions
2 cups bordelaise (brown gravy)

1 cup fresh grated parmesan cheese

• Dice baked potatoes into large pieces with skins on. Sauté potatoes in butter until brown. Add whole cream, salt, pepper, garlic and simmer until cream has thickened. Add remaining ingredients and mix well. Let simmer until thick. Can be served alone or with melted cheddar cheese on top.

Buckingham Broker Restaurant
Scott R. Carter, Exec. Chef
Aurora, CO

Jill McKenzie, Wellington, Co.

148

Candice Hall, Mancos, Co.

Oprah's "Classic" Potatoes

2-1/2 lbs. red potatoes
2-1/2 lbs Idaho potatoes
1-1/4 cup creamy pureed horseradish
10 oz. butter
3/4 quart heavy whipping cream
2-1/2 Tbl. Kosher salt
1-1/2 Tbl. ground black pepper

• Wash potaotes well, leaving skin on. Cut potatoes in half. Place in kettle and fill with water to cover. Bring to a boil, turn down to simmer until potatoes are very tender. Drain all water. Add butter while potatoes are hot and begin to hand mash. Add cream, salt, pepper and horseradish, and mash well until creamy but slightly lumpy.

Oprah Winfrey

Linda's Latkes - Potato Pancakes

2 large peeled potatoes
1 onion
1 egg
1/4 cup flour
1/2 tsp. salt

• Grate together potatoes and onion. Add beaten egg, flour, salt and mix well.
• Heat oil in large frying pan . When hot, spoon 3 inch wide pancakes into oil. Cook slowly to insure the potatoes are cooked in the middle. Turn when browned. When browned on second side place on paper towels.
• Serve hot with applesauce. "YUM"

Linda Powers
State Senator
Crested Butte, CO

149

Jean Marc Mayotte, Ft. Collins, Co.

Summer Rice Jubilee

1 (6 oz.) package long grain & wild rice
1 cup diced celery
1/4 cup sliced onions
1/2 cup diced cucumber
1/2 cup diced tomato

Dressing
1/2 cup mayonnaise
1/2 cup plain yogurt
1/4 tsp. seasoned salt
1/4 tsp. pepper

Sunflower Seeds

• Prepare rice as package directs - cool completely.
• Toss cooled rice with vegetables.
• Mix dressing ingredients, (Mayonnaise, yogurt, salt and pepper). Pour over rice. Chill.
• Scatter sunflower seeds on top before serving.

Cynthia Hessin
Reporter/Anchor
KMGH-TV "Colorado's 7"

Jennifer Macias, Wellington, Co.

Wild Rice Casserole

1 cup wild rice (I prefer Minnesota wild rice)
1/2 lb. chopped bacon
1/2 cup chopped onion
8 oz. fresh mushrooms (chopped)
1 (16 oz.) can chicken or beef broth

• Cook rice three times, changing the water and cooking 15 min. each time. Drain well.
• Sauté the bacon. Remove bacon and brown the chopped onion in 2 tablespoons reserved grease.
• In a 2 quart casserole put cooked rice, chopped bacon, onion, mushrooms and broth. Bake covered 350° for 1 hour. Check for moisture. May have to add more broth if it appears to be too dry.

Armetta Keeney
1992 - Best Cook in the Country

Justin Campesino, Wellington, Co.

Garlic Vermicelli
(For Garlic Lovers!)

1/4 pound thin vermicelli
1/3 cup olive oil
7-10 cloves garlic trimmed and minced or
   ready for garlic press.

• Boil vermicelli. Drain. In separate sauce pan, warm olive oil on medium heat. Mix in vermicelli and press in garlic. Cook at medium heat for 5-10 minutes. Salt and pepper to taste.

Tom Blickensderfer
State Senator
Englewood, CO

Andrea McMickael, Wellington, Co.

Cavatelli Extraordinaire

1 lb. ground beef
1 lb. ground sausage
1 (30 oz.) jar spaghetti sauce
1 (8 oz.) jar taco sauce
1 (4 oz.) can sliced mushrooms
1 package Italian Seasoning
1/2 cup water
1 (24 oz.) packet cavatelli pasta - cooked
1 lb. shredded mozzarella cheese

• Brown beef and sausage. Drain off grease. Divide cooked pasta into 9 x 13 inch and 9 x 9 inch baking dishes. Sprinkle meat evenly over pasta. Combine spaghetti sauce, taco sauce, mushrooms (drained), seasoning, and water. Pour sauce over meat and pasta. Cover with shredded cheese.
• Bake at 350° until cheese browns and sides of dish are bubbly.

(About 20-30 minutes)

Pam Daale
KMGH TV Channel 7
Meteorologist

Kurt Zimmerman, Wellington, Co.

151

Pasta Con Broccoli

1 lb. Olive Garden fresh pasta shells or
    medium dry shells
1/4 cup Olive garden 100% pure olive oil or
    equivalent
12 oz. broccoli florets, 1" diameter
2 tsp. garlic, fresh, chopped
1/4 cup green onions, thinly sliced
1 cup fresh mushrooms, sliced
2 tsp. parsley, fresh, chopped
Parmesan cheese (optional)

Bechamel Sauce

1/4 cup flour
1/4 cup butter or margarine
1 quart milk
2 teaspoons Chicken bouillon, (mashed if in
    cube form)

Bechamel Sauce

• Melt butter or margarine in a 2 quart saucepan
over medium heat. Stir in flour and cook for 1
minute. Add milk and chicken bouillon and stir
vigorously with a wire whip until mixture barely
comes to a boil. Reduce heat and simmer for 5
minutes, whipping frequently. Keep warm.
• Cook pasta according to directions. Drain and
reserve in a strainer.
• Blanch or steam broccoli for one minute. Drain.
Divide broccoli in half. Chop one half of florets
into 1/4 inch pieces. Reserve. Heat a large sauté
pan over medium heat and add olive oil. Add all
the broccoli, garlic, green onions and mushrooms
to the sauté pan. Cook stirring constantly, for two
minutes or until mushrooms begin to turn golden.
•Add the sautéed vegetables and chopped parsley
to the warm bechamel sauce and stir well. Serve
over hot pasta. Pass parmesan cheese at the
table.
• Reheat the pasta by dropping into boiling water
for a few seconds and drain well.

Buono Appetito!

Serves 4-6

The Olive Garden Restaurant
Brad Kirby
Aurora, CO

Meghan Scott, Wellington, Co.

Dustin Dumwald, Wellington, Co.

Rotini with Shrimp and Mushroom Sauce

4 cups tricolor Rotini, Cooked
3 Tbl. olive oil
1/2 onion, chopped
1 garlic clove, minced
6 mushrooms, washed and sliced
1 cup baby shrimp, cooked
16 oz. stewed tomatoes
4 oz. chicken broth
4 oz. red or white wine (optional)
1 Tbl. tomato paste
Pinch of basil
Pinch of cayenne pepper
Salt and pepper
Chopped parsley
3 Tbl. parmesan grated

• Heat oil in sauce pan and sauté onion, garlic and mushrooms several minutes.
• Add other ingredients, except cheese, pasta, and shrimp. Simmer 8 minutes, stirring occasionally.
• Add shrimp and heat through. Drain pasta. Toss well with sauce and cheese and serve.
• You may want to use 2 cups cooked large shrimp instead of baby shrimp.

Gary and Johanne Wayne
Colorado **Rockies'** Pitcher and Wife
Lakewood, CO

Ken Betchel, Wellington, Co.

Chicken and Mushroom Fettuccine

1/2 lb, mushrooms, sliced
1 onion, chopped
1 clove garlic, minced
1/2 cup butter
1/2 lb. egg fettuccine
1/2 lb. spinach fettuccine
2 cups half and half
Salt and pepper
4 chicken breasts, poached and cooled
3/4 cup tomato puree
Grated Parmesan

• Sauté mushrooms, onion and garlic in butter until soft. Cook pasta until al dente and drain. Add half and half and seasoning to pasta. Cut chicken into bite-size pieces. Add chicken, vegetables and tomato puree to the pasta, mixing well. Place in a buttered 9 x 13" baking dish and bake at 350° for 30 minutes. Serve with Parmesan.

Serves 6

Gary and Johanne Wayne
Colorado **Rockies'** Pitcher and Wife
Lakewood, CO

Derek Jekel, Wellington, Co.

Pasta with Garlic and Anchovies
For Anchovy and Garlic lovers

1 lb. pasta (Linguini is best)
5 cans of anchovies
5 fat cloves of garlic
1/3 cup olive oil
Pepper mill

• Note: Some may find 5 cans of anchovies too strong. If so use one less. It is important not to have too much liquid.
• Place oil in saucepan on low flame. Slice garlic cloves wafer thin and brown in oil. When a light, golden brown, remove from saucepan and discard the garlic.
• While above is going on put water on for pasta.
• Allow olive oil to cool for five minutes or more and add the five cans of anchovies (do not throw them into the very hot oil.) When done, strain pasta through colander & place in serving bowl. Add the anchovies - mix well. Servings should have pepper ground on.

Dr. Michael Charney
CSU Forensic Medicine

Jessi Norris, Wellington, Co.

Ty Presgrove, Wellington, Co.

154

Rigatoni con Zucchini

1/3 cup olive oil
1 cup onion, chopped
1 lb. fresh mushrooms
1-1/2 tsp. garlic, finely minced
3 cups crushed tomatoes
1 (16 oz.) can tomatoes diced and drained
1-1/2 cups tomato puree
1 cup black olives sliced and drained
2 teaspoons capers, drained
1/2 tsp. oregano, dried
1/2 tsp. basil, dried
1/4 tsp. black pepper
1/4 tsp. crushed red pepper
1/2 tsp. fennel seeds
1/2 tsp. salt

Zucchini Preparation

4 large zucchini, sliced lengthwise, 1/4 inch
   thick
2 Tbl. olive oil
Basil, dried
Oregano, dried
Salt
Black pepper

1 lb. rigatoni pasta
Parmesan cheese, freshly grated

• Chop onion. Divide mushrooms into 2 equal portions. Cut 1 portion into quarters and reserve. Finely mince remaining portion. Mince garlic. Heat olive oil in a heavy Dutch oven over medium heat. Add onion and minced mushrooms. Cook 10 minutes or until onions are very soft, stirring frequently. Add garlic and mushroom quarters and cook 5 more minutes stirring constantly. Add remaining ingredients, stir and bring to a simmer. Reduce heat and simmer 20 minutes, stirring frequently.
•Bring a large pot of water to a boil. Cook rigatoni according to package directions.

Zucchini Preparation

• Cut ends off of zucchini. Cut lengthwise into 1/4 inch thick rectangular slices. Sprinkle sliced zucchini with salt, pepper, basil and oregano. Heat 1 tablespoon of olive oil in a large skillet over medium heat. Place zucchini slices in one layer in the pan. Sauté about 3 minutes per side just until tender. Remove to heated platter, and cover to keep warm while sautéing remaining zucchini. Add remaining olive oil as needed.
• Drain cooked rigatoni and transfer to a serving platter. Ladle sauce over the pasta. Top with zucchini slices and serve. Pass extra sauce and freshly grated Parmesan cheese. Buono Appetito!
Serves 4-6

The Olive Garden Restaurant
Brad Kirby
Aurora, CO

Travis Bredehoft, Wellington, Co.

Spatzle-German Egg Noodles

2-1/4 cup all purpose flour
1 tsp. salt
2 eggs
1/2 cup water (approx.)

• Mix flour and salt into a medium bowl. Add eggs, mix well. Add water gradually until dough is smooth, light, but firm. Let rest for 10 minutes.
• Cut dough into boiling salted water (or push through potato ricer). When spatzle floats, and has cooked a few minutes, drain in colander - top with browned bread crumbs for a typical "Swabian" delicacy from south western Germany

Mary Weiss
Water Color Painter

Jamie Lindsay, Wellington, Co.

Spaetzle

2-1/2 cups flour
1 egg
1 tsp. salt
Dash nutmeg
1 cup luke warm water

• Mix all ingredients together by hand and beat well. Bring large pot of salted water to boil. Cut dough with table knife from a small wooden cutting board to about Linguine size directly into boiling water. Do not cook more than 1/2 of dough at a time. Stir occasionally and boil rapidly for 2 minutes. Drain into bowl of ice. When entire batch is cooked, drain well, coat with butter and warm in skillet.

Hans T. Wyppler
Chef de Cuisine
The Black Bear Inn
Lyons, CO

Toni Nagy, Wellington, Co.

VEGETABLES

Approximately 75% of commercial dry beans are grown in Northeast Colorado and 95% of seed beans are grown on the Western Slope.

C.S.U. - Dept. of Agriculture

THE VEGETARIAN'S NIGHTMARE
a dissertation on plants' rights

Ladies and diners I make you
A shameful degrading confession.
A deed of disgrace in the name of good taste
Though I did it, I meant no aggression.
I had planted a garden last April
 And lovingly sang it a ballad.
But later in June beneath a full moon
I, forgive me, I wanted a salad!
So I slipped out and fondled a carrot
Caressing its feathery top.
With the force of a brute I tore out the root!
It Whimpered and came with pop!
Then laying my hand on a radish
 I jerked and it left a small crater.
Then with the blade of my TrueValue spade
I exhumed a slumbering tater!
Celery I plucked, I twisted a squash!
Tomatoes were wincing in fear.
I choked the Romaine. It screamed out in pain.
their anguish was filling my ears!
I finally came to the lettuce
As it cringed at the top of the row
 With one wicked slice I beheaded it twice
As it writhed, I dealt a death blow.

I butchered the onions and parsley.
My hoe was all covered with gore.
I chopped and I whacked without looking back
Then I stealthily slipped in the door
My bounty lay naked and dying
So I drowned them to snuff out their life.
I sliced and I peeled as they thrashed and they reeled
On the cutting board under my knife.
I violated tomatoes
so their innards could never survive.
I grated and ground 'til they made not a sound
Then I boiled the tater alive!
Then I took the small broken pieces
 I had tortured and killed with my hands
And tossed them together, heedless of whether
They suffered or made their demands.
I ate them. Forgive me, I'm sorry.
But hear me, though I'm a beginner
Those plants feel pain, though it's hard to explain
To someone who eats them for dinner!
I intend to begin a crusade
For PLANT'S RIGHTS, including chick peas.
The A.C.L.U. will be helping me , too.
In the meantime, please pass the bleu cheese.

Baxter Black
Columnist
"On The Edge of Common Sense"

Vegetable Casserole

1 can white shoe peg corn, drained
1 can French style green beans, drained
1/2 cup chopped onions
1/2 cup chopped celery
1/4 cup chopped green pepper
Salt and pepper
1/2 cup grated sharp cheese
1/2 cup sour cream
1 can cream of celery soup

• Mix together and put in casserole.

Topping
Crumble one stack Ritz Crackers and mix with 1/2 stick melted butter and 1/2 cup slivered almonds.

• Bake at 350°F for 45 minutes.

Byron R. White
Retired Associate Justice
U.S. Supreme Court

Blanca Burgos, Wellington, Co.

Veggie Frittata

2 cups cooked pasta (linguine)
1 egg
Veggies (cauliflower, broccoli, tomatoes, onions, mushrooms)
1/4 cup cheese
1/4 tsp. of each, garlic, spike, aromat.

• Mix together all ingredients in large bowl.
• Warm a 6-8 inch sauté pan with some oil in it.
• Put it all in the pan heat both sides until they slide easily to flip them over.
*Aromat is hard to find. Try the gourmet Dept. at King Soopers and Toddy's.

Kevin Harper, D. J. McCadams
Voted #1 breakfast in Colorado by "Snow Country Magazine"
Vail, CO

Jenny Jones, Mancos, Co.

158

Creamed Corn Deluxe

2 packages (totalling 20 oz.) frozen kernel corn
3/4 cup whipping cream
1 tsp. salt
6 tsp. sugar
Pinch white or cayenne pepper
2 Tbl. flour
2 Tbl. melted butter

• Combine all ingredients except butter and flour, bring to a boil. Simmer 5 minutes. Blend butter and flour. Stir into corn mixture. Simmer a few more minutes until it thickens. Optional: Sprinkle Parmesan Cheese on top before serving.

Gale Norton
Attorney General of Colorado

Fay Becksted, Wellington, Co.

Scalloped Corn

1 can creamed corn
12 crackers (crushed)
1 onion (diced)
2 eggs (beaten)
1 cup milk

• Mix together and bake in an 8 x 8 square baking dish at 375°F. for 1 hour.

Rusti Ruth
Friend of Education
Redding, CA

Dustin Shefferd, Wellington, Co.

159

Ginger Carrots

3 or 4 cups sliced carrots
1 cup orange juice
1/2 cup chicken broth
3 whole cloves
3/4 tsp. ground ginger
1-1/2 tsp. grated lemon rind
3 Tbl. sugar

• Bring all ingredients except sugar to a boil. Stir in sugar and simmer for 30 minutes or until carrots are tender.
• Serves 6.

State Senator
Ray Powers
Assistant Majority Leader
Colorado Springs, CO

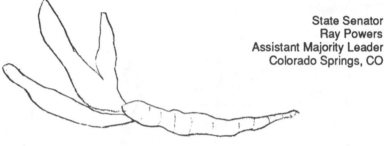

Cassy McDonald, Wellington, Co.

Tanner Baked Beans

2 (30 oz.) cans pork and beans
1 cup (8 oz.) maple syrup
1 large onion, chopped
1 large green bell pepper, chopped
2 stalks celery, chopped
4 Tbl. mustard
4 Tbl. ketchup
8 bacon strips cut in small pieces
1 tsp. garlic powder (optional)

• Put bacon pieces in frying pan and fry until half done. Add onions, bell pepper, chopped celery and cook until done. Place ingredients from frying pan in large baking bowl with beans, maple syrup, mustard, ketchup and garlic powder. Stir thoroughly.
• Bake in oven at 400°F for 1 hour. Excellent side dish for outdoor barbecue.

State Representative
Gloria T. Tanner
Denver, CO

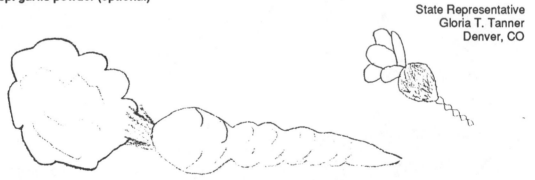

Vanessa Neilsen, Wellington, Co.

Kelley Baked Beans

3 cans baked beans (use a variety)
1 large onion, chopped
3 Tbl. catsup
3/4 cup brown sugar
3 or 4 Tbl. butter, melted
2 Tbl. Worcestershire Sauce
1 dash tabasco
2 tsp. dry mustard
1 cup pecans, chopped
5 strips bacon, fried and crumbled

• Mix all together and bake 1 hour at 350°F.

Dona Kelley
President
Colorado Association for the Education of Young
Children

Buckhorn Baked Beans

1 (16 oz.) can baked beans
5 oz. spicy pork sausage
1 small yellow onion
6 celery stalks including leafy top
1/2 green pepper
1/4 Tbl. chili powder
3/4 tsp. mustard
2 Tbl. ketchup

• Dice celery, green pepper, and onion (1/4 inch).
• Place sausage in large pot, brown sausage over medium heat while stirring to prevent sausage from clumping up.
• When sausage has browned, pour off excess grease. Add diced vegetables and continue to cook until onions are clear.
• Add chili powder, mustard, and ketchup and bring to a boil.
• Add can of beans and mix with spoon to ensure an even distribution of spices and vegetables. Reduce heat and bring to a boil, stirring constantly to prevent scorching.

George Carlberg
Executive Chef, Buckhorn Exchange
Denver, Colorado

Dani Barch, Wellington, Co.

161

Photo of Dolores Vaccaro taken by 4-H photographer, Sarah Vandeberg.

Asparagus Delight

Message to Kids:
"Education is to mankind as nature is to an eagle; it informs the mind, directs the heart, and frees the spirit."

Dolores Vaccaro

Mike McChesney, Wellington, Co.

2 (15 oz.) cans asparagus spears, undrained
3 Tbl. butter or margarine
3 Tbl. all purpose flour
1 cup milk
1/8 tsp. salt
1/4 tsp. white pepper
6 hard cooked eggs, sliced
2 (3 oz.) cans mushroom stems and pieces, drained
2 Tbl. fine, dry bread crumbs

• Drain asparagus, reserving 1 cup liquid; set aside.
• Melt butter in a heavy saucepan over low heat; add flour, stirring until smooth. Cook 1 minute, stirring constantly. Gradually add 1 cup asparagus liquid and milk; cook over medium heat, stirring constantly, until thickened and bubbly. Stir in salt and pepper.
• Spread 1/4 cup sauce in a greased 10 x 6 x 2 inch baking dish. Layer half each of the asparagus, eggs, mushrooms, and sauce. Repeat layers; then sprinkle with bread crumbs.
• Bake at 325°F for 20 to 25 minutes or until bubbly. Makes 8 servings.

Dolores Vaccaro
Blue Ribbon Winner
Colorado State Fair
1993 Homemaker of the Year

Dustin Fuller, Wellington, Co.

PIES

Vanessa Nielsen, Wellington, Co.

Dear Kids:

"I have found that the more I read and listen rather than watch and talk the more knowledgeable I seem to become. Could there be a message in this somewhere?

Of course the message is to be more intent upon educating your mind with worthwhile pursuits. Drugs, gangs, alcohol and other such things are obviously not the ingredients for success. Please remember that nothing good comes easily. The harder you work the luckier you will become. "

> Sincerely yours,
> Hale Irwin

Hale Irwin
GOLF SERVICES, INC.

Pecan Pie

9" pie shell (unbaked)
3 eggs
1/2 cups sugar
1 tsp. vanilla
1 cup dark Karo syrup
3 Tbl. melted butter (not hot)
1-1/2 to 2 cups whole pecans (top quality)
Pinch of salt

• Beat eggs with fork. Add rest of ingredients and mix well.
• Pour in unbaked shell .
• Bake at 350° for 1/2 hour or until set.
• Serve with whipped cream.

Hale and Sally Irwin
Professional Golfer

164

 PIES

Sour Cream Raisin Pie

Filling:
3/4 cup sugar
1/2 tsp. cinnamon
3 egg yolks
1 Tbl. cornstarch
2 Tbl. vinegar
1-1/2 cups raisins
pinch of salt
2 cups sour cream

Meringue
1 Tbl. cornstarch
1 Tbl. sugar
1/2 cup water
3 egg whites
3 Tbl. sugar

• **Filling:** In a sauce pan combine the sugar, cinnamon, egg yolks, cornstarch, vinegar, raisins, salt and sour cream. Cook until thick and cornstarch is cooked. Pour into baked pie shell and top with meringue.
• **Meringue:** Cook the first 3 ingredients until clear. Set aside. Beat egg whites until frothy, add the sugar and beat until stiff, add to cooked mixture and gently mix in. Put on top of pie filling and bake at 350° for 12-15 minutes.

Armetta Keeney
1992 Best Cook in the Country

Rhubarb Custard Pie

2 eggs
2 Tbl. milk, skim
1 cup plus 2 Tbl. fructose
3 Tbl. all-purpose flour
1/2 tsp. nutmeg
3 cups fresh rhubarb, cut up
2 tsp. margarine
2 (9 inch) pie shells

• Beat eggs slightly; add milk. Combine fructose, flour and nutmeg and blend in egg mixture. Fold in rhubarb. Pour into baked 9-inch pie shell. Cover with lattice top. Cover edges of pie with foil. Bake at 400° for 20 minutes. Remove foil and continue baking for another 20 or 30 minutes, or until browned and rhubarb is tender.

* This recipe uses fructose, a naturally occuring sugar in corn. Fructose is 1-1/2 times sweeter than sucrose, so less is needed (which means less calories).

Colorado Corn Administrative Committee

Vanessa Nielsen, Wellington, Co.

 PIES

German Apple Pie

2 eggs
1 cup sugar
6 Tbl. flour
1 tsp. baking powder
1 cup diced apples
1 cup chopped nuts
2 tsp. vanilla

• This recipe makes its own crust.

• Beat eggs until foamy. Gradually add the sugar and lay aside. Combine the flour and baking powder and fold into egg mixture. Fold in the apples and nuts and vanilla. Put in 9" greased pie tin. Bake 350° for 40-45 minutes (until brown).
• Cool in refrigerator overnight or 2-3 days ahead.

Mr. and Mrs. Bryon R. White
Retired Assoc. Justice U.S. Supreme Court

Pie Crust

3 cups flour
1 tsp. salt
1-1/4 cup Crisco
1 Tbl. vinegar
1 egg
8 Tbl. ice water

• Mix flour, salt and Crisco.
• Combine vinegar, egg and water. Add to first mixture.
• Use what you need and prepare pie shells for later and freeze. I thaw the shell out before baking. I put plastic wrap between them and stack them to freeze.
• Makes 3 (9") shells.

Armetta Keeney
1992 Best Cook in the Country

Natasha Walton, Mancos, Co.

 PIES

Strawberry Pie

1/2 pkg. vanilla wafers, crushed
2 pt. fresh strawberries, washed and stemmed
1 can Eagle Brand sweetened condensed milk
1/2 cup fresh lemon juice
1/2 pint (1 cup) whipping cream, whipped
2 Tbl. sugar
1 tsp. vanilla

• Pat crushed vanilla wafers into 9" or 10" pie pan. Mix Eagle Brand sweetened condensed milk and lemon juice thoroughly. Stir in whole strawberries. Spoon strawberry mixture into wafer pie shell. Whip cream with 2 Tbl. sugar and 1 tsp. vanilla. Spoon over top of pie. Sprinkle with vanilla wafer crumbs. Add 2 or 3 strawberries in center for garnish. Chill overnight in refrigerator.

Gail Schoettler
Colo. State Treasurer

Tom McChesney, Wellington, Co.

Chocolate Mint Pie

9" baked chocolate crumb crust
1-1/2 cups vanilla wafer crumbs
6 Tbl. Hershey's cocoa
1/3 cup sugar
6 Tbl. butter or margarine

Pie filling:
1-1/4 cups sugar
1/3 cup cocoa
1/3 cup cornstarch
1/4 tsp. salt
1/2 cup Brach's Starlight Mints (crushed)
3 cups milk
3 Tbl. butter

• For the pie crust, combine crumbs, cocoa, and sugar in a bowl. Stir in butter. Press mixture onto bottom and up the side of a 9" pan. Bake at 350° for 10 minutes. Cool.
• For the pie filling, combine (in a saucepan), sugar, cocoa, cornstarch, salt, mints and milk. Cook and stir over medium heat until mixture boils; cook 3 minutes. Remove from heat; blend in butter and pour in crumb crust.
• Serve with whipped topping.
• Note: You can use graham cracker crust.

Armetta Keeney
1992 Best Cook in the Country

Maurissa Moore, Wellington, Co.

 PIES

Peanut Butter Pie with Merinque

9" baked pie shell

<u>Pie filling:</u>
3/4 cup powdered sugar
1/2 cup peanut butter (creamy)
2/3 cup granulated sugar
1/3 cup cornstarch
3 egg yolks
2-1/2 cups milk
2 Tbl. margarine or butter
1 Tbl. vanilla

<u>Meringue:</u>
1 Tbl. cornstarch
1 Tbl. sugar
1/2 cup water
3 egg whites
3 Tbl. sugar

• Mix powdered sugar and peanut butter together. Set aside. In a saucepan, combine granulated sugar, cornstarch, egg yolks and milk. Cook until thickened. Remove from heat and add margarine and vanilla. In the bottom of baked pie shell, put all but 2 Tbl. of the peanut butter mixture. Pour the pudding over this while hot.
• To make the meringue, cook cornstarch, sugar and water until thick and clear. Set aside. Beat egg whites until frothy. Add sugar and beat until peaks form. Add cooked mixture and mix gently. Put over pudding. • Top with 2 Tbl. of reserved peanut butter mixture and bake at 350° for 12- 15 minutes.

Armetta Keeney
1992 Best Cook in the Country

Furr's Millionaire Pie

2 cups sifted powdered sugar
1/4 lb. (1 stick) margarine or butter, softened
2 large fresh whole eggs
1/8 tsp. salt
1/4 tsp. vanilla
2 baked 9" pie crusts
1 cup heavy whipping cream
1/2 cup sifted powdered sugar
1 cup crushed pineapple, well drained
1/2 cup chopped pecans

• Cream together powdered sugar and margarine with electric mixer. Add eggs, salt and vanilla. Beat until light and fluffy. Spread mixture evenly into baked pie shells and chill. Whip cream until stiff. Blend in powdered sugar. Fold in pineapple and pecans. Spread this mixture on top of the chilled base mixture and chill thoroughly.
Yield: 2 - 9" pies.

William L. Hyde Jr.
Furr's/Bishop Cafeterias

(See raw egg caution pg.175)

Lindsey Hendrix, Colo. Springs, Co.

Lemon Pie

9" baked pie shell

Pie filling:
2 cups sugar
1/2 cup cornstarch
2 cups water
4 egg yolks
Dash salt
2 Tbl. butter
8 Tbl. fresh squeezed lemon juice

Meringue:
1 Tbl. cornstarch
1 Tbl. sugar
1/2 cup water
3 egg whites
4 Tbl. sugar

• In a sauce pan put sugar, cornstarch, water, yolks and salt. Cook until thickened and cornstarch is cooked. Remove from heat. Add butter and lemon juice. Pour in baked shell and top with meringue.
• To make the meringue: Cook cornstarch, sugar and water until thick and clear. Remove from heat. In a separate bowl, beat egg whites until frothy and add sugar. Beat until mixture forms peaks. Add cooked mixture and mix gently.
• Spread on filling and brown in 350° oven for 12 - 14 minutes. This is a no-weep meringue.

Armetta Keeney
1992 Best Cook in the Country

Peanut Butter Pie

Make or buy 9" crumb crust (your favorite flavor)
1 envelope Knox gelatin
4 oz. cream cheese
1 cup powdered sugar
1/2 cup peanut butter
8 oz. Cool Whip

• Prepare crumb crust for 9" pie. Dissolve 1 envelope Knox gelatin in 1/4 cup hot water. Set aside to cool. Mix cream cheese, powdered sugar and peanut butter. Beat well. Mix in Knox gelatin and beat until thoroughly mixed. Fold in Cool Whip. Pour into crust and chill. Enjoy!

Sue Gano
Godfather's Pizza

169

Nicole Bodkins, Wellington, Co.

Lemon Meringue Tart

2 (9") sweet pie shells
1 cup softened butter
1 tsp. salt
3 Tbl. sugar
3-1/2 cups flour
1/2 cup plus 2 Tbl. cold milk
3 Tbl. oil

Pie filling:
4 egg yolks
2 whole eggs
5 Tbl. sugar
Zest of two lemons (grated peel)

Meringue:
4 egg whites
4 oz. powdered sugar

• **Pie Shell:** Combine the butter, salt and sugar in the bowl of a mixer fitted with a dough hook. Mix for 1 minute. Gradually add the flour and mix at low speed until the mixture forms little balls. Mix in enough milk (it should be at room temperature in the wintertime and chilled during the summer) to bring the crumbs together into a compact mass. Add the oil and mix for 1 minute. Gather the dough into a ball, cover and let sit in a cool place for 2 to 3 hours before using. Do not refrigerate. Note: The oil added at the last minute gives the dough a sable, "sandy" or crumbly consistency.
• After the dough has rested, roll the pastry to a thickness of 3/16" and line 9" tart pan with half the mixture. (To transfer dough from pastry marble to the pie pan, roll it up on the rolling pin and unroll it over the pan.) Cut off the excess dough and crimp the edges of the pie with a pastry pincher or with your fingers. Prick the bottom of the crust with a fork.
• Preheat oven to 450° and bake blind for about 15 minutes. Be sure the crust is cooked properly - it should be a light brown. If the dough rises in the middle while cooking, use a fork to prick a small hole to release the steam.
• **Filling:** In a 2-1/2 qt. saucepan, combine all the pie filling ingredients and whip as you would when making a hollandaise or sabayon to get the mixture fluffy. Cook it over a low heat whisking constantly until the mixture thickens and is almost boiling. DO NOT let it boil as it will curdle. Pour into the prebaked pie shell and let cool.
• **Meringue:** Beat the egg whites and powdered sugar until stiff and, using a pastry bag with a star tip, pipe the meringue over the entire lemon mixture. Bake in oven at 425° to brown the top of the meringue, for about 5 minutes.
• For best results, use a copper saucepan as it distributes the heat evenly, otherwise a double boiler may be used.

Liz and Luc Meyer
The Left Bank Restaurant, Vail, CO

Lacey Morris, Mancos, Co.

PIES

Best Apple Pie

2-1/2 lb. cooking apples, pared, quartered, cored and thinly sliced (8 cups)
1/3 cup firmly packed light brown sugar
1/3 cup granulated sugar
1 Tbl. cornstarch or 2 Tbl. flour
1/4 tsp. ground cinnamon
1/4 tsp. ground nutmeg
1/4 tsp. salt
2 Tbl. butter or margarine
Water or milk
Sugar for sprinkling

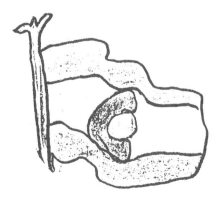

• Place apples in large bowl. Mix sugars, cornstarch or flour; cinnamon, nutmeg, and salt in a small bowl; sprinkle over apples; toss gently to mix. Let stand until a little juice forms, about 10 minutes.
• Put one pie shell into 9" pie plate (1/2" overhang).
• Pile apple mixture into pastry; dot with butter or margarine. Moisten edge of bottom pastry with water. Place second folded pastry on apples so point is on center; unfold. Trim overhang to 1 inch; turn edges under and press together to seal. Pinch to make stand-up edge; flute. Make 3 slits near center of top shell.
• For a crispy-sugary top, brush top of pastry with a little water or milk and sprinkle lightly with sugar.
• Bake pie in hot oven (425°) 40 minutes, or until juices bubble through slits and apples are tender. If edges are browning too fast, cover with a narrow strip of foil. Cool for about an hour and serve with vanilla ice cream.

Governor Roy Romer
Colorado

Nicole Bodkins, Wellington, Co.

Clay's Piquant (Fresh Fruit Tart)

1 pkg. Pillsbury pie crust or homemade crust
1 pkg. dried beans (any type will do)
1 sheet aluminum foil (sized to fit tart pan)

First layer filling:
1/3 cup sugar
3 Tbl. tapioca
3/4 cup pineapple juice
3/4 cup apple juice
1 egg (beaten)
1 tsp. vanilla
1/4 cup coconut rum (optional)
1/2 cup cream cheese

Second layer filling:
3 Tbl. strawberry jelly
1 fresh pineapple cut into 2" wide triangles x
     1/4" thick
1 qt. fresh medium-sized strawberries (hulled
     and halved)

• Place pie crust in tart pan and prick with fork.
Place aluminum foil on top of crust and pour the
entire pkg. of dried beans on top of the foil to keep
the crust flat. Bake the crust for approx. 10-15
minutes at 350°. Remove foil and beans. Let the
crust cool.
• **First layer filling:** Combine sugar, juice, egg
and tapioca in a small sauce pan. Let the mixture
set for 5 minutes. Cook tapioca mixture over
medium heat until it comes to a full rolling boil.
Remove from heat and stir in the vanilla, coconut
rum and the cream cheese. Let cool for approx.
15 minutes.
• **Second layer filling:** Cut the strawberries in
half and cut the pineapple into 2" triangles x 1/4"
thick. Melt all of the strawberry jelly and set aside.
• Assembly: Pour the first layer filling into the
cooked pie crust. Working from the outside edge
of the crust, place a row of strawberries (tip
pointed up) around the crust. Next, take the
pineapple triangles (tip pointed up) and arrange
the next row. Continue this process by alternating
the strawberries and pineapple. Using a pastry
brush, paint the fruit to give the tart a glazed
appearance. Chill for at least 30 minutes and
serve. Clay's Piquant does not store well; it must
be served within three or four hours of assembly.

Jesse Clay
Clay's Black Belt Academy - Ft. Collins, CO
Four Times World Karate Champion

Tom McChesney, Wellington, Co.

 PIES

Maple Pecan Pie

1 (9") uncooked pie shell
3 eggs
1 cup maple syrup
1/4 cup dark corn syrup
1/4 cup sugar
1/4 cup unsalted butter, melted
1 tsp. vanilla
1/4 tsp. salt
1-1/2 cups pecan halves

• Preheat oven to 425°. In a large bowl, beat the eggs until blended. Add the maple syrup, corn syrup, sugar, butter, vanilla and salt. Beat until thoroughly combined. Stir in the pecan halves.
• Pour the pecan mixture into pastry lined pan. Bake 15 minutes, then reduce the heat to 350° and bake about 25 minutes. Serve warm or at room temperature.

Gary and Johanne Wayne
Colorado **Rockies** Pitcher and Wife
Lakewood, CO

Kennan Blehm, Wellington, Co.

Country Apple Pie

1 (9") unbaked pie shell
5 cups thinly sliced apples
3/4 cup sugar
4 Tbl. flour
1/4 tsp. salt
1/2 tsp. cinnamon
1 cup cream (30%)
1Tbl. sugar
1/4 tsp. cinnamon

• Place the apples in a pastry lined pan. Mix together the next 5 ingredients and pour over the apples. Sprinkle mixture of cinnamon and sugar over the top of pie. Bake at 400° for 50-60 minutes. Enjoy!

Gary and Johanne Wayne
Colorado **Rockies** Pitcher and Wife
Lakewood, CO

Wes Fuller

 PIES

Delicious Strawberry Pie

6 cups strawberries
1 cup sugar
3 Tbl. cornstarch
1/2 cup water
1 (3 oz.) pkg. cream cheese
1 (9") pie shell, cooked

• Mash 1 cup strawberries. In a saucepan, put sugar and cornstarch; gradually add water and mashed berries. Heat on medium until boiling (like pudding). Let cool.
• Stir cream cheese until smooth. Spread on bottom of <u>baked</u> pie shell. Fill with the rest of the berries. Pour cooled mixture on top. Chill 3 hours.

Gary and Johanne Wayne
Colorado **Rockies** Pitcher and Wife
Lakewood, CO

Easy Peanut Butter Pie

1 baked pie shell
2 pkgs. vanilla instant pudding
3-1/4 cups milk
1/4 tsp. vanilla
1 cup powdered sugar
1/2 cup peanut butter
1-1/2 cups Cool Whip

• Combine powdered sugar and peanut butter. Blend until the appearance of biscuit mix. Spread half of this mixture on pie shell. Mix pudding with milk. Beat according to pudding pkg. directions. Add vanilla. Pour into prepared pie shell. Top with Cool Whip and sprinkle with remaining peanut butter mixture.

Kim Christiansen
News Reporter /Co-anchor
KUSA-TV Channel 9
Denver, CO

Vanessa Nielsen, Wellington, Co.

Blackberry Cobbler with Godiva Custard

Rosemary Pastry:
2 tsp. granulated sugar
1 cup all-purpose flour
1 Tbl. baking powder
1/2 tsp. salt
4 Tbl. (1/2 stick) unsalted butter
1/4 cup heavy cream
1/2 tsp. fresh rosemary, finely chopped

Blackberries:
3 cups fresh blackberries
1/4 cup orange juice
1/4 cup sugar
2 Tbl. cornstarch
2 Tbl. heavy cream

Godiva Custard:
1 tsp. powdered unflavored gelatin
1/4 cup water, room temperature
1/4 cup brown sugar, packed
2 eggs, separated
Pinch salt
1/2 cup Godiva liquor
1/4 cup sugar
2 cups heavy cream

• Heat oven to 400° Butter four 1 cup ramekins or a 1 qt. casserole. Set aside. To make pastry put flour, sugar, baking powder and salt in a mixing bowl and mix well. Add butter and mix with a fork until it resembles coarse meal. Stir in cream and rosemary. Mix quickly to form a stiff dough. Next roll dough to a thickness of 3/8" (everything should be well floured to prevent sticking) and cut 4 circles 3" in size, set aside.
• Wash berries well, discarding soft or moldy ones. Mix with orange juice and sugar. Let stand 1.5 hours. Next mix in the cornstarch and stir until well mixed. Divide between the ramekins or pour into the casserole. Top with rosemary biscuits and brush the tops with a little cream. Bake for 15-20 minutes, until fruit is thick and bubbly and biscuits are well browned.
• The custard should be made 24 hours in advance. Bloom gelatin in 1/4 cup water. Heat gently to dissolve (no warmer than 125-130°), set aside. Whip brown sugar, egg yolks and salt in mixer until light and fluffy. Add gelatin mixture and mix well. Stir in Godiva liquor and set aside. Whip egg whites until they form a coarse foam and continue to beat until they reach a medium peak stage. Whip cream until stiff. Using a rubber spatula gently fold egg whites into egg yolk mixture, next the whipped cream.
• Garnish each cobbler with Godiva custard.

Tante Louise Restaurant
Denver, CO

Caution: This recipe specifies raw egg. However, pasturized eggs are available at grocery stores and would be the only safe choice as an ingredient in an uncooked pie filling.

 PIES

Quick Apple Crisp

1 Granny Smith apple
Maple syrup or honey
Margarine
Granola cereal

• Pare, core and slice apple. Evenly divide into 2 custard cups. Lightly drizzle maple syrup or honey over apples. Dot with margarine; sprinkle with granola cereal. Microwave 1-1/2 to 2 minutes; let stand. Serve warm with frozen yogurt. Yum!

Washington Apple Growers

Alecia Arevalos, Wellington, Co.

Pecan Rum Pie

1 cup brown sugar
1/4 cup butter
1/2 cup corn syrup
1 Tbl. rum or rum extract
1 Tbl. vanilla
Pinch salt
3 eggs
1-1/2 cups pecans

• Cream butter and brown sugar together. Add corn syrup, vanilla and rum. Mix one minute. Add salt and eggs - one at a time. Mix until creamy and eggs are fully incorporated. Add half of the pecans and mix until combined. Pour into unbaked 9" pie shell. Bake at 400° until crust is golden and center is firm, about 40-50 minutes. Add the rest of the pecans and bake another 10 minutes.
Variation: Walnut rum pie: substitute 1-1/2 cups chopped walnuts for pecans.

Judy Van Dyke
The Castaways Restaurant
Manitou Springs, CO

The Three "P's": Pleasing Peach Pie

Pie filling:
1 cup sugar
2 Tbl. cornstarch
3 Tbl. vanilla tapioca pudding pie mix
2 Tbl. white corn syrup
6 cups peeled, sliced Palisade, CO fresh
    peaches
1 Tbl. butter flavored Crisco
1 Tbl. lemon juice

Pie Crust:
2-1/4 cups unbleached flour
1 tsp. salt
3/4 cup plus 2 Tbl. chilled butter flavored
    Crisco
7 Tbl. ice water
1 egg white, beaten
(Milk, sugar)

• **Pie filling:** Combine sugar, cornstarch, tapioca pudding pie mix and white corn syrup. Put in peaches gently. Put in microwave and heat thoroughly.
• **Pie crust:** Combine flour and salt in a bowl. Cut in Crisco using a pastry blender until flour is blended to form pea-sized chunks. Sprinkle with water, a little at a time and toss lightly with a fork until dough forms a ball. Press down and make two even balls. Roll dough between two sheets of waxed paper. Roll dough into circle to form bottom crust and place in pie dish. Trim one inch larger than pie pan. Brush bottom with beaten egg white. Moisten pastry edge with milk. Fill bottom crust with cooled peach filling leaving excess liquid out. (Amount depends on juice peaches have created). Roll top crust same as bottom crust. Put top crust onto filled pie plate. Fold top edge under bottom crust, then flute. Brush top with milk and sprinkle sugar on lightly. Cover edges of pie with foil.
• Bake at 425° for 20 minutes, then reduce heat to 375°. Bake for 30 minutes more. Remove foil and continue baking until all is nicely browned.

Dolores Vaccaro
Winner - Colorado State Fair

Chance Tarr, Wellington, Co.

Blueberry Sour Cream Pie

9" unbaked pie shell

Filling:
2 cups drained blueberries
1 cup sugar
1/2 cup flour
1/4 tsp. salt
1/2 tsp. vanilla
1 egg, beaten
1 cup sour cream

Topping:
1/3 cup sugar
1/3 cup flour
1/4 cup softened butter
1 tsp. cinnamon

• **Filling:** Combine all filling ingredients in bowl. Mix well. Pour into a 9" unbaked pie shell. Bake at 400-425° for 15 minutes. Reduce heat to 325° and bake another 30 minutes.
• **Topping:** Combine ingredients in bowl, cutting in butter. Sprinkle on top of pie and bake 15 minutes more at 350°.
Variation: Sour cream apple pie: substitute 2 cups of peeled, cored and diced apples for blueberries.

Judy Van Dyke
The Castaways Restaurant
Manitou Springs, CO

Ty Presgrove, Wellington, Co.

Easy Custard Pie

9" unbaked pie shell
2-1/2 cups milk
4 eggs
2/3 cup sugar
1/4 tsp. salt
1 tsp. vanilla
Nutmeg

• Put pie shell in the oven and turn oven to 475°. Scald milk while you partially bake shell.
• In bowl put eggs, sugar, salt and vanilla. Add scalded milk and mix well. Pour into partially baked pie shell and sprinkle with nutmeg. Bake 5 minutes at 475°. Reduce heat to 425° for 10-15 minutes. Chill.

Armetta Keeney
1992 Best Cook in the Country

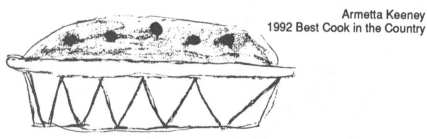

Nicole Shepherd, Colo. Springs, Co.

☀ BARS - BROWNIES ☀

Tom McChesney, Wellington, Co.

Marvelous Marbled Brownies

Cake:
5 bars (1.3 oz. each) DOVE Dark Chocolates
1/2 cup butter
3/4 cup granulated sugar
1/4 tsp. salt
1/2 tsp. vanilla extract
2 large eggs
1/2 cup all-purpose flour

Filling:
3 oz. cream cheese
1 oz. Irish cream liqueur
1 Tbl. granulated sugar
1 Tbl. all-purpose flour
1/2 large egg

1 quart vanilla ice cream

Hot Milk Chocolate Sauce:
5 bars (1.3 oz. each) DOVE Milk Chocolate
2 Tbl. butter
2 Tbl. heavy cream
2 Tbl. water

Prep. Time: 1 hr. (cake)
Prep. Time: 15 minutes (sauce)
• Preheat oven to 350°. Prepare pans by brushing lightly with melted butter and dusting with flour.
• **Cake:** Melt chocolate and butter over a hot water bath. Place mixture in a small mixer bowl with paddle attachment. Add the sugar and salt; mix until combined. Add the vanilla extract and the eggs, one at a time, until well blended. Add the flour and mix until incorporated; set aside.
• **Filling:** In a small mixer bowl with whisk attachment, combine the cream cheese and liqueur until smooth. Add the sugar, flour, vanilla extract and egg; whisk until combined. Set aside.
• Fill prepared pan(s) with chocolate brownie mixture. Pipe the cream cheese mixture on the top of the brownie mixture; swirl with a toothpick or skewer.
• **Sauce:** Melt chocolate and butter over a hot water bath. Add heavy cream and water; stir until combined. Makes about 1 cup.
• Bake approximately 30 minutes for the 10-inch tart OR 20 minutes for the six 4-1/2 inch tarts. Place pieces of brownie tarts on serving plates; top with vanilla ice cream and Hot Milk Chocolate Sauce.
• Yield: one 10-inch tart or six 4-1/2 inch tarts

M&M/MARS
Recipe developed by students at
theCulinary Institute of America

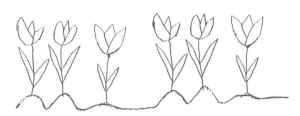

Amy Westover, Wellington, Co.

My Favorite Brownies Anywhere

2 sticks butter (1 cup)
1 cup semi-sweet chocolate bits
4 squares unsweetened chocolate
4 eggs
2 cup sugar
1 cup flour
2 tsp. vanilla
1 cup pecan bits, chopped
1 cup miniature marshmallows

• Melt together butter, semi-sweet chocolate bits, and unsweetened chocolate squares over low heat. Remove from heat and cool. In large mixer, beat the eggs well. Add the sugar slowly and beat well. Add the melted chocolate mixture, (cooled) and blend. Add the flour and blend lightly. Add the vanilla and blend. Add the marshmallows and pecans and blend thoroughly. Grease a 9x13 pan and pour in the mixture. Bake in a preheated 350° oven for 30 minutes or until done. These should not be dry. Cool and cut into squares for serving. They do not need icing.

Pat Miller
Gabby Gourmet

Mari Burgos, Wellington, Co.

Congo Squares

3/4 cup sugar
3/4 cup margarine
1 tsp. vanilla
2 eggs
3 cups flour
2 tsp. baking powder
1/2 tsp. salt
1/2 cup milk
6 oz. pkg. chocolate chips

• Blend first four ingredients. Add dry ingredients, alternating with milk. Fold in chips. Pour into greased pan. Bake at 350° for 40-45 minutes.

Representative Maryanne "Moe" Keller
Colorado State Representative
Wheatridge, CO

Bryon Butzin, Colorado Springs, Co.

181

Potato Brownies

3 oz. unsweetened chocolate
3/4 cup margarine
1-2/3 cups sugar
1 tsp. vanilla
1/4 tsp. salt
4 eggs
1 cup mashed potatoes
1 cup flour
1/2 tsp. baking powder
1/2 cup chopped nuts

• Melt chocolate and margarine in saucepan on top of stove or in glass dish in microwave. Cool. Cream sugar, vanilla and eggs. Mix well. Add chocolate mixture, potatoes, flour, baking powder and nuts. Beat until creamy. Pour into greased and floured 9x11" cake pan. Bake at 350° about 30 minutes or until done. Use with following icing.
• Icing: 1 cup powdered sugar, 2 Tbl. hot coffee, 1 Tbl. cocoa, 1 tsp. vanilla. Mix together and spread on top of brownies.

State Representative Lewis H. Entz
Hooper, CO

Schaye's Favorite Brownies/Candy Bar Mix

4 large eggs, lightly beaten
2 cups sugar
3/4 cup butter or margarine, melted
2 tsp. vanilla
1-1/2 cups flour
1/2 tsp. baking powder
1/4 tsp. salt
1/3 cup cocoa
4 (2.07 oz.) chocolate-coated caramel peanut
    nougat bars, coarsely chopped
3 (1.55 oz.) milk chocolate bars, finely chopped

• Combine eggs, sugar, butter and vanilla in a large bowl. Combine flour, baking powder, salt and cocoa. Stir into egg mixture. Fold in chopped nougat bars. Spoon into a greased 9x13 pan. Sprinkle evenly with chopped milk chocolate bar. Bake at 350° for 30 - 35 minutes.

Olympian Wendy Lucero Schaye
and Ex-Nugget Danny Schaye

182   *Tom McChesney, Wellington, Co.*

Nancy Reagan's Brownies

3 oz. semi-sweet chocolate squares
2 oz. unsweetened chocolate squares
12 oz. unsalted butter
6 eggs
2 cups superfine sugar
2/3 cup cake flour
1 tsp. salt
1 tsp. baking powder
1 Tbl. vanilla
2 cups pecans, finely ground

Variation
Substitute 1 cup honey for the 2 cups of sugar and reduce vanilla to 1-1/2 tsp. This will halve the number of calories.

• Preheat oven to 350°
• In glass measuring cup, place chocolates with butter. Microwave at full power (100%), about 90 seconds to melt. Or, in insert of double boiler over hot water on medium heat, stir to melt chocolates and butter. Cool mixture.
• In food processor with metal blade and motor running, add eggs through funnel attached to feed tube. Add sugar in same manner. Process until light lemon colored and mixed well. With motor running, pour chocolate mixture through funnel. Process to mix.
• In a bowl, sift together flour, salt and baking powder. Add to chocolate mixture through funnel. Process to mix. Add vanilla and nuts. Pulse to mix. Pour into prepared pan (9-3/4"x14" jelly roll pan, buttered, and dusted with cocoa). Bake 30 minutes. Cool. Cut into squares. Sprinkle with powdered sugar if desired.

Katie Stapleton
Host of KOA's "Cooking with Katie"

Paula Woodward's Brownies

2 sq. unsweetened chocolate
1/2 cup butter or margarine
2 eggs
1 cup sugar
1/2 tsp. pure vanilla
1/2 cup flour

• Melt chocolate and butter on low heat. Mix together eggs, sugar and vanilla. Add flour. Add chocolate mixture. Bake in wax paper lined 8" square pan at 325° for 30 minutes. Remove from pan and cover with powdered sugar. Cut in squares. Enjoy!

Paula Woodward
KUSA Channel 9 Anchor
"Nine Wants to Know" Reporter

Mike McChesney, Wellington, Co.

Double Fudge Saucepan Brownies

2/3 cup all-purpose flour
1/4 tsp. baking soda
1/4 tsp. salt
1/2 cup sugar
2 Tbl. butter or margarine
2 Tbl. water
2 cups (12-oz. pkg.) *HERSHEY'S semi-sweet
    chocolate chips, divided
2 eggs, slightly beaten
1 tsp. vanilla extract
1/2 cup chopped nuts (optional)

· High altitude directions: Increase flour to 3/4 cup; decrease sugar to 1/3 cup plus 2 Tbl.; increase water to 3 Tbl.

* Hershey, Mini Chips, and Reese's are registered trademarks. Recipes courtesy of the Hershey kitchens, and reprinted with permission of Hershey Foods Corporation.

• Heat oven to 325°. Grease 9-inch square baking pan. In bowl, stir together flour, baking soda and salt. In medium saucepan, combine sugar, butter and water. Cook over low heat, stirring constantly until mixture comes to boil. Remove from heat; immediately add 1 cup chocolate chips, stirring until melted. Stir in eggs and vanilla until blended. Gradually add flour mixture, blending well. Stir in remaining 1 cup chips (and nuts, if desired). Pour batter into prepared pan. Bake 25 to 30 minutes or until brownies begin to pull away from sides of pan. Cool completely in pan on wire rack. Cut into squares. About 1-1/2 dozen brownies.

Hershey Foods Corporation

Death By Chocolate

Brownie mix
8 oz. Cool Whip
1 pkg. of treat-size or 3 (1.4 oz. size) Heath bars
1/2 cup pecans, chopped
1 large size chocolate pudding mix

• Layer 1: Make brownie mix according to directions. Cool. Divide in half and break or tear each section into bite size pieces. Layer 1 is 1/2 of these pieces.
• Mix large pkg. chocolate pudding according to directions and pour on top of brownie pieces. Spread on Cool Whip. Sprinkle with crushed Heath bars. Sprinkle with chopped pecans. Layer remaining 1/2 of brownie pieces on top. Cover bowl and allow flavors to blend overnight.

Mark Koebrich
Channel 9 - "Good Afternoon Colorado"

Tom McChesney, Wellington, Co.   184

Katie Stapleton's Denver Brownies

3/4 cup flour, sifted
1 tsp. baking powder
1/8 tsp. salt
1/2 cup superfine sugar
2 Tbl. water
6 oz. semi-sweet chocolate chips
2-1/2 oz. unsalted butter
1 tsp. vanilla
2 eggs
1/2 cup coarsely ground walnuts or pecans
    (optional)
1 oz. bourbon

• Preheat oven to 325°.
• Sift together flour, baking powder, and salt. Set aside. In pan over medium heat, combine sugar with water. As you stir constantly, heat mixture to just under a boil. Remove pan from heat and stir in chocolate chips, butter and vanilla. Beat in eggs, one at a time. Add flour mixture. Add nuts if you wish. Pour into prepared baking pan (8" square baking pan, buttered and dusted with cocoa). Bake 25 to 30 minutes.
• Remove pan from oven and sprinkle with bourbon. Cool.

White Frosting

4 oz. unsalted butter, softened
1 tsp. vanilla
2 cups powdered sugar, sifted

• In food processor with metal blade, combine butter and vanilla. Process until smooth. With motor running, pour powdered sugar through a feed tube with funnel. Process until mixed and creamy. Wait until brownies are cool, then frost. Chill.

Chocolate Glaze

6 oz. semi-sweet chocolate chips
1/2 cup hot water
1/2 oz. (1 Tbl.) butter

• Put chocolate chips in a bowl and cover with hot water. Chocolate will melt almost instantly. In about 30 seconds, quickly pour off all liquid. Stir until chocolate is creamy and add butter. Chocolate will shine. Cool glaze and spread over white frosting. Chill until firm or freeze. (Denver Brownies freeze beautifully.) To serve: cut to make 25 brownies. Serve at room temperature.

Katie Stapleton
Host of KOA's "Cooking with Katie"

Jenifer Foote, Wellington, Co.

185

Blonde Rocky Road Brownies

1 pkg. (20 oz.) refrigerated sliceable sugar
    cookies
48 KRAFT caramels
2 Tbl. water
1 cup Baker's semi-sweet real chocolate chips
1 cup peanuts
2 cups KRAFT miniature marshmallows

• Prep. time: 10 min. Cooking time: 20 min.
• Heat oven to 350°. Press cookie dough onto bottom and sides of 13x9-inch baking pan. Bake 15 to 18 minutes or until lightly browned. Microwave caramels and water in medium microwavable bowl on HIGH 2 to 3 minutes or until smooth, stirring every minute. Pour caramel mixture over crust; top with chips, peanuts and marshmallows. Heat broiler. Broil 5 inches from heat for 1 minute or until marshmallows are lightly browned. Cool; cut into bars. Makes 24.
• Variation: Substitute refrigerated sliceable peanut butter cookies for sugar cookies.

KRAFT Creative Kitchens

O'Henry Bars

4 cups (about 8-3/4 oz.) quick oatmeal
1 cup brown sugar, sifted
1/2 cup dark Karo syrup
1/2 cup melted margarine
1 tsp. vanilla
2 cups semi-sweet chocolate chips
1/2 cup peanut butter (use either creamy or with
    nuts)

• Preheat oven to 350°. In a medium bowl, mix oatmeal with brown sugar. Add syrup, melted margarine and vanilla. Pat mixture into 9x13 baking pan. (This is an enormous pain as you have to work patiently with a spatula, spreading it into the far corners of the pan.) Bake only 15 minutes. Remove pan from oven and cool.
• In a heavy pan over medium heat, melt chocolate chips with peanut butter. Stir constantly to melt and mix. Be wary of scorching! When chocolate is melted and sauce is smooth, spread on top of oatmeal mixture in pan. Cut when chocolate is set to make about 30 bars. Yum, yum!

Katie Stapleton
From Larry Cox's "KOA's National Recovery Act
Cookbook"

Eddie Rodrigues, Wellington, Co.

Mini-Chip Blondies

2 cups all-purpose flour
1 tsp. baking powder
1/4 tsp. baking soda
1/4 tsp. salt
3/4 cup (1-1/2 sticks) butter or margarine, softened
1-1/2 cups packed light brown sugar
2 eggs
2 Tbl. milk
1 tsp. vanilla extract
2 cups (12 oz. pkg.) *HERSHEY'S MINI CHIPS semi-sweet chocolate

* Hershey, Mini Chips, and Reese's are registered trademarks. Recipes courtesy of the Hershey kitchens, and reprinted with permission of Hershey Foods Corporation.

• Heat oven to 350° Grease 13x9x2-inch baking pan. In bowl, stir together flour, baking powder, baking soda and salt. In large mixer bowl, beat butter and brown sugar until light and fluffy. Add eggs, milk and vanilla; beat well. Gradually add flour mixture, beating well. Stir in small chocolate chips. Spread into prepared pan. Bake 30 to 35 minutes or until lightly browned. Cool in pan on wire rack. Cut into bars. About 3 dozen bars.
• High altitude directions: increase flour to 2 cups plus 2 Tbl.; decrease baking powder to 3/4 tsp.; decrease packed light brown sugar to 1-1/4 cups; increase milk to 1/4 cup. Bake at 350° for 27 to 32 minutes.

Hershey's Foods Corporation

Energy Bars

Bars:
2 eggs, lightly beaten
1/2 cup chunky peanut butter
3/4 cup firmly packed light brown sugar
2/3 cup instant nonfat dry milk
1/4 cup all-purpose flour
1/4 cup melted margarine
3 cups rolled oats
1 cup raisins (optional)
Icing:
1 cup carob chips
1 Tbl. softened margarine

• Combine eggs, peanut butter and sugar in large bowl. Add dry milk, flour and margarine; mix until well blended. Stir in oats and raisins. Mix until evenly coated. Spread into an 8 or 9 " square non-stick pan (or lightly greased). Press down firmly. Bake at 350° for 25 minutes.
• Sprinkle 1 cup carob chips on warm bars. Cover pan with foil to melt chips adding 1 Tbl. margarine (softened) to ease in spreading melted chips. Cool. Cut into 20 bars.

Kitty Fassel, wife of Jim Fassel (Bronco Offensive Coordinator) and experienced tailgater!

Tom McChesney, Wellington, Co.

Frosted Peanut Butter Brownies

1 cup butter or margarine
1/3 cup cocoa
2 cups sugar
1-1/2 cups all-purpose flour
1/2 tsp. salt
4 large eggs
1 tsp. vanilla extract
1 (12 oz.) jar chunky peanut butter
1/2 cup butter or margarine
1/4 cup cocoa
1/3 cup milk
10 large marshmallows
1 (16 oz.) pkg. powdered sugar, sifted

• Combine 1 cup butter and 1/3 cup cocoa in a saucepan over low heat; cook, stirring frequently until butter melts. Remove from heat and cool slightly.
• Combine sugar, flour and salt in large mixing bowl. Add chocolate mixture and beat at medium speed with an electric mixer until blended. Add eggs and vanilla, mixing well. Spread into a well-greased 13x9x2-inch pan. Bake at 350° for 20 to 25 minutes or until a wooden pick inserted in center comes out clean.
• Remove lid from peanut butter jar; microwave at MEDIUM (50% power) 2 to 3 minutes or until peanut butter melts, stirring at 1 minute intervals. Spread over warm brownies. Chill about 30 minutes or until set.
• Combine 1/2 cup butter and next 3 ingredients in a saucepan over medium heat; cook, stirring frequently, until marshmallows melt. Remove from heat, and add powdered sugar, stirring until smooth.
• Spread over peanut butter, and chill until set. Store in refrigerator. Freeze in airtight containers for up to 3 months.
• Yield: 4 dozen.

Patty Vann
Assistant Test Kitchen Director
Southern Living Magazine

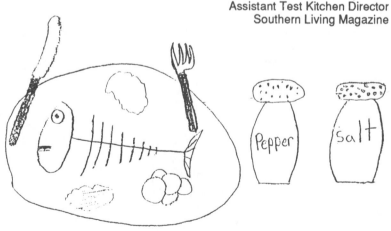

Dever Weskamp, Wellington, Co.

BARS - BROWNIES

Salted Peanut Bars

3 cups flour
1 cup butter or margarine
1-1/2 cups light brown sugar
1/4 tsp. salt
2 small or 1 big pkg. butterscotch chips
3 Tbl. butter
3 Tbl. water
1/2 cup light corn syrup
3 cups salted Spanish peanuts (about 1 lb.)

• Mix first 4 ingredients like pie crust. Put in jelly roll pan (pan approx. 17" x 13"). Bake 10 minutes at 350°. Melt next 4 ingredients. Add Spanish peanuts. Spread mixture over crust as soon as it is out of oven. Bake 8 minutes more. Yield: 60 bars.

Jeane Faatz
State Representative
Southwest Denver

Almond Chocolate Buttercrunch

3/4 cup toasted almonds, coarsely chopped
4 oz. unsalted butter
3/4 cup packed brown sugar
1 cup (5-3/4 oz.) chocolate morsels

• Sprinkle chopped almonds to cover bottom of baking pan, (one 8"x8" or smaller baking pan, generously buttered). Set aside.
• In small, heavy pan over low-medium heat, melt butter. Whisk in brown sugar which dissolves at once. Bring to boil over medium heat. As you stir constantly, boil 7 minutes. Pour mixture over almonds. Let set about 3 to 5 minutes. • Quickly sprinkle with chocolate morsels. Use spatula to expedite melting and smooth over entire brown sugar mixture. Refrigerate about 20 to 25 minutes. With a sharp knife, cut into squares. Under no circumstances, either refrigerate longer or freeze as that will change the complexion of the chocolate. Serve at room temperature or keep in tins until your Valentine presentation to a grateful lover who will love you all the more.

Katie Stapleton
Host of KOA's "Cooking with Katie"

Ruben Cabral, Wellington, Co.

Peanut Butter Chips and Jelly Bars

1-1/2 cups all-purpose flour
1/2 cup sugar
3/4 tsp. baking powder
1/2 cup (1 stick) cold butter or margarine
1 egg, beaten
3/4 cup grape jelly
1-2/3 cups (10 oz. pkg.) *REESE'S peanut butter
    chips, divided

* Hershey, Mini Chips, and Reese's are
registered trademarks. Recipes courtesy of the
Hershey kitchens, and reprinted with
permission of Hershey Foods Corporation.

• Heat oven to 375°. Grease 9-inch square baking
pan. Stir together flour, sugar and baking powder;
with pastry blender or fork, cut in butter until
mixture resembles coarse crumbs. Add egg;
blend well. Reserve half of mixture; press
remaining mixture onto bottom of prepared pan.
Spread jelly evenly over crust. Sprinkle 1 cup
peanut butter chips over jelly. Stir together
remaining crumb mixture with remaining 2/3 cup
chips; sprinkle over top. Bake 25 to 30 minutes or
until lightly browned. Cool completely in pan on
wire rack. Cut into bars. About 16 bars.
• High altitude directions: Increase flour to 1-1/2
cups plus 1 Tbl. Add 1 Tbl. water with egg. Do
not change baking time or temperature.

Hershey Foods Corporation

Creamy Fudge Candy

1 can evaporated milk
4 cups sugar
3 small pkgs. (6 oz.) chocolate chips
1 cup butter or oleo
28 (about 1/2 bag) large marshmallows
2 tsp. vanilla
4 cups nuts

• Boil evaporated milk and sugar for 10 minutes.
Remove from the stove and add chocolate chips,
butter, marshmallows, vanilla and nuts. Pour into
buttered 9x13 dish. Let cool and set in refrigerator
for 24 hours. Makes about 5 lbs.

Rusti Ruth
Friend of Education

Vanessa Neilsen, Wellington, Co.

Peanut Butter Chocolate Bars

3 oz. bittersweet chocolate, broken into pieces
1 cup unsalted roasted peanuts
4 oz. unsalted butter cut into 8 pieces (1 Tbl. each)
1-1/4 cups firmly packed dark brown sugar
2 large eggs
1/2 tsp. vanilla
1-1/4 cups flour

This is a perfect treat for a kid's gathering.

• Preheat oven to 350°.
• In food processor with steel blade, place chocolate pieces. Pulse 4 times. Then, process until chopped finely, about 1 minute. Remove from food processor and reserve.
• In same food processor, place 1/4 cup peanuts and process to chop coarsely, about 5 seconds. Remove and set aside.
• In same food processor, process remaining 3/4 cup peanuts to smooth paste, about 2 minutes. Add butter and sugar and process until combined, about 30 seconds. Scrape down food processor bowl when necessary. Add eggs and vanilla and process until combined, about 10 seconds. Add flour and 1/2 of chopped peanuts and process to combine, about 5 seconds. Scrape down bowl when necessary.
• Spread batter evenly in 9 x 13 pan. Thump pan on kitchen counter to fill corners of pan. Batter is very thin. Place in oven and be sure pan is level. Bake 25 minutes or until an inserted toothpick in center comes out clean.
• Remove pan from oven and sprinkle with reserved chocolate. Let stand until melted. With spatula, spread chocolate over top to make a smooth coating. Sprinkle top with remaining 1/2 of chopped peanuts.
• Refrigerate to cool and harden. Cut into 2 x 1-1/4 inches bars with a sharp knife. Store in refrigerator to crisp.

Katie Stapleton
Host of KOA's "Cooking with Katie"

Lacey Morris, Mancos, Co.

Cream Cheese and Jam Dream Bars

1/2 cup nuts - ground
1-1/4 cups flour
1/2 cup firmly packed brown sugar
1/2 cup margarine
1/2 cup oatmeal
1 (8 oz.) pkg. cream cheese
1/3 cup granulated sugar
1 egg
1 tsp. vanilla
1-1/2 cups cherry jam
1/2 cup nuts - ground for topping

• Preheat oven to 350°. Grease 9x13 pan.
• **Crust:** Combine flour and brown sugar. Add margarine and cut in flour mixture until crumbly and well mixed. Add 1/2 cup of finely chopped nuts and oatmeal. Mix well. Reserve 1/2 cup of this mixture for topping. Press remaining crumb mixture into bottom of pan. Bake at 350° for 12 - 15 minutes.
• **Filling:** Beat cream cheese, sugar, egg and vanilla until smooth. Spread over hot baked crust and bake 10 more minutes. Spread a thin coat of cherry jam over cheese layer. Sprinkle reserved crumbs and the 1/2 cup of nuts over the top. Return to the oven and bake 5 minutes. Cool and cut into squares. Enjoy!

Nancy Horton
1992 1st Place Winner of Sure Jell Contest at
Colorado State Fair with this recipe

Marshmallow Treats

1 pkg. Kraft caramels
1 can Eagle Brand milk
1 sq. margarine (2 Tbl.)
About 65 lg. size marshmallows
Toothpicks
1 box of crisp rice cereal

• In a double boiler melt caramels, Eagle Brand milk and margarine. Stick toothpicks in marshmallows and dip in sauce. Roll in crisp rice cereal and set on wax paper.
Makes about 65 treats (if caramel is used sparingly).

Dennis Brimhall, CEO
Univ. of Colo. Health and Science Center

Bryce Hall, Wellington, Co.

CAKES

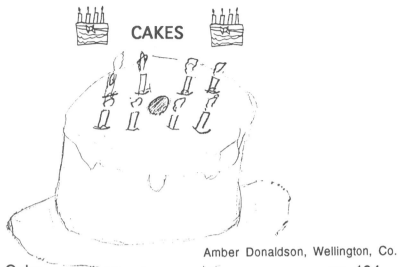

Amber Donaldson, Wellington, Co.

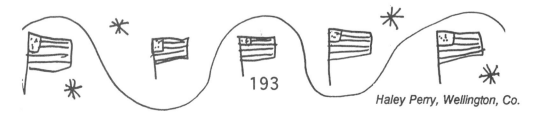

Haley Perry, Wellington, Co.

Best Two Egg Cake

1/2 cup shortening or margarine
1 1/2 cup sugar
1 tsp. vanilla
2 eggs
2-1/4 cups flour
2-1/2 tsp. baking powder
1 tsp. salt
1 cup + 2 Tbl. milk

• Stir shortening to soften. Gradually add sugar and cream together. Add eggs and vanilla, mix. Add dry ingredients and mix with milk. Pour into pan. Bake at 375° for 25 minutes. Frost if desired.

Ann Azari
Mayor of Ft. Collins, CO

Toffee Cake

1 cup sugar
1 cup brown sugar
2 cups flour
1 tsp. soda
1/2 cup butter
1 cup buttermilk
1 egg
1/2 tsp. vanilla
5 oz. chocolate covered toffee bars (chopped)
1/2 cup chopped pecans

• Put sugars in large mixing bowl. Sift in dry ingredients, stir to mix. Cut in butter (as for pie crust). Remove a 1/2 cup of the mixture and set aside. To remainder add buttermilk, egg and vanilla. Beat thoroughly and turn into greased 9x13 pan. Combine reserved dry mixture with chopped candy and nuts. Sprinkle over batter. Bake at 350° for 30 minutes. Serve from baking pan.
Yield: 12 servings.

Ray Powers
State Senator
Colorado Springs, CO

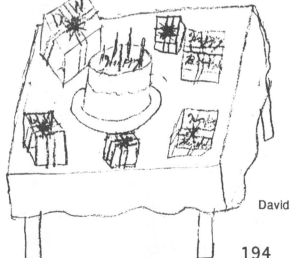

David Waldo, Wellington, Co.

CAKES

Strawberry Shortcake

Sliced fresh strawberries
Sugar

Shortcake:
1 cup sifted flour
1-1/3 Tbl. sugar
1-3/4 tsp. baking powder
1/2 tsp. salt
2 Tbl. margarine
1 Tbl. shortening
1/3 - 1/2 cup milk
Non-dairy whipped topping

Shortcake
• Sift 1st four ingredients.
• Cut in next 2 ingredients.
• Stir in milk.
• Knead lightly.
• Form into 4 flattened-top shortcakes. Bake on lightly greased cookie sheet at 400° for 8 minutes. They freeze well after cooking.

Strawberries
• Prepare at least 6 hours in advance. Can be day before. Slice strawberries. Sprinkle plenty of sugar over berries, cover and refrigerate, (allow to "juice") Spoon over shortcake. Top with non-dairy whipped topping.

Jeanne Faatz
State Representative
Southwest Denver

Date Cake

1 cup brown sugar
3 Tbl. butter
1 cup dates (cut fine)
1 tsp. soda
1/2 cup nuts (cut fine)
1 egg
1 cup boiling water
1 tsp. vanilla
1-1/2 cup flour

• Pour boiling water over dates. Mix sugar, egg and butter together. Put flour in sifter and add soda. Combine egg mixture to dates. Sift in flour and add nuts and vanilla.
• Bake 45 minutes at 350°.

Rusti Ruth
Friend of Education, Redding, CA

Olivia Stull, Wellington, Co.

 CAKES

Kathy Walsh's Sister's Irish Cream Cheesecake

1 (8-1/2 oz) pkg. chocolate wafer crumbs
1/2 tsp. cinnamon
1/2 cup butter or margarine (softened)
3 (8 oz.) pkg. cream cheese (softened)
1 cup sugar
1 tsp. vanilla extract
3 eggs
8 oz. semi -sweet chocolate (melted)
2/3 cup Irish cream liquer
2-2/3 cups heavy cream

• Combine crumbs, cinnamon and butter or margarine; press into bottom of 10 inch spring form pan; chill 2 hours. Beat cream cheese and sugar; gradually add vanilla extract and eggs; blend. Stir in chocolate, liquer and heavy cream; mix well. Pour into chilled crust. Bake at 350° for 1 to 1-1/4 hours.
• Cool. Refrigerate overnight.
• Makes one 10-inch cheesecake.
• To serve when frozen: thaw, unwrapped, in refrigerator overnight.

Kathy Walsh
News 4 Anchor and Reporter

Philly 3 Step Chocolate Chip Cheesecake

2 (8 oz.) pkgs. Philadelphia brand cream cheese, softened
1/2 cup sugar
1/2 tsp. vanilla
2 eggs
3/4 cup mini semi-sweet chocolate chips, divided
1 ready-to-use graham cracker crumb crust (6 oz. or 9-inch)

Prep. time: 10 min. Cooking time: 40 min.
• MIX cream cheese, sugar and vanilla with electric mixer on medium speed until well blended. Add eggs; mix until blended. Stir in 1/2 cup of the chips.
• POUR into crust. Sprinkle with remaining 1/4 cup chips.
• BAKE at 350° F, 40 minutes or until center is almost set. Cool. Refrigerate 3 hours or overnight.
• Yield: 8 servings

KRAFT Creative Kitchens

Karl Whitman, Wellington, Co.

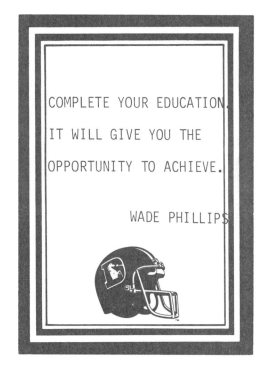

```
COMPLETE YOUR EDUCATION.

IT WILL GIVE YOU THE

OPPORTUNITY TO ACHIEVE.

            WADE PHILLIPS
```

Brownie Cheese Cake

Layer 1:
1 pkg. German chocolate cake mix
1 egg
1/3 cup margarine, softened

Layer 2:
2 packages (8 oz.) cream cheese, softened
2 eggs
3/4 cup sugar
2 tsp vanilla

Layer 3:
2 cups sour cream
1/4 cup sugar
1 Tbl vanilla

• **Layer 1:** Mix cake mix, 1 egg and 1/3 cup margarine on low speed until crumbly. Press into 9x13 pyrex dish.
• **Layer 2:** Beat cream cheese, 2 eggs, 3/4 cup sugar and 2 tsp. vanilla until smooth and fluffy. Spread over cake mixture. Bake 350° for 20 to 30 minutes.
• **Layer 3:** Mix well the sour cream, 1/4 cup sugar and 1 Tbl. vanilla. Spread over cake. Refrigerate 8 hours. Cut into small pieces.
• May wish to drizzle chocolate sauce or candies on top to decorate.

Wade Phillips
Head Coach
Denver Broncos

197

Miniature Cheesecakes

1/2 cup graham cracker crumbs
2 Tbl. butter or margarine, melted
1 (8 oz.) pkg. cream cheese, softened
1/4 cup sugar
1 egg
1/2 tsp. vanilla extract
1 (10-oz.) jar cherry preserves

• Combine graham cracker crumbs and butter, mixing well. Line one 3/4-inch muffin pans with miniature paper liners. Spoon 1 tsp. graham cracker mixture into each liner; gently press into bottom.
• Beat cream cheese with electric mixer until light and fluffy; gradually add sugar and mix well. Add egg and vanilla, beating well. Spoon mixture into liners. Bake at 350° for 10 minutes.
• Place cherry preserves in a small saucepan; heat just until preserves melt. Spoon about 1 tsp. preserves over each cheesecake. Chill thoroughly. Makes 2 dozen.

Dolores Vaccaro
Colorado State Fair
First Prize Champion

Cream Cheese Frosting

3 oz. cream cheese, softened
1/2 cup butter
2 cups powdered sugar
2 Tbl. cocoa (omit if want white frosting)
1 tsp. vanilla
2 - 3 tsp. or more cream to make right
　　consistency to spread

• Mix ingredients and spread.

Darlene Miller
Friend of Education from Battle Mt., NV

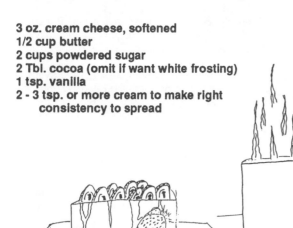

Nathan Griffin, Wellington, Co.

198

CAKES

Chocolate Chip and Oat Snackin' Cake

Vegetable cooking spray
1 cup packed light brown sugar
2/3 cup butter or margarine, softened
3 egg whites
1 cup skim milk
2-1/4 cups all-purpose flour
2-1/4 cups rolled oats
1/2 tsp. baking soda
1/2 tsp. salt
2 cups (12-oz. pkg.) HERSHEY'S Semi-Sweet
    Chocolate Chips

ORANGE GLAZE:
Stir together 2 Tbl. softened butter or
margarine, 3/4 cup powdered sugar, 1/2 to 1
tsp. freshly grated orange peel and 1 Tbl.
orange juice; beat until smooth.

• Heat oven to 350°
• Spray 13x9x2-inch baking pan with vegetable
cooking spray. In large bowl, stir together brown
sugar, margarine and egg whites; stir in milk. Stir
in flour, oats, baking soda, salt and chocolate
chips. Spread in prepared pan. Bake 25 to 30
minutes or until light golden brown and center
feels firm when touched lightly. (Do not
overbake.) Immediately spread with ORANGE
GLAZE. Cool completely. 12 to 15 servings.
HIGH ALTITUDE DIRECTIONS (3500 to 6500
feet): Heat oven to 375° F.

"Hershey, Mini Chips and Reese's are
registered trademarks. Recipes courtesy of
the Hershey Kitchen and reprinted with
permission of Hershey Foods Corporation."

Hershey Foods Corporation

The Best Pound Cake Ever

1 lb. butter, softened
3 cup sugar
6 eggs
4 cup unbleached white flour
1 cup milk
2 tsp. vanilla, almond or lemon extract
2 tsp. baking powder

• Preheat oven to 350° .
• Spray bundt pan with cooking spray. Cream
butter and sugar. Beat in eggs. Add 2 cups flour
and beat well. Mix in milk and extract. Combine
baking powder and remaining two cups of flour,
add to butter. Beat well. Pour batter into bundt
pan. Bake about an hour until knife inserted into
center comes out clean. Delicious with
raspberries and whipped cream.

Nancy Richards
Majic 100.3 KMJI
FM News Director

Chris Clark, Wellington, Co.

199

KEZW Pumpkin Cake

Cake:
4 jumbo eggs
2 cups sugar
1 cup melted Crisco
1 can (16 oz.) pumpkin
2 cups flour (spooned into cup)
2 tsp. baking powder
1 tsp. baking soda
3/4 tsp. salt
1/2 tsp. ground ginger
2 tsp. cinnamon (rounded)
1/4 tsp. ground clove
1/2 cup dark raisins soaked in boiling water, then drained

Frosting:
1/4 cup butter flavored Crisco
2 cups powdered sugar
1 tsp. vanilla
3 Tbl. evaporated milk

• **Cake:** In large bowl of mixer, beat together eggs, sugar, melted shortening and pumpkin. Beat in flour, baking powder, soda, salt, cinnamon, ginger and cloves. Stir in raisins. Pour batter into greased and floured 9x13 inch baking pan. Tap pan on counter to release air bubbles. Bake center shelf in preheated 375° oven 40 to 45 minutes or until wooden pick inserted in center comes out clean. Ice with frosting.

• **Frosting:** Place shortening in small sauce pan over very low heat until golden colored. Watch that it doesn't smoke or burn. Remove from heat. Add sugar and vanilla. Add enough milk for spreading consistency.

Rick Crandall
Radio Announcer
KOSI and KEZW Radio

Yum, Yum Cake

1 cup flour
2 cups brown sugar
1 tsp. soda
1 egg
1 tsp. vanilla
1 (16 oz.) can fruit cocktail including juice

• Mix flour, brown sugar and soda. Add remaining ingredients. Bake in a greased
8-inch pan at 350° for 40 minutes. Serve warm with whipped cream.
• Much better hot out of the oven.

Rusti Ruth
Friend of Education
Redding, CA

Jeremiah Jones, Wellington, Co.

 CAKES

Light As A Cloud Sponge Cake

Beat in a large bowl until stiff:
6 jumbo egg whites
1/2 tsp. cream of tartar
1/2 tsp. salt

Beat in another large bowl until thick (about 5 min.):
6 jumbo egg yolks
1 cup sugar
1 cup Softasilk cake flour
1/4 cup cold water
1 tsp. lemon extract and 1 tsp. lemon peel
1 tsp. orange extract and 1 tsp orange peel

• **Cake:** Fold the egg white mixture into the yolk mixture and cut all together. Pour into ungreased 10 x 4 inch tube pan. Bake at 375° for 30 minutes, then at 350° for 10 minutes. Cool on inverted heat-proof funnel.

• **Glaze:** In a small mixing bowl, combine powdered sugar, 1 tsp lemon flavoring and enough milk to make glaze of drizzling consistency. Drizzle over cake.

Dolores Vaccaro
State Fair Winner
Pueblo, CO

White Fruit Cake

1 lb. butter
2-1/2 cups sugar
6 eggs
1-1/2 oz. lemon juice
4 cups flour (save 1/4 cup to add to fruit)
1 tsp. baking powder
1 lb. white raisins
2 (8 oz.) can candied cherries
1 (8 oz.) can candied pineapple
4 cups pecans

• Mix butter, eggs, sugar and lemon. Add flour and baking powder. Add the fruit and flour mixture. Gently fold in pecans and pour into greased tube pan.
• Bake at 275° for about 2 hours. Wrap tightly in foil. Bake 4 weeks before holiday to improve (makes it moist.)

Rusti Ruth
Friend of Education
Redding, CA

Andrew Kisner, Wellington, Co.

"Good luck and great success with the cookbook. All good wishes to you, and God bless."

Willard Scott

Brown Sugar Pound Cake

Cake:
2 sticks butter
1/2 cup Crisco shortening
5 eggs
1 lb. and 1 cup light brown sugar
3-1/2 cups plain flour
1/2 tsp. baking powder
1 cup milk

Frosting:
1 stick butter
1 cup chopped pecans
1 box confectioner's sugar
Milk to thin

• **Cake:** Let eggs and butter "sit" till they're room temperature. Cream together 2 sticks butter and 1/2 cup Crisco. Add 5 eggs one at a time, creaming after each. Add 1 lb. and 1 cup light brown sugar. Sift together 3-1/2 cup plain flour and 1/2 tsp. baking powder. Add flour, baking powder mixture alternately with 1 cup milk to sugar mixture. Bake in greased and floured tube pan for 1-1/4 to 1-1/2 hours at 325°.
• **Frosting:** Toast 1 cup chopped pecans in 1 stick butter in thick broiler pan till they brown well. Let cool a little, then add 1 box confectioner's sugar. Add enough milk to thin to spreading consistency. Spread on top of cake. Some should "drip" down sides and center, but should not be spread anywhere except on top.

Willard Scott
NBC Today Show

Tom McChesney, Wellington, Co.

Chocolate Torte

12 bars (1.3 oz. each) DOVE Dark Chocolate,
    broken into pieces
1-1/4 cups granulated sugar, divided
2 cups (1 lb.) unsalted butter
1 cup strong brewed coffee (flavored coffees
    may be used)
10 large eggs, beaten

• Prep. Time: 30 min., + 90 min. baking
• Preheat oven 300°. Prepare a 10-inch springform pan by coating the inside with vegetable oil spray and dusting with 1/4 cup sugar; discard excess sugar. Wrap pan with foil to make it water tight.
• In a double boiler, melt chocolate, 1 cup sugar and butter. Pour mixture into large mixing bowl; add coffee and blend well. Add in beaten eggs, making sure all ingredients are well combined. Pour batter in prepared pan. Set pan in 1-inch water bath and bake 90 min. (center of torte will appear semi-liquid). Chill thoroughly before unmolding.
• Garnish torte with whipped creme rosettes and fresh berries. Serve slices of torte on vanilla sauce, if desired.
• Yield: 8 - 12 servings

M&M/MARS

Bjana Barella, Wellington, Co.

Flourless Chocolate Torte

1 lb. semi-sweet chocolate
14 oz. butter
2-1/2 oz. strong coffee
10-1/2 oz. sugar
9 eggs
5 oz. sugar

• Melt chocolate and butter together in a hot water bath. Combine coffee and 10-1/2 ounces of sugar. Whip eggs and 5 ounces of sugar for 7 minutes on high. Slowly add coffee mixture. Mix one minute. Scrape bowl and mix one minute longer. Pour into a buttered and sugared 9 inch spring form pan. Bake in a water bath for approximately 1 - 1-1/2 hours at 300° until firm. Cool in pan. Invert and refrigerate for 3 - 4 hours. Dust lightly with cocoa powder and serve with whipped cream.

Ronald Pehoski
Pastry Chef
Scanticon Denver Hotel

Sara Foote, Wellington, Co.

203

 CAKES

High Altitude Chocolate Cake

3 eggs
1 cup cooking oil
1/2 cup buttermilk
1 tsp. vanilla
2 cups sugar
1-3/4 cup cocoa
1 tsp. salt
1 tsp. baking soda
1 tsp. cinnamon
2 cups unsifted flour
1 cup boiling water

• Combine the eggs, oil, buttermilk and vanilla. Mix together until smooth. Sift together the sugar, cocoa, salt, baking soda, cinnamon and flour. Add to egg mixture, mix together until smooth. Pour in the boiling water and mix. (Batter will be very thin.) Pour into a greased 8-inch round cake or bundt pan. Bake at 350° for 30 minutes. Let cool for 20 minutes and frost.

Congressman Scott and Lori McInnis

Yummie Chocolate Zucchini Cake

1/2 cup butter
1/2 cup cooking oil
1-3/4 cup sugar
2 eggs, beaten
2 tsp. vanilla
1/2 cup sour milk
2-1/2 cup sifted flour
1/2 tsp. baking powder
2 tsp. soda
4 Tbl. cocoa
1/2 tsp. cloves
2 cup zucchini
1/4 cup chocolate chips

• Cream together the butter, oil, and sugar. Add beaten eggs and vanilla and sour milk. Sift together dry ingredients and add to egg mixture. Add grated zucchini and chocolate chips.
• Bake in a greased 9x13 pan in a 350°F oven for 45 to 50 minutes.

Darlene Miller
Friend of Education from Battle Mt., NV

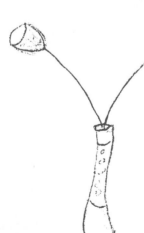

204 Jennifer Ehrlich, Wellington, Co.

Wacky Cake

1-1/2 cups flour
1 cup sugar
1 tsp. baking soda
1/4 cup cocoa
1 tsp. vanilla extract
1 tsp. cider vinegar
6 Tbl. acceptable margarine, melted
1 cup water

Preheat oven to 350°
• Use an ungreased 8-inch cake pan. In the pan, sift and mix together flour, sugar, soda and cocoa.
• Make three wells in flour mixture. Put vanilla in first, vinegar in second, and melted margarine in the third.
• Pour 1 cup of water over all and mix with a fork until ingredients are entirely moist.
• Bake 30 minutes.

Richard P. Brennan
Exec. Director
American Heart Association of Colorado

Punch Bowl Cake

1 chocolate cake mix
1 large vanilla instant pudding
2 cans cherry pie filling
2 small or 1 large can crushed pineapple (do not drain)
1-1/2 cup nuts
1 large container Cool Whip

• Bake cake according to box directions. After cake has cooled cut into small squares; starting with cake, layer ingredients as listed in punch bowl. Should make two layers depending on size of bowl.
• A white cake can be used with strawberry pie filling.

State Representative Mike Coffman
Aurora, CO

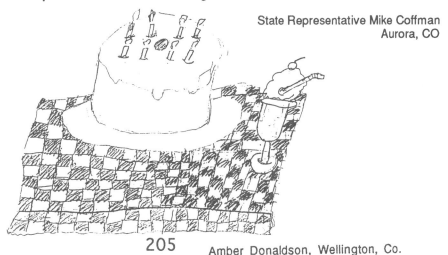

Amber Donaldson, Wellington, Co.

Dad's Favorite Chocolate Cake

1/2 cup margarine
4 Tbl. (heaping) cocoa
1 cup water
2 cup + 2 Tbl. flour (unsifted)
2 cups granulated sugar
1 tsp. soda
1/2 tsp. salt (optional)
1 tsp. vanilla
2 eggs
1/2 cup sour milk (see below)

Frosting
1/2 cup sour milk
4 Tbl. cocoa (heaping)
1/2 cup margarine
1 box powdered sugar
1 Tbl. vanilla
3/4 cup chopped nuts

To sour milk combine:
1 cup milk
1 Tbl. vinegar or 1 Tbl. lemon juice

• Heat in small sauce pan margarine, cocoa, and water. Stir frequently till boiling. Remove from heat.
• In a large bowl combine flour, sugar, soda, and salt. Add first mixture. Beat until smooth. Add vanilla, eggs, and sour milk. Beat until smooth. Bake at 350° for 20-25 minutes. Do not over cook. Bake in 15x10x1 inch jelly roll pan.
• Cool for 5-10 minutes and then frost with frosting.

Frosting instructions

• Heat sour milk, cocoa, and margarine in sauce pan over med heat till boiling, stirring frequently to prevent scorching. Remove from heat and add powdered sugar to thicken. Add vanilla and nuts. Beat till evenly mixed. Spread on cake while quite warm. Enjoy!

Nancy Horton
1992 State Fair Winner

Jenifer Foote, Wellington, Co.

Cookies

Cookies

Crystal Hunt, Wellington, Co.

Colorado produces the equivalent of 2.6 million hundred-pound bags of pure sugar each year from sugar beets.

C.S.U. Dept. of Agriculture

207

Kathern O'Brien, Wellington, Co.

Fresh Peaches Stuffed with Macaroons

6 firm ripe peaches
5 stale macaroons, crushed in a blender to = 1
   cup crumbs
2 Tbl. sugar
4 Tbl. unsalted butter
2 egg yolks

• Preheat oven to 375°. Blanch peaches, 2 at a time in boiling water for about 20 seconds. Lift them out with a slotted spoon, plunge them into cold water and peel off the skins. Cut the peaches in half and remove the pits. Scoop enough peach pulp out of each half to make a deep space in the center. Add this pulp to the crushed macaroons. Then stir in sugar, butter and egg yolks. Stuff the peach halves with the mixture. Arrange the peach halves in a buttered baking dish and bake them for about 25 min. or until they are just tender. Baste with sugar syrup from the pan during baking. Serve hot or cold with raspberry sauce.

Hans Wyppler - Chef de Cuisine
The Black Bear Inn

Bjana Barella, Wellington, Co.

Cherry Nut Surprises

2-1/2 cups all purpose flour
1 Tbl. dry milk
1 tsp. baking powder
1/4 tsp. salt
3/4 cup butter or margarine, softened
1 cup sugar
1 egg, unbeaten
1/4 cup Dr Pepper
1 tsp. vanilla
1/2 cup maraschino cherries, finely chopped,
   well drained
2 cups flake coconut
1 cup almonds, blanched and chopped

• On wax paper, sift together flour, dry milk, baking powder and salt. Cream butter and sugar, add egg and mix until light and fluffy. Mix in Dr. Pepper and vanilla. Add flour mixture about 1/2 at a time, mixing well after each addition. Stir in cherries, coconut and nuts. Drop by teaspoonfuls about two inches apart on greased cookie sheet. Bake at 350° for 10 to 12 minutes. Remove from baking sheet to cooling rack immediately. For crisp cookies, do not store in tight container.
• Yield: 6 dozen cookies

Elizabeth R. Guest
Dr Pepper/Seven-Up Company

Merissa Bartels, Wellington, Co.

Go To School Zucchini Drop Cookies

1 cup zucchini, grated
1 tsp. soda
1 cup sugar
1/2 cup margarine
1 egg, beaten
2 cups flour
1 tsp. cinnamon
1/2 tsp. cloves
1/2 tsp. salt
1 cup chopped nuts
1 cup raisins

• Thoroughly combine zucchini, soda, sugar and margarine. Add egg. Combine flour mixture, nuts and raisins to zucchini mixture. Drop by spoonfuls onto greased baking sheet. Bake at 375° for 12 to 15 minutes. Makes about 3 dozen cookies.

Darlene Miller
Friend of Education
Battle Mt., NV

Lacey Morris, Mancos, Co.

Reese's Cookies

2 cups all-purpose flour
1 tsp. baking soda
1 cup shortening OR 3/4 cup (1-1/2 sticks)
    butter or margarine, softened
1 cup granulated sugar
1/2 cup packed light brown sugar
1 tsp. vanilla extract
2 eggs
1-2/3 cups (10 oz. pkg.) - REESE'S Peanut
    Butter Chips
2/3 cup HERSHEY'S Semi-Sweet Chocolate
    Chips or Milk Chocolate Chips

* Hershey, Mini Chips and Reese's are
    registered trademarks. Recipes courtesy
    of the Hershey kitchens, and reprinted
    with permission of Hershey Foods
    Corporation.

• Heat oven to 350°. Stir together flour and baking soda. In large mixer bowl, beat shortening, granulated sugar, brown sugar and vanilla until creamy. Add eggs; beat well. Gradually add flour mixture, beating well. Stir in chips. Drop dough by rounded teaspoonfuls onto ungreased cookie sheet. Bake 8 to 10 minutes or until lightly browned. Cool slightly; remove from cookie sheet to wire rack. Cool completely. About 5 dozen cookies.

High Altitude Directions:
• Increase flour to 2 cups plus 2 Tbl. Decrease baking soda to 3/4 tsp. Decrease granulated sugar to 3/4 cup. Add 1 Tbl. water with flour. Bake at 350° 7 to 9 minutes.
Yield increases to about 6 dozen.

Hershey Foods Corporation

The Best Chocolate Chip Cookies

1/2 lb. butter, softened
1/2 cup solid vegetable shortening
1-1/3 cups granulated sugar
1 cup firmly packed brown sugar
4 large eggs
1 Tbl. vanilla
1 tsp. lemon juice
3 cups flour
2 tsp. baking soda
1-1/2 tsp. salt
1 tsp. cinnamon
1/2 cup rolled oats
2 (12-oz. each) packages semi-sweet chocolate
   morsels
2 cups chopped walnuts or pecans
2 baking sheets, lightly greased

• Preheat oven to 325°.
• In large bowl of electric mixer or with electric beaters, beat butter, shortening, granulated sugar and brown sugar on high speed until very light and fluffy, about 5 minutes. Add eggs, one at a time. Beat well after each addition. Beat in vanilla and lemon juice.
• In another bowl, stir together flour, baking soda, salt, cinnamon and oats. Gradually add to butter mixture. Mix thoroughly. Stir in chocolate morsels and nuts.
• Using about a scant 1/4 cup dough for each cookie, drop onto prepared baking sheet. Space cookies about 3-inches apart.
• For SOFT cookies, at 325°, bake about 20 minutes until light golden brown.
• For CRISP cookies, at 350°, bake 16 to 18 minutes until golden brown.
• Transfer cookies to racks to cool. Serve or if surprisingly any of these delicious cookies remain, hide them in airtight tins.

Katie Stapleton
KOA's Host of "Cooking with Katie"
Author of the cookbook, "Denver Delicious"

Rafe Gracey, Wellington, Co.

Grandma's Mandelbrot - German Cookie

3 eggs
1 cup sugar
3/4 cup oil
1 tsp. vanilla
1 cup chopped walnuts
3 cups unsifted flour
1 tsp. baking powder

• Combine all ingredients. Knead dough into three long strips. Grease cookie sheet and bake at 350° for 30 minutes or until brown. Slice into 1/2 inch slices. Can place slices side down on greased pan and put under broiler for two or three minutes until toasted.

Marcy Morrison
Legislator and former El Paso County
Commissioner

Graham Cracker Specials

15 graham crackers (doubles)
6 oz. unsalted butter, cut up
1 cup brown sugar
1 cup nuts, chopped (optional)

• Preheat oven to 350°. Cover entire baking sheet with whole graham crackers. In small pan, cream butter with sugar. Boil mixture over medium heat, 2 minutes. Pour over graham crackers. Sprinkle nuts over top if desired. Bake 15 minutes. Cool cookies and break into 4 fingers. Place immediately in cookie tin, lined with wax paper. Also, layer cookies with wax paper. Have wax paper on top of cookies for added protection. Cookies will begin to crisp after four hours, but will be even crispier the following day. Good luck lasting that long.

Katie Stapleton
KOA's Host of "Cooking with Katie"
Author of the cookbook, "Denver Delicious"

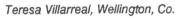

Teresa Villarreal, Wellington, Co.

211

Nut Butter Balls A La James Beard

1 cup flour
1 cup nuts such as walnuts, pecans, hazelnuts
    or almonds (use only one kind)
2 Tbl. superfine sugar
4 oz. butter, cut into 8 pieces
2-4 Tbl. powdered sugar for coating
1 baking sheet, unbuttered

• Preheat oven to 325°.
• Into food processor with metal blade, place flour, nuts, sugar and butter. Process until blended, 30 seconds. Scrape sides of bowl. Process until dough forms a ball, about an additional 15 to 30 seconds.
• Using a teaspoon of dough for each cookie, roll into balls and place on baking sheet. Bake 12 to 15 minutes, until golden brown.
• Remove from oven. Let cool on baking sheet, 5 minutes, to prevent crumbling.
• While still warm, drop a few at a time into a bag of powdered sugar to coat, or sift powdered sugar over cookies on a wire rack with a piece of wax paper underneath to catch the excess.

Katie Stapleton
KOA's Host of "Cooking with Katie"
Author of the cookbook, "Denver Delicious"

Everything-in-the-Cupboard Cookies

1 cup white sugar
1 cup brown sugar
1 cup butter or margarine
1 egg
1 pkg. chocolate chips (6 oz.)
1 cup Rice Krispies
1 cup oatmeal
3-1/2 cups flour
1/2 tsp. baking soda
1/2 tsp. salt
1/2 cup chopped nuts

• Mix white and brown sugar with butter. Add egg and beat until fluffy. In seperate bowl mix flour, baking soda and salt. Add to sugar mixture. Add chips, Rice Krispies, oatmeal and nuts and mix well.
• Drop by tablespoon onto greased cookie sheet and bake 10 minutes in 350° oven.

Pam Daale
KMGH-TV Meteorologist - Channel 7

Tom McChesney, Wellington, Co.

Fabulous Fudgies

2 cups sugar
1/4 cup cocoa
1/2 cup milk
1 stick butter
1/2 cup peanut butter
3 cups oatmeal

• Boil together sugar, cocoa, and milk for one minute in a pan or in the microwave. Add the rest. Stir until blended. Let set 5 minutes. Drop by spoonfuls onto waxed paper. Let cool and enjoy.

Dr. Suzanne Barchers
Children's Museum of Denver

Oatmeal Chewy Surprise Cookies

1 cup firmly packed light brown sugar
3/4 cup Butter Flavor Crisco
1/2 cup granulated sugar
1/4 cup water
1 egg
1 tsp. vanilla
1 cup all-purpose flour
1 tsp. salt
1/2 tsp. baking soda
1 cup flaked coconut
1-1/2 cups butterscotch bits
3 cups old fashioned (not quick) oats,
    uncooked

• Combine brown sugar, shortening, granulated sugar, water, egg and vanilla in large bowl. Beat on medium speed of mixer until well blended. Add flour, salt and baking soda at low speed. With a spoon stir in, one at a time, coconut, butterscotch bits and oats. Drop by rounded teaspoonful, 2 inches apart onto baking sheet which has been covered with foil. Bake in preheated 350° oven 12 to 14 minutes or just until set and just beginning to brown. Do not overbake. Cool 5 minutes before removing to cooling rack. Makes about 2-1/2 dozen cookies.

Lindsey and Linda Holzrichter
1st Place 1992 Colorado State Fair

Stacey Dumwald, Wellington, Co.

Chewy Oatmeal Cookies

8 oz. unsalted butter, chunked
1/2 cup superfine sugar
1-1/2 cups packed brown sugar
2 large eggs
1-1/2 tsp. vanilla
1-1/2 cups flour
1/4 tsp. salt
1 tsp. baking soda
1/4 tsp. ground allspice
1/2 tsp. ground nutmeg
1/4 tsp. ground cloves
1-1/2 tsp. ground cinnamon
3 cups regular or quick-cooking oats
1 cup raisins
3/4 cup chopped walnuts
Two 12" x 15" - baking sheets, buttered

• Preheat oven to 375°
• In food processor with metal blade, place butter with sugars. Process to cream. With motor running, through feed tube, add eggs and vanilla. Pulse after each addition to mix.
• In medium bowl, mix all dry ingredients except oats. Remove cover from food processor bowl and add to egg mixture. Return cover and process to blend well.
• In same manner, add oats, raisins and walnuts all together and pulse to mix.
• Drop a rounded tablespoon of dough onto prepared baking sheet. Space about 2 inches apart. Bake until cookies are golden, but centers are still soft, 10 to 12 minutes. If using a single oven, switch baking sheets halfway through cooking. Transfer cookies to racks to cool. Serve or store in airtight tin can or plastic bag, up to 3 days.
• VARIATION: Omit all spices, raisins and walnuts to make a simple yet tasty oatmeal cookie.

Katie Stapleton
KOA's Host of "Cooking with Katie"
Author of the cookbook, "Denver Delicious"

Justin Campesino, Wellington, Co.

Sugar Bunnies

6 oz. unsalted butter
6 oz. powdered sugar
1 small egg
1-1/2 tsp. vanilla
1-1/2 cups sifted flour (measure with 1/3 cup
    dry measurer)
1/4 tsp. Salt

Wax paper
Two baking sheets, ungreased

Frosting:
1-3/8 cups powdered sugar
2 Tbl. unsalted butter, softened
2 egg whites
1/4 tsp. salt
Additional powdered sugar or milk
Food Colorings

• In bowl, cream butter with sugar. Beat in egg and vanilla, then flour and salt until well blended. Divide dough in half. Wrap each dough half in a sheet of wax paper and flatten into a 3/4-inch round. Refrigerate one hour or until firm.
• Preheat oven to 325°.
• On floured surface, roll dough half to 1/8-1/4-inch thick. Repeat procedure with remaining dough half. Using a bunny head pattern (a round face with a pair of protruding ears), cut out bunnies from dough and place on baking sheets. Bake until lightly colored, about 12 minutes. Cool.
• **Frosting:** In a bowl, cream powdered sugar with butter, egg whites and salt until smooth and glossy. If mixture is too thin, add additional powdered sugar. But if too thick, add a few drops milk.
• **To color:** Divide frosting into separate bowls. Stir in separate food coloring into each until frosting is desired shade. Cover bowls with damp cloths to prevent drying out.
• **To pipe onto bunny faces:** spoon into a pastry bag fitted with small writing tip.
• Everyone's heard about Playhouse Bunnies. But here we have the original Sugar Bunnies. The great distinction is that Sugar Bunnies have the cutest faces you can dream up.
• Decorate these cookie faces with or without colored frosting, and use any old candy you have around the house even my favorite, candy corn for downward eyes and nose.

Katie Stapleton
KOA's Host of "Cooking with Katie"
Author of the cookbook, "Denver Delicious"

Tracie Alexander, Ft. Collins, Co.

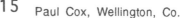

215 Paul Cox, Wellington, Co.

Strawberry Bonbons

"Just a couple of lush strawberries semi-covered with dark or white chocolate hardened crust makes a stupendous dessert. Or be experimental and try dipping other fruit in chocolate. Actually fruit dipped in chocolate will last a couple of days, refrigerated. What a surprise!!"

4 oz. semi-sweet chocolate, chunked
(or 4 oz. white chocolate, chunked - if you
desire a white dip)
1 (1 pt.) basket strawberries with stems
1 heavily buttered baking sheet

<u>Variations</u>
Try dipping other firm, unblemished fruit such as slices of pear (peeled and cored), kiwi slices (peeled) or bunches of grapes (dip individually and reassemble bunch).

• **Chocolate tempering instructions:**
Place in double boiler insert over hot, not boiling water. Use rubber spatula to stir and speed up melting. When chocolate is about three-fourths melted, remove insert from pan and keep stirring until completely melted. Let chocolate cool about 15 minutes or if you have a candy thermometer, let cool to 82° and reheat chocolate to 86°. Continue to use rubber spatula to stir. Again let chocolate cool about 10 minutes. You will achieve a shiny texture.
• **To dip fruit:** Wash strawberries and let dry. Dip each strawberry in chocolate to semi-coat. Use a quick twisting motion to coat only bottom half of each strawberry. Place it at once on prepared baking sheet. Refrigerate as soon as possible to harden chocolate. Keep in refrigerator until ready to serve.
• Note: Gauge the amount of chocolate by the amount of fruit you wish to dip. 4 oz. melted chocolate is enough for a 1 pint basket of strawberries.

Katie Stapleton
KOA's Host of "Cooking with Katie"
Author of the cookbook, "Denver Delicious"

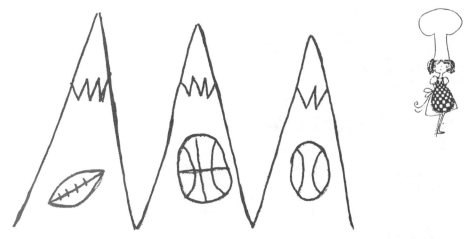

216   *Mike McChesney, Wellington, Co.*

Microwave Double Chocolate Cookies

3/4 cup unbleached flour
1/4 cup unsweetened cocoa
1/2 tsp. baking soda
1/2 tsp. salt
6 Tbl. honey, warmed, or 1/2 cup granulated
    sugar
1/4 cup brown sugar
4 oz. unsalted butter, chilled, cut up
1 egg
1 tsp. vanilla
1/2 cup semi-sweet chocolate morsels (from 6-
    oz. pkg.)
1/2 cup pecans, chopped (optional)

• Sift together flour, cocoa, baking soda and salt.
• Into food processor bowl fitted with steel blade, pour honey or granulated sugar. Add brown sugar, chilled butter, egg and vanilla. Process to mix. Attach funnel to feed tube of food processor and pour flour mixture through funnel, as motor continues to run. Process to mix. Pour into a separate bowl. Add chocolate morsels. Add pecans, if desired. Wrap dough in plastic wrap and refrigerate at least 30 minutes.
• To microwave: cover a piece of stiff cardboard (can be round or oblong to fit microwave oven) with waxed paper. With a teaspoon, drop cookies carefully on waxed paper in a circle. (Each cookie should be about 1/2 teaspoon of dough.)
• Microwave baking time (60%) will vary:
8 cookies - 2-1/2 minutes at bake
Turn cardboard: add 30 seconds
Turn cardboard: add 20 seconds
6 cookies - 2 minutes at bake
Turn cardboard: add 20 seconds
Turn cardboard: add 10 seconds
3 cookies - 1 minute at bake
• Look to see if an additional 10 seconds is needed
• Caution: Microwaving these cookies on a paper plate covered with waxed paper, instead of cardboard, does not work!
Cool cookies at least 8 minutes before removing from waxed paper. Remember microwave cooking time continues a few minutes after cookies are removed from microwave.

Katie Stapleton
KOA's Host of "Cooking with Katie"
Author of the cookbook, "Denver Delicious"

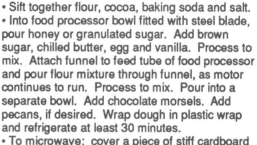

Tom McChesney, Wellington, Co.

217

Peanut Blossoms

1-3/4 cups Pillsbury's BEST All Purpose or
    Unbleached Flour
1/2 cup sugar
1/2 cup firmly packed brown sugar
1 tsp. baking soda
1/2 tsp. salt
1/2 cup shortening
1/2 cup peanut butter
2 Tbl. milk
1 tsp.vanilla
1 egg
Sugar
About 48 milk chocolate candy kisses

• Heat oven to 375° F. Lightly spoon flour into measuring cup; level off. In large bowl, blend flour, 1/2 cup sugar, brown sugar, baking soda, salt, shortening, peanut butter, milk, vanilla and egg at low speed until stiff dough forms. Shape into 1-inch balls; roll in sugar. Place 2 inches apart on ungreased cookie sheets.
• Bake at 375° for 10 to 12 minutes or until golden brown. Immediately top each cookie with a candy kiss, pressing down firmly so cookie cracks around edge; remove from cookie sheets. About 4 dozen cookies.

Pillsbury Company

Robert Morris, Wellington, Co.

Oatmeal Cookies "the Best"

3 eggs, well beaten
1 cup raisins
1 tsp. vanilla extract
1 cup butter
1 cup brown sugar
1 cup white sugar
2-1/2 cups flour
1 tsp. salt
1 tsp. ground cinnamon
2 tsp. baking soda
2 cups oatmeal (substitute 1/2 cup wheat germ
    for more healthful cookies)
3/4 cup chopped pecans

Combine eggs, raisins and vanilla and let stand for one hour, covered with plastic wrap. Cream together butter and sugars. Add flour, salt, cinnamon and soda to sugar mixture. Mix well. Blend in egg-raisin mixture, oatmeal, wheat germ and chopped nuts. Dough will be stiff. Drop by heaping teaspoons onto ungreased cookie sheet or roll into small balls and flatten slightly on cookie sheet. Bake at 350° for 10 to 20 minutes or until lightly browned.
• Note: Delicious. Secret is soaking of raisins.
• Yield: 6 dozen

From The Jr. League of Denver's
Top Cookbook "Colorado Cache"

Toni Nagy, Wellington, Co.

ICE CREAM

Christina Lucardie, Wellington, Co.

In 1991, total cash receipts of Colorado dairy products exceeded 166 million dollars.

C.S.U.- Dept. of Agriculture

Bjana Barella, Wellington, Co.

219

 ICE CREAM

Tim's Best-Ever Ice Cream

6 eggs
4 cups sugar
1 cup sour cream
1 (20 oz.) raspberries (fresh or frozen)
1-1/2 Tbl. vanilla
1 can evaporated milk
1 qt. heavy whipping cream

• Beat eggs in large mixing bowl. Add raspberries and beat for 1 minute. Combine all the remaining ingredients. Blend together well. Add to raspberries and egg mixture. Pour into ice cream maker. Freeze and turn until set.

Tim Foster
Colorado State Representative
Grand Junction, CO

Christina Lucardie, Wellington, Co.

Rhubarb Topping

4 cups chopped rhubarb
2 cups water
1 cup sugar
1 (3 oz.) pkg. strawberry jello

Ice Cream
OR Whipped cream and angel food cake

• Cook 4 cups of rhubarb in 2 cups of water. Put 1 cup sugar into 3 oz. pkg. of strawberry jello. Add to hot rhubarb. Dissolve. Cool.

•Serve with ice cream or whipped cream over angel food cake.

Ruth Gjelsness
Reynolds, ND

Chris Clark, Wellington, Co.

 ICE CREAM

Golden Orange Ice Cream Topping

4 oranges peeled & sectioned
3 Tbl. whole butter
1/4 cup Brandy
1/4 cup triple sec
1/4 cup honey
1/4 cup brown sugar
1/4 cup cream

• Sauté oranges (sectioned with all membranes removed) in whole butter. Add brandy and triple sec. Flame this mixture with a match or over a gas stove. Let simmer. Add remaining ingredients and cook on low heat until thickened.
• Serve warm over vanilla ice cream. Don't worry about the alcohol - it all cooks out leaving only the taste of the liqueur.

Scott R. Carter
Executive Chef of the Buckingham Broker

Meghan Scott, Wellington, Co.

Frozen Fudge Sundae

1 (12 oz.) pkg. chocolate chips
30 regular size marshmallows
1/2 gal. vanilla ice cream
1 box vanilla wafers
1 (13 oz.) can evaporated milk
1/2 cup chopped pecans

• In top of double boiler, melt chocolate chips, marshmallows and evaporated milk. Cool until lukewarm. Lay vanilla wafers on bottom of 9x13 pan. Slice ice cream into 12 equal slices using 6 to a layer. Lay 6 slices of ice cream over wafers. Spoon 1/2 fudge sauce over ice cream. Lay remaining 6 slices , top with rest of fudge sauce. Top with nuts. Freeze. Thaw 10 minutes before serving. Serves 15-16.

Brig. General Patrick K. Gamble
Commandant, USAFA

Meghan Scott, Wellington, Co.

 ICE CREAM

"TCBY" Peanut Butter & Jelly Shake

1 cup "TCBY" frozen peanut butter yogurt
1/3 cup lowfat or whole milk
2 Tbl. crunchy peanut butter
2 Tbl. strawberry jam or grape jam
Chopped peanuts or whole strawberries to
   decorate (optional)

• Place frozen yogurt and milk in container of blender or small food processor and mix on high for 10 seconds. Add peanut butter and jelly and mix on high for 15 seconds or until slushy. Pour into a tall (14 oz.) glass and sprinkle with chopped peanuts or strawberries, if desired.

Sara Wilson
New Product Development Manager
"TCBY" - The Country's Best Yogurt

Amsbry Ball, Wellington, Co.

"TCBY" Shiver

3 medium-size scoops (6-7 oz.) "TCBY" Frozen
   Yogurt
2 Tbl. candy, chopped fruit OR nuts

• Place scoops of frozen yogurt in large mixing bowl. Blend together with a spoon and soften slightly. Add candy, fruit or nuts and mix thoroughly with a spoon. Serve in a medium-size (10 oz.) glass.

Sara Wilson
New Product Development Manager
"TCBY" - The Country's Best Yogurt

penguin Pocket-knife

Kyle Korby, Wellington, Co.

222

 ICE CREAM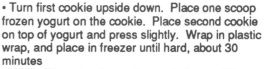

"TCBY" Yogwich

2 cookies of your favorite variety such as chocolate chip, oatmeal or sugar (NOTE: do not use cookies that have a filling, such as Oreos)
1 scoop "TCBY" frozen yogurt for each Yogwich (NOTE: scoop size depends on size of cookie)

• Turn first cookie upside down. Place one scoop frozen yogurt on the cookie. Place second cookie on top of yogurt and press slightly. Wrap in plastic wrap, and place in freezer until hard, about 30 minutes
NOTE: These treats may be made in quantities ahead of time, to be available to enjoy anytime!

Sara Wilson
New Product Development Manager
"TCBY" - The Country's Best Yogurt

Johnathan Schulein, Wellington, Co.

Tangy Raspberry Pops

2 cups cold water, divided
1 pkg. (0.3 oz.) sugar-free raspberry gelatin
1 cup buttermilk
1 bag (12 oz.) frozen unsweetened whole raspberries, thawed OR 2 cups fresh raspberries
12 paper cups (3 oz. each)
12 flat wooden sticks

• Place 1 cup water in 2-cup microwavable measuring cup. Microwave in HIGH (100%) 2-1/2 to 3 minutes, or until boiling. Place gelatin in large mixing bowl. Stir in boiling water until gelatin is dissolved. Stir in 1 cup cold water, buttermilk and raspberries. Mix well. Freeze until slightly thickened, about 1 hour. Stir twice. Pour into paper cups; insert wooden sticks. Freeze until firm. Peel off paper cup before eating. These can be frozen up to 2 weeks. Cover with plastic wrap if freezing more than 1 day.
Serving size: 1 Calories per serving: 25
Protein 1 g, fat 0g, carbohydrate 5g
Calcium 30 mg, riboflavin (B2) .06mg

American Dairy Association
Thornton, CO

Vanessa Nielsen, Wellington, Co.

ICE CREAM

Yogurt Fruit Pops

1 pkg. (0.3 oz.) sugar-free cherry flavor gelatin
3/4 cup boiling water
1 cup milk
1 carton (8 oz.) cherry flavor yogurt

Dissolve gelatin in boiling water in small bowl; chill until consistency of unbeaten egg whites. Beat until light and fluffy. Add milk and yogurt; beat until well blended. Divide evenly between 8 (3-ounce) paper cups. Place wooden stick in each. Freeze several hours. (If keeping longer than overnight, wrap individually in plastic wrap.) To serve, peel cup off "pop."
NOTE: Other fruit flavors of gelatin and yogurt may be used.
Serving size: 1 pop
Calories per serving: 50
Protein 3g, fat 1 g, carbohydrate 7g
Calcium 79 mg, riboflavin (B2) .10 mg

American Dairy Association
Thornton, CO

I SCREAM YOU SCREAM
WE ALL SCREAM FOR

Maurissa Moore, Wellington, Co.

Rhubarb Strawberry Sauce

4 cups fresh rhubarb, cut-up
2/3 cup crystalline fructose
1 Tbl. cornstarch
1/2 cup water
1 cup strawberries, halved

• **This recipe uses fructose, a naturally occuring sugar from corn, fruit and honey. Fructose is 1-1/2 times sweeter than sucrose, so less is needed and there are less calories.**

Combine rhubarb, crystalline fructose, cornstarch and water in 1-1/2 quart glass dish. Cover. Microwave 8 minutes on HIGH. Stir once. Add strawberries, cover and cook 4 minutes or until thick and bubbling. Chill until ready to serve. If desired, add additional cup of berries. Can be eaten like pudding.
Yield: 5 cups
* Crystalline fructose can be found at King Soopers and Alfalfa's.

Colorado Corn Administrative Committee

Maurissa Moore, Wellington, Co.

224

RECImimes FOR KIDS

Ruben Cabral, Wellington, Co.

Apples are Colorado's major fruit crop. Sales are centered on the Western Slope.

C.S.U. - Dept. of Agriculture

Alecia Arevalos, Wellington, Co.

Peanut Butter & Jelly Sandwich

First you take peanuts and crunch 'em.
Then you take your grapes and you squish
    'em.
Then you take your bread and you spread it for
    your peanut butter and jelly sandwich.
Then you take your sandwich and you eat it.
'Cause it's good...peanut butter and jelly!

• Barney has many favorites: He likes snacks
such as peanut butter, carrot sticks, and celery
sticks.

                        Barney

Jesse Noland, Mancos, Co.

 **RECIPES FOR KIDS**

Caramel Apple Dip

Cream cheese
Caramel ice cream topping
Chopped nuts
Apples

• Spread softened cream cheese on serving plate. Drizzle with caramel ice cream topping and sprinkle with chopped nuts. Use apple slices to "scoop up" some fun!

 Washington State Apple Growers

Green Eggs and Ham

Eggs
Green food coloring
Sliced ham

• Dr. Seuss's Favorite Meal:
• Scramble eggs as usual. Have your child add green food coloring to a light green color. Fry sliced ham and serve with cooked green eggs.
• When everyone has finished eating, sit down together and read Dr. Seuss's classic book, "Green Eggs and Ham". Have fun reading together, this is a meal your whole family will enjoy!

Dr. Seuss

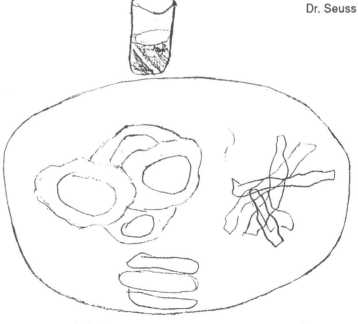

227   *Ron Betts, Wellington, Co.*

You'll Love 'Em Brownies

3/4 cup margarine or butter
1 package "M&M's" semi-sweet chocolate
    candies, divided (found in baking section)
1-3/4 cup sugar
3 eggs, lightly beaten
1/2 tsp. vanilla extract
1 cup all-purpose flour

• Preheat oven to 350°F. Grease and flour 13x9-inch baking pan. In medium saucepan over medium heat melt margarine.
• Add 3/4 cup "M&M's" Semi-Sweet Chocolate Candies.
• Cook mixture over low heat, stirring constantly with a metal spoon, and pressing candies with back of spoon to break up. (Chocolate mixture will be melted and small pieces of color coating will remain.) Remove from heat.
• Stir sugar into chocolate mixture. Mix in eggs and vanilla until well blended. Stir in flour. Spread in prepared baking pan. Sprinkle remaining 3/4 cup "M&M's" Semi-Sweet Chocolate Candies over top of brownies.
• Bake 30 to 35 minutes, or when wooden pick inserted in center comes out clean. Do not overbake. Cool in pan on wire rack. Cut into squares.
• Makes approx. 24 brownies.
• Recipe for ages 8 and up.

M&M's "Me and Mom N' Dad Cookbook"
MARS, Incorporated

Amy Westover, Wellington, Co.

Choco-Nutter Squares
(Ages 8 and up)

2 eggs
1 cup firmly packed light brown sugar
1/3 cup peanut butter
1/4 cup margarine or butter, melted
1/2 tsp. vanilla extract
1 cup all purpose flour
1/2 tsp. baking powder
1/8 tsp. baking soda
1 package "M&M's® Semi-Sweet Chocolate Candies*, divided
*Found in baking section

• Preheat oven to 350°F. In electric mixer at high speed beat eggs 2 - 4 minutes*, or until thick and fluffy. Beat in sugar. Blend in peanut butter, margarine, and vanilla extract.
• Add combined flour, baking powder, and baking soda; mix well. Stir in 3/4 cup "M&M's"® Semi-Sweet Chocolate Candies
• Spread batter into greased 9 inch square baking pan.
• Sprinkle remaining 3/4 cup "M&M's"® Semi-Sweet Chocolate Candies over top of squares.
• Bake 25-30 minutes. (Do not overbake) Cool in pan on wire rack. Cut into squares.
*(For chewy-moist squares, beat eggs about 2 minutes, for cake-like squares beat eggs about 4 minutes.)
• VARIATIONS: For one 15-1/2 x 10-1/2 inch pan of bars, double all ingredients; bake for 25-28 minutes
Yield: 1 to 1-1/2 dozen squares

M&M's "Me and Mom N' Dad Cookbook"
MARS, Incorporated

Chance Tarr, Wellington, Co.

Jumbo Crunchy Sandwich Cookies
(Ages 5 and up)

2 cups "M&M's"® Semi-Sweet Candies *
    divided (approx. 1-1/2 packages)
6 Tbl. margarine, softened, divided
1/3 cup sugar
1 egg
2-1/2 cup all purpose flour
1/2 tsp. salt
1/4 tsp. baking soda
1 can vanilla frosting
***Found in baking section**

• Preheat oven to 400°F. In a small saucepan over low heat, stir 1 cup "M&M's"® with 2 tablespoons margarine just until margarine melts. (Mixture will not be smooth.) Set aside.
• In mixer, with small bowl, beat remaining 4 tablespoons margarine and sugar until light. Add egg, beat well.
• Stir in chocolate mixture just until combined. Mix together flour, salt and soda. Stir into chocolate mixture.
• Shape level tablespoonful of dough into balls. Place 2 inches apart on ungreased baking sheet. Butter the bottom of a glass, dip in sugar then flatten dough until 1/4 inch thick.
• Bake 5 to 7 minutes until cookies spring back when touched lightly in center. Remove from baking sheet to baking rack and cool completely.
• Spread one cookie with heaping teaspoon of filling; sprinkle with "M&M's"®. To make sandwich, spread frosting on bottom of second cookie and gently press against first cookie to hold together.
• Frost around cookie sandwich edge.
• Roll edge in remaining "M&M's"® to coat. Repeat to make 18 sandwiches. Place on rack to set.
Yield: 18 cookies

M&M's "Me and Mom N' Dad Cookbook"
MARS, Incorporated

Ruben Cabral, Wellington, Co.

Double Surprise Cookies

(Age 6 and up)

1/3 cup sugar
2/3 cup butter or margarine
2 egg yolks
1/2 tsp. vanilla
1/8 tsp. almond extract
1-1/2 cup all purpose flour
1/4 tsp. salt
36 "M&M's® Peanut or Peanut Butter or Almond
    Candies
1/4 cup confectioners' (powdered) sugar
1-1/2 tsp. water
3/4 cup "M&M's® Semi-Sweet Chocolate
    Candies*
*Found in baking section

• Preheat oven to 350°F. In mixer beat margarine 30 seconds. Gradually add sugar and beat until light and fluffy. Add egg yolks, vanilla and almond extract; beat thoroughly.
• Stir together flour and salt. Add to creamed mixture and mix well.
• Cover and chill at least one hour.
• For each cookie: With floured hands shape a rounded teaspoonful dough around an "M&M's® Chocolate Candy to form a ball about 1 inch in diameter. Place 1 inch apart on ungreased baking sheet.
• Bake 12 to 15 minutes until dough springs back when touched and cookie is lightly browned at bottom. Remove to wire rack; cool completely.
• To decorate, mix together confectioners sugar and water until smooth. Spread on tops of cookies and immediately sprinkle generously with "M&M's® Semi-Sweet Chocolate Candies, pressing lightly.
Yield: 36 cookies

M&M's "Me and Mom N' Dad Cookbook"
MARS, Incorporated

Rori Wright, Wellington, Co.

Mini Granola Bites
(Ages 6 and up)

3/4 cup margarine or butter, softened
1 cup light brown sugar (firmly packed)
1 large egg
1 tsp. vanilla
1-1/2 cup all purpose flour
3/4 tsp. baking soda
1/2 tsp. ground cinnamon
3/4 cup quick-cook oats
1/2 cup chopped walnuts (optional)
3/4 cup granola cereal with raisins
1 package "M&M's® Semi-Sweet Chocolate
    Candies* divided
*Found in baking section

• Preheat oven to 350°F. Using mixer with small bowl, beat margarine about 30 seconds. Beat in brown sugar. Add egg and vanilla; beat well. Stir together flour, baking soda and cinnamon; gradually add to margarine mixture.
• Place granola in a plastic bag and crush with rolling pin to break big chunks. Stir crushed granola, oatmeal, nuts and 1 cup "M&M's® Semi-Sweet into dough. Mix well.
• Drop by tablespoonfuls 1 inch apart onto lightly greased baking sheet. Place 2-3 "M&M's® on each cookie.
• Bake 7 to 9 minutes until just browned. Remove to wire rack; and cool completely.
Yield: 10 dozen bite size or 5 dozen 2-inch cookies.

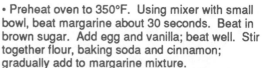

M&M's "Me and Mom N' Dad Cookbook"
MARS, Incorporated

Choco-Nut Dip

Chocolate chips
Peanut butter
Apples

• Combine equal parts of chocolate chips and peanut butter. Microwave until melted; stir. Serve with a variety of your favorite Washington state apples.

Washington State Apple Growers

Scott Peterson, Wellington, Co.

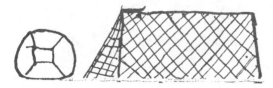

232

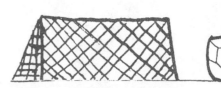

Justin Latham, Wellington, Co.

Frozen Heavenly Hash
(Ages 6 and up)

1 quart chocolate ice cream, ice milk or frozen
    yogurt
3/4 cup marshmallow cream
2/3 cup chopped toasted almonds**, or granola
    cereal
1 cup "M&M's® Semi-Sweet Chocolate Candies*
*Found in baking section
NOTE: All recipe ingredients double easily to
    make 1/2 gallon ice cream.

• Place ice cream in large mixing bowl to soften.
Let stand for 6-8 minutes, or until slightly soft.
Beat with wooden spoon until thick, and of
spoonable consistency. (Return to freezer if
mixture becomes too soft, or slightly melted.)
• Add marshmallow cream to softened ice cream;
mix in with fork to form swirls.
• Fold in nuts or granola cereal and "M&M's®
Semi-Sweet Chocolate Candies.
• Return to original ice cream container or plastic
freezer container. Freeze 6-8 hours or overnight
until firm. Serve in cones or dessert dishes.
• **To toast chopped almonds; place single layer
in 13 x 9 inch baking pan. Bake at 300°F. for 15-
20 minutes, or until lightly toasted.
Yield: 1 quart

M&M's "Me and Mom N' Dad Cookbook"
MARS, Incorporated

Space Balls

1/4 cup wheat germ
1/4 cup dry milk
1/4 cup peanut butter
2 Tbl. honey

• Mix together, roll into balls.
• Great in the classroom for kids' cooking class!

Kitty and Jim Fassel
Bronco Offensive Coordinator

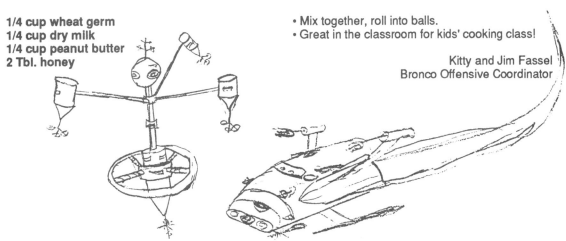

Tom McChesney, Wellington, Co.

Chocolate Pumpkin Mini-Muffins
(Ages 8 and up)

1-2/3 cup all purpose flour
3/4 cup sugar
1 Tbl. pumpkin pie spice
1 tsp. baking soda
1/4 tsp. baking powder
1/4 tsp. salt
2 eggs
1 cup canned pumpkin
1/2 cup vegetable oil
1 cup "M&M's® Semi-Sweet Chocolate Candies*
    divided
*Found in baking section

• Preheat oven to 350°F. Grease miniature muffin cup pan, or line with small paper baking cups.
• In large bowl, stir together flour, sugar, pumpkin pie spice, baking soda, baking powder and salt with egg beater.
• In a small bowl use egg-beater to beat eggs, pumpkin and oil; pour into dry ingredients. Stir just until moistened. Stir in 1/2 cup "M&M's® Semi-Sweet Chocolate Candies.
• Spoon slightly rounded tablespoonful of batter into prepared muffin cups. Top with remaining 1/2 cup "M&M's® Semi-Sweet Chocolate Candies.
• For mini muffins, bake 15-20 minutes. For standard size muffins, bake 20 minutes. Bake until springy to touch. Remove from pan and cool on wire racks.
Yield: 36 mini muffins or 12 standard size muffins.

M&M's "Me and Mom N' Dad Cookbook"
MARS, Incorporated

Bjana Barella, Wellington, Co.

Johnathan Schulein, Wellington, Co.

 SCHOOL COOK-OFF

Kelly Smith, Mancos, Co.

These recipes are the winners of our Statewide competition. We awarded $100.00 in prizes for "The Best Thing to Bring to a School Party." If you would like to enter next year's competition, send your favorite recipe to: Eyestone PTO, P.O. Box 69, Wellington, CO 80549.

Lazy Daisy Cake

Cake
2 eggs
1 cup sugar
1 cup flour
1 tsp. baking powder
1/2 tsp. salt
1/2 tsp. vanilla
1/2 cup milk
1 Tbl. butter

Icing
1/4 cup butter
1/4 cup sour cream
1 cup brown sugar
1 cup coconut

Cake • Beat 2 eggs until thick, add sugar beating well. Add sifted flour with baking powder, salt and vanilla. Put milk and butter on stove and bring to a boil. Add to first mixture. Bake in 8" square pan about 30 minutes at 350°.

Icing • Mix butter, sour cream and brown sugar together. Put on stove until butter melts and then add coconut. Pour onto hot cake and put under broiler for 5 minutes to brown.

Tracy Alexander
Werner Elementary School
Fort Collins, CO

Bouncing Ball Punch

3 packages (10 oz. each) frozen melon balls
1 can (46 oz.) your favorite fruit punch
1 can (6 oz.) frozen lemonade concentrate
Water

• About 40 minutes before you want to serve punch, remove the frozen melon balls from freezer. Let stand at room temperature about 20 minutes for easier opening.
• Mix the fruit punch drink, lemonade concentrate and two 6-oz. cans water (use the lemonade can) in punch bowl. Add the frozen melon balls and let stand 15 minutes. Stir and serve.

Dolores Vaccaro
Pueblo, CO

Stephanie Pfaff, Wellington, Co.

Kennan Blehm, Wellington, Co.

Chocolate Gobblers

Oreo Cookies
Chocolate Icing
Candy kisses
Red hot candy
Candy corn

• For each turkey use an Oreo cookie for the base. Frost cookie with chocolate icing. Place one candy kiss for turkey's head. Stick wattle in place with small amount of chocolate icing. Arrange a tail of candy corns.

Great for Thanksgiving!

Kylee and Ruth Smylie
Eyestone Elementary
Wellington, CO

Butterscotch Spider Cookies

12 oz. bag of butterscotch pieces
(1-1/2 cup)
1/2 cup peanut butter
14 oz. bag Chow Mein Noodles

• Microwave butterscotch and peanut butter to melt. Then stir in noodles. Put on cookie sheet by spoonfuls and refrigerate.

Tom McChesney
Eyestone Elementary
Wellington, CO

Tom McChesney, Wellington, Co.

237

Sugar Cookies

2/3 cup shortening
3/4 cup sugar
1/2 tsp. grated orange peel
1/2 tsp. vanilla
1 egg
4 tsp. milk
2 cups sifted all-purpose flour
1-1/2 tsp. baking powder
1/4 tsp. salt

Icing
3 egg whites
4 cups powdered sugar
1/2 tsp. cream of tartar

Tips
• Can be stored up to 3 weeks on counter in sealed container.
• Best to use pate colors (bought at Michael's) Keep moist towel over opened icing container, will harden fast.
• Let decorated cookies set 1/2 day to overnight before stacking in cookie tins.

• Thoroughly cream shortening, sugar, orange peel, and vanilla. Add egg; beat till light and fluffy. Stir in milk. Sift together dry ingredients; blend in creamed mixture. Divide dough in half. Chill 1 hour. Cut in desired shapes with cutters on lightly floured surface. Bake 6 to 8 minutes at 375°.
• Makes 2 dozen.

Icing Instructions
• Mix together. Beat 7 to 10 minutes till fluffy. (should be stiff).

Marie Crettet
Eyestone Elementary
Wellington, CO

Gideon Dione, Wellington, Co.

Ham and Cheese Roll-ups
School Cook-off Winner

1 can refrigerated crescent rolls
1 cup chopped turkey ham
1 cup shredded cheddar cheese
Butter

• Cut each cresent roll in half.
• Roll out flat.
• Spread with butter and sprinkle with turkey ham and cheese. Roll up, tucking in ends as you do.
• Bake 400° 10-12 minutes.

Makes 16 rolls.

Lois Grenier
Eyestone Elementary
Wellington, CO

Crab-Mushroom-Cheese Quiche

1 cup cream
3 eggs (room temperature)
1 tsp. dry mustard
dash of nutmeg
1 can crab meat (I use artificial crab meat 1/2 lb.) Great for people who are allergic to shell fish.
3/4 cup fresh mushrooms, sautéed (optional)
1/2 sliced onion, sautéed
1 unbaked pie crust (9 inch)
1-1/2 cup grated Swiss cheese

Pie Crust
3 cup flour
1-1/4 tsp. salt
1 cup Crisco
Milk

• Prepare pie shell. Beat eggs, add cream, salt, nutmeg and dry mustard. Add sautéed onion and mushrooms. Add grated Swiss cheese and crab meat. Put in baked pie shell and bake for 45 minutes at 350°.

Pie Crust Instructions
• Mix flour and salt. Add Crisco. Mix with pastry blender or 2 knives until it looks like corn meal. Add milk 1/4 cup at a time until all flour is moist and stays in a ball.

Marie Crettet
Eyestone Elementary
Wellington, CO

Nicole Bodkins, Wellington, Co.

Lemon Cream Cheese Coffee Cake

2 1/2 cup flour
3/4 cup sugar
3/4 cup butter
3/4 cup sour cream
1/2 tsp. baking powder
1/2 tsp. baking soda
1/4 tsp. salt
1 egg
1 tsp. almond extract

Filling
1 package (8 oz.) cream cheese softened
1/4 cup sugar
1 egg
*Lemon sauce

Topping
1/2 cups chopped walnuts
Reserved 1 cup crumbs

Filling
• In small bowl mix nuts and crumbs, sprinkle over top. Bake at 350° for 55-60 minutes or until cream cheese filling is set and crust is a deep golden brown. Cool 15 minutes. Remove sides of pan. Serve warm or cool. Cover and refrigerate leftovers.

• In large bowl, combine flour and sugar. Cut in the butter using a pastry blender until mixture resembles coarse crumbs. Remove 1 cup for topping. To remaining crumb mixture add baking powder, soda, salt, sour cream, egg and almond extract; blend well. Spread batter over bottom and 2 inches up side of greased and floured 9 inch spring form pan. (Batter should be 1/4 inch thick on sides.)

Filling Instructions
• In small bowl combine cream cheese, 1/4 cup sugar and egg. Blend well. Pour over batter in pan.

Lemon Sauce
• (May use canned lemon pie filling (3/4 cup) or Mix 3/4 cup sugar, 4 Tbl. cornstarch, 1/4 tsp. salt in sauce pan. Gradually stir in 1/2 cup water, cook, stirring constantly until mixture thickens and boils. Boil and stir 5 minutes. Remove from heat. Stir in 1/2 cup lemon juice, 4 drops yellow food color. May make ahead and refrigerate.
• Carefully spoon lemon sauce evenly over cheese filling.

Jill Becksted
Eyestone Elementary
Wellington, CO

Adam Scripture, Wellington, Co.

Sugar Cookies

4-1/2 cup flour
1 tsp. baking powder
1 tsp. baking soda
1-3/4 cup sugar
2 cups butter
3 eggs slightly beaten
1 tsp. vanilla

Butter Cream Icing

1-1/2 cup shortening
1/2 cup water or evaporated milk
1/2 Tbl. meringue powder (if water is used)
2 lbs. powdered sugar
1 tsp. vanilla
1/2 tsp. almond flavoring
1/2 tsp. salt.

• Mix dry ingredients. Add butter by cutting in with pasty blender. Add eggs and vanilla. Chill overnight. Roll and cut into desired shapes. Bake at 350° 8 to 10 minutes.

Icing Instructions

• Whip shortening at high speed until fluffy. Add 1/2 of the powdered sugar. Mix at low speed until blended, then at high speed until thoroughly blended. Add water or milk and mix at low speed until blended. (Add flavoring and salt at this time.) Mix at medium speed until thoroughly blended. Add balance of powdered sugar, blend at low speed then whip at high speed until fluffy.

Kendra Caffee
Eyestone Elementary
Wellington, CO

Microwave Fudge

1/2 cup cocoa
1 lb. powdered sugar
1/4 lb. margarine
1/4 cup milk
1 tsp. vanilla
1 cup chopped nuts

• Mix cocoa and sugar in microwave pan. Slice margarine over the top. Pour on the milk, but <u>do not mix.</u> Cover and cook in microwave 2 minutes on high power.
• Add vanilla and nuts. Mix well. Pour into 8" greased pan. Chill 1 hour

Tracy Alexander
Werner Elementary School
Fort Collins, CO

Kylee Smylie, Wellington, Co.

Megan's Magical M & M Munchies

2 cups all purpose flour
3/4 tsp. baking soda
3/4 tsp. salt

1 cup (8 oz.) softened butter
2/3 cup sugar
1/2 cup brown sugar
1 egg
1 tsp. vanilla
1 (12 oz.) package M & M baking pieces
Chocolate Bark

• Mix flour, baking soda and salt in small bowl and set aside.
• In separate bowl combine the butter, sugars and beat until fluffy. Add the egg and vanilla. Gradually add the flour mixture. Stir in M & M's. Drop by teaspoonful on ungreased cookie sheet. Bake at 375° 8-11 minutes.
• Cool cookies completely.
• Heat 4 pieces of chocolate bark in microwave. Dip one-half of cookie in melted bark. Refrigerate 1/2 hour.
Makes 5 dozen cookies.

Patti Gallegos
Eyestone Elementary
Wellington, CO

Magic

Fruit Pizza

Tom McChesney, Wellington, Co.

1 (18 oz.) roll refrigerated slice and bake sugar
    cookies
1 (8-oz.) package Philadelphia Brand cream
    cheese, softened
1/3 cup sugar
1/2 tsp. vanilla
Assorted fruits*
1/2 cup Kraft orange marmalade, peach or
    apricot preserves
2 Tbl. water
*Sliced peaches or nectarines, blueberries,
strawberry and grape halves, makes a colorful
pizza. You can use almost any fruit. You will
need 3-4 cups of sliced fruit.

• Cut cookie dough into 1/8-inch slices. Cover bottom of pan with slices, overlapping slightly. Bake at 375°, 12 minutes or until crust is light golden brown. Cool completely on wire rack.
• In Bowl, combine cream cheese, sugar and vanilla. Mix until well blended. Spread mixture evenly over crust.
• Arrange fruit over cream cheese in an attractive design.
• Combine marmalade and water in bowl. Mix well. Using teaspoon, spoon mixture evenly over pizza, covering all fruit. Chill. Cut into wedges to serve

Dolores Vaccaro
Pueblo, CO

242

Chance Tarr, Wellington, Co.

Holiday Rocky Roads

12 double graham crackers
2 cups miniature marshmallows
1 (6 oz.) package semisweet chocolate chips
1 (6 oz.) packet (mini) M & Ms
1/2 cup salted peanuts
1/2 cup butter or margarine
1/2 cup firmly packed brown sugar
1 tsp. vanilla extract

• Preheat oven to 350°. Arrange graham crackers in a single layer in a 15 1/2 x 10 1/2 x 1 inch jelly-roll pan. Sprinkle with marshmallows, then chocolate chips, M & Ms and peanuts.
• In small sauce pan, combine butter and sugar. Cook over low heat, stirring constantly, until sugar is dissolved. Add Vanilla. Drizzle evenly over prepared graham crackers.
• Bake 10 minutes. Cool. Cut into 2 x 1 inch bars.
• Makes 48 cookies

Lois Grenier
Eyestone Elementary
Wellington, CO

The Perfect Fall Harvest Party Mix

2 cups raisins
2 cups goldfish or guppy crackers
1 (7-1/2 oz.) mini Oreos
2 cups Candy corn
2 cups lightly salted peanuts (12 oz).

• Mix in a large airtight container.

• Stores well!

Terri Gutierrez
Eyestone, Elementary
Wellington, CO

Damien Bennett, Wellington, Co.

Dirt Cake

1 (1 lb. 8 oz.) package Oreo cookies (crushed)
2 small packages vanilla pudding
1 (8 oz.) cream cheese
8 oz. whipped topping
3 cups milk
Gummy worms

• In a mixer bowl, mix pudding, milk, cream cheese until smooth. Set aside. Layer cookies, cream cheese mixture, and cool whip in a flower pot or small pail. Before the last addition put gummy worms in mixture.

Jill Becksted
Eyestone Elementary
Wellington, CO

Tom McChesney, Wellington, Co.

Peanut Butter Bonbons
School Cook-off Winner

2 cups peanut butter
1/2 cup butter or margarine
4-1/2 cups sifted powdered sugar
3 cups crisp rice cereal, crushed
1 (6-oz.) package butterscotch pieces (1 cup)
1 (6-oz.) package semisweet chocolate pieces
(1 cup)

• Melt peanut butter and butter. Mix sugar and rice cereal. Pour butter mixture over cereal mixture. Blend together with hands. Form into 1/2 inch balls. Chill till firm. Melt butterscotch pieces in top of double boiler over boiling water. Dip half the candies in coating; swirl tops. Place on waxed-paper-lined baking sheet. Chill till firm. Repeat melting and dipping process with chocolate pieces and remaining candies. Chill till firm. Makes 100

Dolores Vaccaro
Pueblo, CO

Andrea Gutierrez, Wellington, Co.

Old-Fashioned Molasses Cookies

1-1/2 cups sugar
1 cup shortening
2 eggs
1/2 cup light or dark molasses
3 tsp. baking soda
1/2 cup water
5-1/2 cups all-purpose flour
1-1/2 tsp. ground cinnamon
1 tsp. ground ginger
1 tsp. ground cloves
1 tsp. salt
Frosting (below)

Frosting

2 envelopes unflavored gelatin
1-1/2 cup cold water
1-1/2 cup granulated sugar
3-1/2 cup powdered sugar
2 tsp. vanilla
1-1/2 tsp. baking powder
1/4 tsp. salt

• Mix sugar, shortening, eggs and molasses. Dissolve baking soda in water; stir into molasses mixture. Stir in remaining ingredients except frosting. Cover and refrigerate at least 2 hours.

• Heat oven to 375°. Roll dough 1/4 inch thick on lightly floured cloth-covered board. Cut with floured 2 3/4-inch round cookie cutter or other favorite cutter. Place about 2 inches apart on lightly greased cookie sheet. Bake until light brown, 8 to 10 minutes. Cool; generously frost bottoms of cookies with frosting. Let stand 2 to 3 hours before storing to allow frosting to dry. Makes about 6 dozen cookies.

Frosting Instructions
• Sprinkle gelatin on cold water in 2-quart saucepan to soften; stir in granulated sugar. Heat to rolling boil; reduce heat. Simmer uncovered 10 minutes. Pour hot mixture over powdered sugar in large mixer bowl; beat until foamy, about 2 minutes. Beat in remaining ingredients on high speed until very stiff but not dry, 12 to 15 minutes.

Dolores Vaccaro
Pueblo, CO

Gabe Kintzley, Wellington, CO.

Crystal Hunt, Wellington, Co.

Caramel Cereal Pops

1 (14-oz.) package (about 48) vanilla caramels
1/4 cup milk
4 cups crisp rice cereal
1 cup salted peanuts
Shortening

• Unwrap the caramels and put them into a heavy 3-quart saucepan. Measure the milk and add it to the pan with the caramels. Put the pan onto the burner. Turn the burner to low heat. Cook and stir with a wooden spoon till caramels are melted and smooth. This will take about 15 minutes.
• Turn burner off. Take pan off burner. Measure the crisp rice cereal and peanuts. Stir the cereal and peanuts into the pan. Keep stirring till the cereal and peanuts are well coated with the melted caramel mixture.

• Grease an 8 x 8 x 2 inch baking pan by putting a little bit of shortening on a folded paper towel. Spread the shortening evenly over the bottom and sides of the pan. Spoon the cereal mixture into the pan. Use the back of the wooden spoon to press the cereal mixture into the pan. Let the mixture stand about 1 hour or till firm.
• Use a table knife to cut the firm cereal mixture into 2-inch squares. Use the table knife or a narrow metal spatula to remove the 2-inch squares from the pan. Insert a wooden stick into one end of each square.

Makes 16 pops.

Dolores Vaccaro
Pueblo, CO

Golden Crisp Cereal Squares

1/4 cup (1/2 stick) Parkay Margarine
1 package (10 1/2 oz.) Kraft Miniature
    Marshmallows
8 cups Post Golden Crisp Cereal

Prep time: 10 minutes
Microwave cooking time: 3 minutes
Range top cooking time: 10 minutes
Range Top Instructions
• Melt margarine in large sauce pan over low heat. Add marshmallows; stir until melted and well blended. Remove from heat stir in cereal until well coated. Continue as above for cutting.

Microwave Instructions
• Microwave margarine in large microwave-safe bowl on HIGH (100 %) 45 seconds or until melted. Add marshmallows; toss to coat with margarine. Microwave on High
1-1/2 minutes or until smooth when stirred, stirring after 45 seconds. Immediately add cereal; toss until well coated. Press firmly into greased 13x9 in pan. Cool; cut into squares. Makes about 2 dozen.

Dolores Vaccaro
Pueblo, CO

Brittney Morgan, Wellington, Co.

 SCHOOL COOK-OFF

Choco-Mallow Pizza

1 package (12 oz) Baker's semisweet Real
    Chocolate Chips
1 lb. white almond bark, divided
2 cups Kraft Miniature Marshmallows
1 cup crisp rice cereal
1 cup peanuts
1 jar (6-oz.) maraschino cherries, drained, cut
    in half
3 Tbl. green maraschino cherries, drained,
    quartered
1/3 cup Baker's Angel Flake Coconut
1 tsp. oil

• Microwave chips and 14 oz. almond bark in 2-quart microwave-safe bowl on high 2 minutes; stir. Microwave 1 to 2 minutes or until smooth; stir every 30 seconds. Add marshmallows, cereal and nuts. Pour onto greased 12 inch pizza pan. Top with cherries and coconut. Microwave remaining almond bark with oil on high 1 minute; stir. Microwave 30 to 60 seconds or until smooth; stir. Drizzle over top; refrigerate. Serves 10 to 12.
Prep time: 15 minutes plus refrigerating.
Cooking time: 6 minutes

Dolores Vaccaro
Pueblo, CO

Deluxe Chocolate Marshmallow Bars

3/4 cup butter or margarine
1-1/2 cup sugar
3 eggs
1 tsp. vanilla extract
1-1/3 cups all-purpose flour
1/2 tsp. baking powder
1/2 tsp. salt
3 Tbl. baking cocoa
1/2 cup chopped nuts (optional)
4 cups miniature marshmallows

TOPPING
1-1/3 cups (8 oz.) chocolate chips
3 Tbl. butter or margarine
1 cup peanut butter
2 cups crisp rice cereal

• In a mixing bowl, cream butter and sugar. Add eggs and vanilla; beat until fluffy. Combine flour, baking powder, salt and cocoa; add to creamed mixture. Stir in nuts if desired. Spread in greased jelly roll pan. Bake at 350° for 15-18 minutes. Sprinkle marshmallows evenly over cake, return to oven for 2-3 minutes. Using a knife dipped in water, spread the melted marshmallows evenly over cake. Cool. For topping, combine chocolate chips, butter and peanut butter in a small saucepan. Cook over low heat, stirring constantly, until melted and well blended. Remove from heat; stir in cereal. Spread over bars. Chill. Yield: about 3 dozen,

Dolores Vaccaro
Pueblo, CO

Denis Suarez, Wellington, Co.

Applesauce Spice Cake

2-1/2 cups all-purpose flour*
2 cups sugar
1-1/2 tsp. baking soda
1-1/2 tsp. salt
3/4 tsp. ground cinnamon
1/2 tsp. ground cloves
1/2 tsp. ground allspice
1/4 tsp. baking powder
1-1/2 cups applesauce
1/2 cups water
1/2 cup shortening
2 eggs
1 cup raisins
1/2 cup chopped walnuts
Browned Butter Frosting (below)

*Do not use self-rising flour in this recipe.

Browned Butter Frosting
1/3 cup margarine or butter
3 cups powdered sugar
1-1/2 tsp. vanilla
About 2 Tbl. milk

• Heat oven to 350°. Grease and flour rectangular pan, 13 x 9 x 2 inches, or 2 round pans, 8 or 9 x 1-1/2 inches. Beat all ingredients except frosting in large mixer bowl on low speed, scraping bowl constantly, 30 seconds. Beat on high speed, scraping bowl occasionally, 3 minutes. Pour into pan(s).

• Bake until wooden pick inserted in center comes out clean, rectangular 60 to 65 minutes, layers 50 to 55 minutes. Cool layers 10 minutes; remove from pans. Cool completely. Frost rectangular or fill and frost layers with Browned Butter Frosting.

Frosting Instructions
Heat the margarine or butter over medium heat until delicate brown. Mix in powdered sugar. Beat in the vanilla and milk until smooth and of spreading consistency.

Dolores Vaccaro
Pueblo, CO

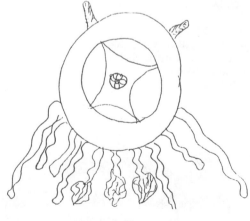

Yesenia Cabral, Wellington, Co.

Meagan Finch, Wellington, Co.

 FRONTIER

Recipes from Colorado's Past

 FRONTIER

Part One: The Indians

When white men first came to Colorado, they learned much about survival from the Indians. The Native Americans taught the frontiersmen which plants and animals were safe to eat and how to dry meats (jerky), fruits and vegetables so that they would store almost indefinitely. Before learning to dry foods, most white men preserved meat by packing it in salt, and preserved fruits and vegetables by canning. Dried foods were easy to prepare and lighter to carry. They could be eaten as a snack on the trail or added to stews. Here's a recipe for Jerky and for stew using dried ingredients.

Beef Jerky

1 cup of brown sugar dissolved in 1/4 cup water
1 tsp. allspice
1/2 tsp. red pepper
1 Tbl. Morton's Curing salt
2 lbs. beef round steak (or venison, elk) cut 1-1/2 by 1/2 inch thick.

• Combine the first four ingredients and mix well.
• Put the steak into a glass or plastic bowl.
• Pour the sauce over the round steak and place in the refrigerator for 36 hours. Turn the meat over about every 8 hours.
• After 36 hours, drain the sauce off of the meat.

• Dry in food dehydrator or place meat on cookie sheet and place in 200° oven for 10-12 hours. Leave oven door open. Turn the meat over about every 2 to 3 hours. Cook until completely dry or jerky will absorbe odors
• Do not refrigerate. Store on a plate or wax paper for several days. When completely dry, place in paper sack.

Betty & Robert Wood
Submitted by Robbyn Wood
Friend of Education
Wellington, CO

Sioux Washtunkala (Indian Stew)

2 lbs. JERKY (beef, deer or buffalo) broken into bite-size pieces
2 onions, cut up (even better, 8 small wild onions)
4 cups kernel corn, if dried, reconstituted with water
24 prairie potatoes*, soaked overnight if dried
OR 24 little new potatoes, soaked overnight if dried

*Prairie potatoes taste somewhat like turnips and are often strung like garlics by the older Sioux people.

• Cook together and add no salt or pepper if you want the true Indian taste.

Sam'l P. Arnold,Owner
The Fort Restaurant, Morrison, CO
Wonderful historian and author specializing in foods of the American fur trade era. He has hosted nationally syndicated food & and cooking shows on radio & T.V.

 FRONTIER

European immigrants were accustomed to using wheat flour. However, in America corn was much more plentiful and was used extensively by the Indians. Early settlers had to learn to make and use cornmeal in order to survive. Here is a recipe for one of the most essential breads baked by settlers. Johnny Cake is so named because cornmeal breads were "Johnny constant", that is ,"always there".

Johnny Cake

1/2 cups cornmeal
1 cup white flour
1/4 cup sugar
1/2 tsp. soda
1 egg
1 cup sour milk*
1 Tbl. melted butter

* See page 206

• "Combine cornmeal, white flour, sugar and soda. Sift all together and then add 1 egg beaten and 1 cup of sour milk and 1 Tbl. melted butter. Bake in a moderately hot oven."

•This recipe was found in a turn of the century cookbook from the First Congregational Church of Cripple Creek.

Submitted by Erik Swanson
Director of The Cripple Creek District Museum

Anna Ostertag, Wellington, Co.

Andrea Gutierrez, Wellington, Co.

 **FRONTIER**

Indians were the first to discover popcorn. Today, we still adore this snack and should thank our Indian ancestors for a fantastic discovery. Pumpkins were also an Indian discovery and were used in many ways, mostly for stews. Indians also used pumpkin juice for a sweetener (as they had no sugar), and roasted pumpkin seeds for snacks.

Indians learned many things from the settlers as well. Molasses, sugar, wheat flour and metal pans were soon favorite items of the Indians. They would trade for them with the many wagon trains that brought these goods west. A traditional food of the Apaches, Indian Fry Bread, was one result of white man's influence.

Indian Fry Bread - Apache

4 cups unsifted flour
1-3/4 Tbl. baking powder
2 Tbl. oil
1-1/2 tsp. salt
2 Tbl. sugar (can be omitted to use as regular bread)
warm water

• Mix first 5 ingredients together in a large bowl.
• Add enough warm water to make a firm dough. Knead well. Let rest for 20 minutes in a warm place. Roll flat into pieces according to size wanted. Deep fry in hot oil or shortening.
• This recipe doubles well after you have made it a few times. You need to learn to "feel" the dough so it is the right "soft/firm" texture. It should not stick to your hands.
• This bread is and has been a staple of the Indian people. It traveled well, and so was packed along everywhere. It also tasted good and so was fed to visitors. Try omitting the sugar and sprinkle cinnamon and sugar on it or put honey on it.

Charlotte Ortega Van Horn
10 yr. participant in
PR1 School District Rendevous

Nick Tucker, Wellington, Co.

Natasha Walton, Mancos, Co.

252

FRONTIER

Indian Tacos are a variation of Indian Fry Bread that makes a complete and good tasting meal.

Indian Tacos

Prepare pinto beans and after they are done, mash lightly with a small amount of juice. Leave the beans "chunky".

Green Chili
3 or 4 pork steaks, cubed and browned in vegetable oil.
1/4 tsp. each: basil, oregano and parsley
1/2 cup flour
1 clove minced garlic
4 cans tomatoes
1 can jalapenos (Iif you like it hot)
4 cans diced green chilies

Garnishes
Diced onion
Diced tomato
Lettuce
Cheese
Sour cream

Green Chili:
• After browning pork, add spices, flour and garlic. Stir and mix well, coating cubes of pork. Add 4 cans tomatoes, 1 can jalapeños and 4 cans diced green chilies. (I use 1/4 can jalapenos and it is not quite as hot). Simmer about 1 hour, stirring to prevent scorching and to help thicken. If you don't like HOT chili, use 5 cans mild diced green chili.
• Cut bread dough (omit sugar) into 4 - 6 inches circles (smaller ones for kids).
• Fry and let drain.
• Put beans, chili, diced onion, tomato, lettuce, cheese and sour cream in small amounts on fry bread.
• Furnish lots of napkins as they are a bit "messy". These can be served hot or cold. The chili can also be used with eggs or burritos. I also fill flour tortillas with beans, sprinkle with left over cheese and cover with chili.

Charlotte Ortega Van Horn
10-year participant in
PR1 School District Rendevous

Allison Hain, Wellington, Co.

253

Nicole Bodkins, Wellington, Co.

 FRONTIER

From the Hopi Indians we have a ceremonial bread that was made to resemble the Sun God, with the fingers representing the rays of sunlight.

Pueblo Indian Bread

1-1/2 cups water
3 Tbl. butter or margarine
1 Tbl. sugar
3 tsp. salt
2 pkg. dry yeast
1/2 cup very warm water
6-1/2 cups sifted all-purpose flour

• Combine water, butter or margarine, sugar and salt in sauce pan. Heat slowly until butter or margarine melt. Cool to lukewarm. Sprinkle yeast over 1/2 cup very warm water in a large bowl. Stir until dissolved and add butter mixture. Beat in 4 cups flour until smooth. Beat in enough remaining flour to make a soft dough. Turn out on a lightly floured surface. Knead until smooth and elastic, about 5 minutes, using only as much flour as needed to keep dough from sticking. Place in a lg. greased bowl; turn to coat all over with shortening; cover with a clean towel. Let rise in a warm place, away from drafts, 1-1/2 hours or until doubled in bulk.
• Punch down dough; turn out on lightly floured surface and knead a few times.
• Divide dough into 3 parts. Shape each part into a ball. Cover and let rest 10 minutes. You can shape into 3 round loaves or make as follows:

• On floured surface, roll each half into a 9" circle. Fold each circle almost in half. Top circular edge should be about 1" from bottom circular edge. With kitchen scissors make 6 gashes in the dough, cutting from circular edge toward the folded edge (about 2/3 the way). Spread the "fingers" of dough apart so they will not touch each other while baking. Do this to the remaining two balls. Cover and let rise in a warm, draft-free place 1 hour or until double in bulk. (Before cutting, place folded dough on a greased cookie sheet. Large sheets will hold all 3 breads. Bake 50 minutes at 350° or until golden brown and sound hollow when "thumped".
• The "shape" of the split breads are made to resemble the "Sun God" with the fingers representing the "rays". It is served during ceremonials. (I have often put raisins or chopped dried fruits that have been soaked in boiling water, in the dry ingredients.)

Charlotte Ortega Van Horn
10-year participant in
PR1 School District Rendevous

254

Genesis Dionne, Wellington, Co.

Ty Presgrove, Wellington, Co.

After the Pueblo Indians were introduced to Catholicism, the feast day of St. John the Baptist became one of their time-honored celebrations. Many Indian recipes included pine nuts (pinion), readily found in Colorado.

Scott Clark, Wellington, Co.

Indian Feast Day Cookies

1-1/2 cups sugar
1 cup shortening
1 beaten egg
1/4 cup milk
1 tsp. vanilla
2 cups all-purpose flour
1 cup whole wheat flour
1/2 cup finely chopped pine nuts
1 tsp. baking powder
1/4 tsp. salt

• Beat together sugar and shortening till light and fluffy. Combine egg, milk and vanilla. Stir together flours, pine nuts, baking powder and salt; add to creamed mixture alternately with liquid, beating well after each. On lightly floured surface roll half of the dough at a time to a 12x6-inch rectangle. Cut into eighteen 2-inch squares. Make 3/4-inch cuts about 1/2 inch apart into each side of the cookie. Gently lift sections apart, making a two-sided fan shape. Place on ungreased cookie sheet. Bake in 350° oven for 15 to 16 minutes. Remove from cookie sheet; cool on rack. Makes 3 dozen cookies.

Coors Brewing Company
Golden, CO

Drew Bivens, Wellington, Co.

Reggan Blehm, Wellington, Co.

FRONTIER

Part Two: The Military Soldiers and Scouts

Out on the field a soldier would typically carry one days supply of coffee, hardtack, brown sugar and salt pork. Salt pork (or "Old Ned" as it was called) was a main staple. It was usually boiled first to remove some of the salt taste, then fried or cooked on a stick over an open campfire.

Hard tack is a hard flour cracker that was so durable it could withstand being packed in a saddle bag, plus it could be stored for long periods without spoiling.

Hardcrackers, or Hard Tack

4 to 5 cups flour
2 cups water
2 pinches salt

• Knead flour, water and salt; roll out on greased 12x13-inch pan; cut into fifteen pieces; pierce each piece with sixteen holes. Bake for 30 minutes at 425° F, 15 minutes on each side. Reduce temperature to 200° F and bake until all moisture is removed from crackers (approximately 8 to 24 hours. Crackers will not burn in a 200° F oven, so may remain in oven almost indefinitely.)

Recipe from Sam'l P. Arnold
The Fort Restaurant - Denver, CO

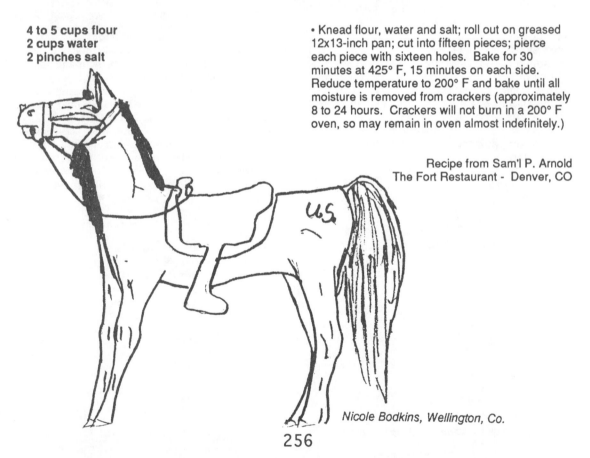

Nicole Bodkins, Wellington, Co.

Tom McChesney, Wellington, Co.

Carlos Garcia

Eating only dry hardtack must have become tiresome because inventive soldiers would take hardtack, dampen it, then fry it in salt pork drippings and sprinkle it with brown sugar for a dessert.

Fresh and dried apples were a basic staple at the forts. But supplies would often run out due to late or sporadic deliveries. Here is an amazing recipe for a mock apple pie. It tastes like an apple pie, but has no apples in it!

Mock Apple Pie

Pastry for double-crust 9-inch pie
2 eggs
25 saltine crackers, broken (about 1-1/2 cups)
1-1/2 cups milk
1 cup sugar
2 tsp ground cinnamon
1 tsp. finely shredded lemon peel
1/2 tsp. ground nutmeg
Vanilla ice cream or light cream (optional)

• Prepare and roll out pastry. Line 9-inch pie plate with half of pastry. Trim pastry to edge of plate. In large bowl beat eggs with fork. Stir in crackers, milk, sugar, cinnamon, lemon peel and nutmeg. Turn into pastry-lined pie plate.
• Cut slits in top crust; place atop filling. Seal and flute edge. Brush with milk and sprinkle with sugar. To prevent overbrowning, cover edge of pie with foil. Bake in 375° oven 20 minutes. Remove foil; bake 25 to 30 minutes more or till crust is golden. Serve warm with ice cream, if desired. Makes one 9-inch pie.

Coors Brewing Company

Natasha Walton, Mancos, Co.

257

John Skibo, Wellington, Co.

Ft. Carson, Colorado is named for the famous frontiersman, Kit Carson. Kit Carson was a trapper on the frontier for 15 years, and then served as a guide for the U.S. government. He was a noted Indian fighter, and ended his career as superintendent of Indian Affairs for the Colorado Territory.

Here is one of Kit Carson's favorite recipes:

Bowl of the Wife of Kit Carson

1/4 cup cooked chicken or turkey meat in bite-sized pieces
1/4 cup cooked rice
1 cup rich chicken broth
1/4 cup cooked garbanzos
Pinch leaf oregano
1/4 chopped chipotle pepper (or leave whole to remove later). Canned chipotle peppers may be found in Mexican grocery stores.
1/4 avocado, sliced
1/4 cup cubed Monterey Jack or Muenster cheese

• Heat broth to boiling and add chicken, garbanzos, chipotle pepper, rice and oregano. Simmer 5 - 10 minutes - remove chili pepper. Serve in large individual bowls, and add cheese pieces and avocado just when serving.

Miss Lona Wood -
grandaughter of Kit Carson
From the recipe collection of
Sam'l P. Arnold

258

FRONTIER

Part Three: Recipes from the Trail

Most wagon trains carried the following provisions: flour, cornmeal, dried apples, potatoes, lard and bacon (salt pork).

These foods would not turn rancid during a long journey. They were supplemented with fresh game, nuts, berries and vegetables whenever possible. You can imagine from this diet how important their bread was. Journey cake was one of the most popular recipes from the trail. It was made enroute by an evening fire and cooked on a flat, wooden shingle called a "journey board". Journey cake contains no milk or eggs as they were too hard to transport.

Journey Cake

1-1/2 cups sugar
3/4 cup butter
1-3/4 cups apple cider
4-1/2 cups flour
1 tsp. each: soda, cinnamon and cloves

• Combine all ingredients. Bake at 375° for 30 minutes or until golden brown in a 9x13 pan.

Sue Ashbaugh - Education Coordinator
The Hiwan Homestead Museum in Evergreen

FRONTIER

Many travelers would include a small keg of sourdough starter in their wagons as the packages of dry yeast we enjoy today did not exist then.

The following are recipes for sourdough starter and bread. The bread may be made more authentically by omitting the "store bought" yeast. If the sourdough starter is "alive" the loaf <u>will</u> rise. However, the dough will require much more time to proof.

Sourdough Starter

1 pkg. active dry yeast
1 cup warm water (110°)
2 cups all-purpose flour
1 (12 oz.) can Coors beer (non-alcohol)
1 Tbl. sugar

• Soften yeast in warm water. Stir in flour, beer and sugar. Beat till smooth. Place in a wide-mouth jar. Cover loosely with cheesecloth; let stand at room temperature 5 to 10 days, stirring 2 to 3 times a day. Mixture will foam and bubble. (Time required to ferment depends on room temperature: if room is warm, let stand a shorter time than if room is cool.) Cover loosely and refrigerate till ready to use.
• To keep *Starter* going: For each 1 cup Starter used, add 3/4 cup water, 3/4 cup all-purpose flour and 1 tsp. sugar to remainder. Let stand at room temperature till bubbly, at least a day. Cover loosely and refrigerate for later use. If not used within 10 days add 1 tsp. sugar. Maintain starter by adding sugar every 10 days (if not used for bread).

Coors Brewing Company

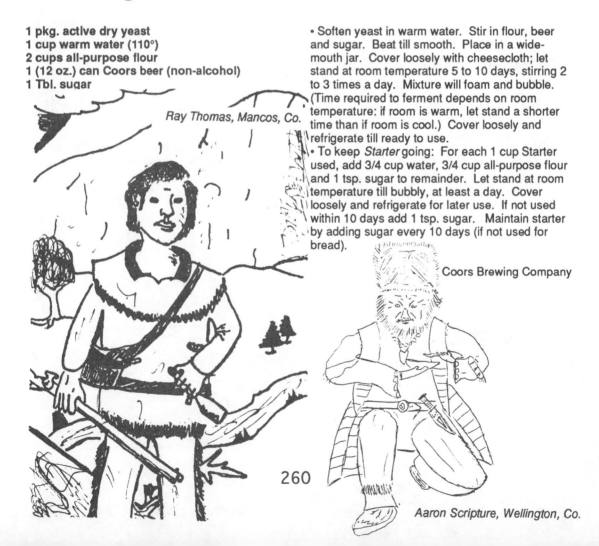

Ray Thomas, Mancos, Co.

260

Aaron Scripture, Wellington, Co.

Sourdough French Bread

1 pkg. active dry yeast
1 (12 oz.) can Coors (non-alcoholic) beer, warmed to 110°
5 to 5-1/2 cups all-purpose flour
1 cup Coors sourdough starter at room temperature
3 Tbl. sugar
2 Tbl. butter or margarine, softened
2 tsp. salt
1/2 tsp. baking soda
Yellow cornmeal

Soften yeast in warm Coors. Blend in 2 cups of the flour, the sourdough starter, sugar, butter and salt. Combine 1 cup of the flour and the soda; stir into flour-yeast mixture. Stir in as much of the remaining flour as you can with a spoon. Knead in enough remaining flour to make a moderately stiff dough that is smooth and elastic (5 to 8 minutes total). Place in greased bowl; turn once. Cover; let rise till double, 1 to 1-1/2 hours. Punch down; divide in half. Cover; let rest 10 minutes. Shape into 2 oblong or round loaves. Place on baking sheet sprinkled with cornmeal. Cover, let rise till almost double, about 1 hour. Brush with a little water. Make diagonal slashes across tops. Bake in 375° oven for 30 to 35 minutes. Makes 2 loaves.

Coors Brewing Company

Beth Mitzushima, Wellington, Co.

Jennifer Fox, Wellington, Co.

 FRONTIER

Some travelers tied a dairy cow to their wagon so they could have fresh milk. This was especially important if they had children. The Spanish-American influence can be seen in this drink that was a favorite along the trail.

Mexican Chocolate

2 squares sweet chocolate
1 quart milk or cream
1 egg*
1/2 tsp. vanilla
1/4 tsp. cinnamon
Pinch nutmeg
Pinch ground, dry orange peel

* May want to use pasteurized eggs (such as egg beaters).

• MEXICAN CHOCOLATE is different in that it has both cinnamon and a bit of vanilla in it, plus egg for festival occasions such as Christmas Eve. You can make it very easily yourself.
• Simply add hot milk or cream to sweet chocolate, add egg, vanilla and cinnamon. Blend for 2 minutes. Start blender at slow speed, or the hot milk will jump at you! I like to add just a pinch of ground orange peel. Be sure, however when you make it, to beat or blend until frothy. Top cups with a sprinkle of nutmeg.

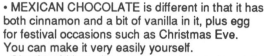

From the collection of Sam'l P. Arnold

Denis Suarez, Wellington, Co.

Matt Lowry, Wellington, Co.

262

Mexico expanded the Spanish frontier in the 1840's by granting huge land grants as far north as Colorado. Mexico feared U.S. aggression, and so it tried to create a "buffer zone" with their own settlers. Our state was named "Colorado" which means **red** or **ruddy** by these Spaniards. Another favorite recipe on the trail with a Spanish background was Capirotada or Spotted Dog. This dish is a bread pudding with raisins and said to date back to medieval days.

Capirotada (Spotted Dog)

6 cups toasted bread pieces
2 cups crushed piloncillo or brown sugar
1 cup water in a small pan
1 medium-sized onion, chopped in small pieces
4 eggs
2 cups sliced apples
3 cups milk
1 cup sultana raisins
1/2 lb. butter or margarine
2 Tbl. cinnamon
1 tsp. nutmeg
1 cup grated yellow cheddar-style cheese
Heavy cream

Boil the sugar and water to make a syrup approximately the consistency of maple syrup. When syrup has thickened slightly, add the onion pieces, letting them cook together. In a bowl, stir eggs and milk together. Don't beat! In a large baking dish, layer broken bread, then syrup, egg mixture, raisins, apples, butter, cinnamon and nutmeg until dish is filled. Bake approximately 45 minutes at 350° F. After 40 minutes, remove from oven and spread cheese over the top. Replace in oven for 5 minutes, or until cheese is melted. Serve hot. Pour a little cold heavy cream over each portion. Serves eight hungry people. (The grizzled American mountain men sometimes had difficulty with Spanish words. Because of the raisins in this bread pudding, it was affectionately dubbed "spotted dog" by the early westerners.)

From Wendy Gordon
Boulder Museum of History
With permission from Sam'l P. Arnold

Genesis Dionne, Wellington, Co.

Jean Marc Mayotte, Ft. Collins, Co.

FRONTIER

Part Four: The Settlers

Almost every family coming west brought kegs of molasses. It was often their only sweetener. As soon as they reached their destination they would make vinegar from their molasses. A popular recipe, especially liked by children, was Vinegar Pie.

Vinegar Pie

Filling:
1-1/2 cups sugar
3 Tbl. cornstarch
3 Tbl. all-purpose flour
1-1/2 Cups water
3 beaten egg yolks
2 Tbl. butter
3 to 4 Tbl. vinegar
1 (9-inch) baked pie shell
Meringue

Meringue:
3 egg whites
1/2 tsp. vanilla
1/4 tsp. cream of tartar
6 Tbl. sugar

• *Filling:* Combine sugar, cornstarch and flour. Stir in 1-1/2 cups water. Cook and stir until mixture boils. Reduce heat; cook and stir 2 minutes more. Remove from heat. Gradually stir about 1 cup hot mixture into egg yolks; return all to saucepan. Cook and stir 2 minutes more. Stir in butter. Gradually stir in vinegar. Pour in pastry shell.
• *Meringue:* In mixing bowl, beat egg whites, vanilla and cream of tartar until soft peaks form. Gradually add sugar, beating to stiff peaks. Spread meringue over hot filling, sealing to pastry. Bake in 350° oven for 12 to 15 minutes. Cool; chill. Makes 1 pie.

Coors Brewing Company
Golden, CO

Scott Lesser, Wellington, Co.

264

 FRONTIER

Children on the frontier did not have candy. Can you imagine their delight when everyone got together for a Molasses Taffy Pull! These parties were usually held in the winter when families had more idle time, and food was less diverse.

Molasses Taffy

1 cup unsulphured molasses
1/2 cup water
1-1/2 cups dark brown sugar
1-1/2 Tbl. cider vinegar
1/4 tsp. salt
5 Tbl. butter
1/8 tsp. baking soda
Confectioner's sugar

• Place the molasses, water, brown sugar, vinegar, salt and butter in a heavy saucepan. Bring to a boil, stirring until sugar dissolves. Boil without stirring until the mixture registers 250° - 280° F on a candy thermometer or forms a hard ball when a little is dropped into cold water. Stir in the baking soda and pour onto a buttered marble slab or heat-proof platter.
• When taffy is cool enough to handle, pull it with both hands to a spread of about 18 inches. Fold the taffy back on itself and continue pulling, twisting slightly until ridges of twists retain their shape (about 15 minutes). Form into a long rope on a surface sprinkled with confectioner's sugar. Cut into bite-sized pieces.
Yield: about 1 pound.

From Wendy Gordon
Boulder Museum of History
with permission from Sam'l P. Arnold

Chelsea Lunders, Mancos, Co.

265

Jennifer Fox, Wellington, Co.

The following are several popular recipes from early Colorado.

Old-Fashioned Pound Cake

2-1/2 sticks butter
1 cup sour cream
6 large eggs - separated
3 cups sugar
3 cups plain flour
1 Tbl. vanilla
1/4 tsp. baking oda
Pinch salt

• Preheat oven to 300°.
• Cream butter and sugar together thoroughly. Add egg yolks one at a time. Beat well after each. Dissolve soda in sour cream. Add alternately with flour (about 1 cup at a time) to the sugar - butter - egg mixture. Add vanilla. Beat egg whites and fold into flour mixture.
• Grease and flour an angel food cake pan. Place a piece of wax paper in bottom. Pour in pound cake batter. Bake for about 2 hours at 300°.

This recipe is over 150 years old.

Peggy Reeves
Colorado State Representative
Fort Collins, CO

Chess Charvat, Wellington, Co.

Scott Clark, Wellington, Co.

266

Mama Hefley's Homemade Ice Cream

8 - 10 med. size eggs, lightly beaten
4 cups sugar (can adjust to your taste)
1 qt. milk (2% works fine)
2 cups diced fruit (Peach or strawberry are my
    favorites but any fresh fruit can be used.)
2 cans evaporated milk (i.e. Columbine, Pet,
    Milnot, etc.)
1 Tbl. vanilla

Mix eggs, sugar and milk thoroughly. Place in microwave* bowl and cook on HIGH for 3 minutes. Stir and repeat 5-6 times (approximately 15 - 18 minutes total) until thickens as making a custard. Remove and cool completely! Place in ice cream freezer container in the following order: cooled custard; 2 cups diced (or blended for smoother cream) fruit; evaporated milk; vanilla and the freezer paddle. Turn paddle a few times to mix. Add just enough milk (2%) to cover the top edge of paddle. Now proceed as usual on freezing the ice cream.

* Original recipe was cooked and stirred constantly on a stove top. This is an old family recipe from the late 1800's.

Congressman Joel Hefley
U.S. Representative from the 5th District,
Colorado Springs, CO

267

Jolene Charvat, Wellington, Co.

Clint Reeve, Wellington, Co.

White Sugar Gingerbread

2 cups all-purpose flour
1 tsp. baking powder
1 tsp. ground ginger
1/2 tsp. salt
1/2 tsp. baking soda
1/4 tsp. ground nutmeg
1/2 cup butter or margarine
1 cup sugar
2 eggs
1 cup buttermilk
Vanilla ice cream, whipped cream or fresh fruit
    (optional)

• Grease and lightly flour 9x9x2-inch baking pan; set aside. In mixing bowl combine flour, baking powder, ginger, salt, baking soda and nutmeg; set flour mixture aside.
• In large mixer bowl beat butter with eletric mixer about 30 seconds. Add sugar and beat tuntil well combined. Add eggs, one at a time, beating till fluffy. Add flour mixture and buttermilk alternately to beaten mixture, beating on low speed after each addition until just combined. Turn batter into prepared pan. Bake in 350° oven 35 to 40 minutes or until done. Cut into squares. Serve warm with ice cream, if desired. Makes 9 servings.

Coors Brewing Company
Golden, CO

Amanda Flores, Wellington, Co.

 FRONTIER

Stack Cake was a traditional pioneer wedding cake that was put together right at the wedding! Each guest brought a layer of cake. Applesauce was spread between layers, and all the layers were stacked. A bride's popularity could be measured by the number of layers she received. This simple molasses cake was typical.

Stack Cake (Pioneer Wedding Cake)

1 cup butter
1 cup sugar
1 cup molasses
3 eggs
4 cups all-purpose flour
1 tsp. baking soda
1 tsp. salt
1 cup Coors beer (non-alcoholic)
2 (15 oz.) jars chunk-style applesauce
1/2 tsp. ground cinnamon
Whipped cream
Sliced apples

• Grease and flour three 8 x 1-1/2 inch round baking pans; set aside. In large mixing bowl cream butter and sugar until light and fluffy. Beat in molasses; add eggs, one at a time, beating well after each. Stir together flour, baking soda and salt; add to creamed mixture alternately with Coors, beating after each addition. Pour 1-1/3 cups batter into each prepared pan. (Refrigerate remaining batter.) Bake in 375° oven about 15 minutes or until cake tests done. Cool in pans 5 minutes; remove from pans and cool on wire racks. Wash pans; grease and flour. Repeat baking with remaining batter. Combine applesauce and cinnamon; spread between cooled cake layers. Spread whipped cream on top; garnish with sliced apples. Serve with additional whipped cream. Makes 20 to 24.

Coors Brewing Company
Golden, CO

Jill McKenzie, Wellington, Co.

Justin Latham, Wellington, Co.

FRONTIER

Calamity Jane (Martha Jane Burke) was a famous frontier woman and friend of Wild Bill Hickok (James Butler Hickok). Here is her recipe for a Twenty Year Cake.

Calamity Jane's Twenty Year Cake

8 eggs (beaten separate)
1-2/3 cups sugar
1-2/3 cups butter
3-1/3 cups flour
1/2 tsp. cloves
1 tsp. cinnamon
4 tsp. mace
4 tsp. nutmeg
2/3 tsp. yeast powder
OR 2/3 tsp. soda and 1 tsp. cream of tartar
2-1/2 lb. seeded raisins
1/2 lb. citron (cut very fine)
1-2/3 lb. currants

Mix butter, eggs and sugar. Add flour, cloves, cinnamon, mace, nutmeg and yeast (or soda & cream of tartar). Then fold in fruit. Bake 275° for 2 hours or until done. Makes 1 (8 lb.) cake.

Submitted by Rusti Ruth
Friend of Educ. from California

Old West Ranch Baked Beans

1 (20 oz.) can kidney beans
1 (20 oz.) can small red beans
1 (20 oz.) can great northern beans
1/2 cup brown sugar
2 Tbl. Dijon mustard
1 lb. chorizo sausage
1 cup diced onion
2 tsp. red chili powder
1 (20 oz.) can diced tomato
1 cup black molasses (or to taste)

Cook sausage and onion together in fry pan until browned. Drain all cans and mix with sausage and onion in a dutch oven. Add all other ingredients, mix well. Place uncovered in a 325° oven for 45 min. - 1 hour. Serve with cornbread and butter.

Robert Starekow
Chef of Silverheels Southwest Grills,
Summit County & Golden, Colorado

270

Amanda Liukko, Mancos, Co.

 FRONTIER

Part Five: The Gold Rush

In 1859, gold was discovered in Colorado . The gold rush began as hundreds of people headed to Colorado crying: *"Pikes Peak or Bust!"* Gold was first panned from rivers and later mined from famous mother lodes in the mountains. Mrs. Eveitte Swanson's grandmother, Johannah, was a mine camp cook in Alma, Colorado, from 1895-1920. Here are two of her favorite recipes:

Swedish Chokladbrod

1 cup butter
3/4 cup sugar
1 egg
2 Tbl. cocoa
2 tsp. vanilla extract
1-3/4 cups sifted all-purpose flour
1/4 tsp. baking powder
1 egg white, slightly beaten
1/4 cup chopped nuts
3 Tbl. sugar

Cream the butter with the sugar, then mix in the egg, cocoa and the vanilla. Sift the flour and baking powder together then add the creamed mixture and blend well. Spread the batter on buttered cookie sheets so that you have long strips 1-1/2 inches wide and about 1/4 inch thick. (Leave about 3" between strips.) Brush with egg white and sprinkle with chopped nuts and sugar. Bake in moderate oven about 10 to 12 minutes. Then leave them on the cookie sheet to cool. After about 2 mintues cut strips into bars about 1-1/2 inches wide. Do not remove from the sheet until the cookies are cool and crisp.
Makes about 60 cookies.

Mrs. Eveitte Swanson
Submitted by Erik Swanson, Director
Cripple Creek District Museum
Cripple Creek, CO

Greg Cummings, Mancos, Co.

Chase Preuit, Wellington, Co.

Kennan Blehm, Wellington, Co.

Swedish Coffee Cake (Gott Vetebrod)

2 pkg. of dry yeast (or compressed yeast)
1/4 cup warm water
2/3 cup butter
1/3 cup sugar
2 tsp. crushed cardamon seeds
1/2 tsp. salt
3/4 cup scalded milk
1 egg
3-1/2 to 4 cups sifted all-purpose flour
3/4 cup raisins (optional)

Soften the yeast in warm water (110°) then mix the butter, sugar, cardamom, salt and hot milk. Let it cool. Add egg, yeast and 2-1/2 cups of flour - stir. Add enough of the remaining flour to make a soft dough. Turn out dough on lightly floured surface and knead until smooth and elastic. Put dough in a lightly buttered bowl, turn once to grease the surface then cover and let rise in a warm place until it has doubled in bulk (about 1-1/2 hrs.). When light, punch down and knead lightly again. Form dough into various shapes, let rise and bake at 375° for 20 to 25 minutes.

Mrs. Eveitte Swanson
Submitted by Erik Swanson, Director
Cripple Creek District Museum
Cripple Creek, CO

 FRONTIER

A favorite lunch for the miners around Central City was cornish pasties, especially good after being warmed over a lantern.

Cornish Pasties

Crust:
2 cups sifted flour
1 tsp. salt
1/2 cup water
1-1/4 cups finely chopped suet
1/2 cup lard
Or you can substitute 1 cup shortening for suet and lard. Original recipe was with suet and lard.

Filling:
2-1/2 cups flank steak, cut into thin strips
1-1/2 cups diced potatoes
3/4 cup chopped onions
3/4 cup chopped rutabagas
1-1/2 Tbl. suet or butter
Salt and pepper

Crust: Sift together flour and salt, cut in shortening until like corn meal. Roll dough thin and cut into 6x6 in. squares.
Filling: Put in center of pastry square, meat and veggies, season, sprinkle with 1 Tbl. water. Fold pasty over center and crimp edges together with fork to seal.
Bake: 350° for 45 minutes to an hour, until browned (on greased cookie sheets).
For Suet Crust: After adding suet and lard, blend well. Cut in with pastry blender. Add water a little at a time. Put on board and knead thoroughly before rolling.
• This recipe was given to me from a neighbor in Denver, whose family resided in Central City in the late 1800's.

Frances Beyer
Gilpin County Historical Society
Central City , CO

Of the thousands that searched for gold in Colorado, only a few found their fortunes. The most famous of these is Molly Brown. Our final recipes are from "The Unsinkable Molly Brown Cookbook".

Snickerdoodles

1 cup sugar
3/4 cup butter
4 eggs
1 cup sifted flour
1 tsp. baking powder
1/4 tsp. salt
1 cup hickory nuts or pecans
Cinnamon

• Melt butter, stir in sugar, add eggs slightly beaten. Sift flour, salt and baking powder together and add to egg mixture. Spread batter thinly on buttered cookie pan. Sprinkle cinnamon and chopped hickory nuts over batter. Bake 350° until lightly brown. Cut into squares immediately. Unless you are fortunate enough to live near a hickory grove, pecans will have to do.

Molly Brown House Museum
Denver, CO

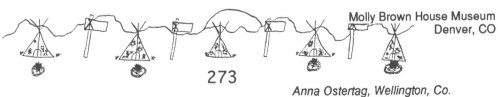

273

Anna Ostertag, Wellington, Co.

Miner's Casserole

2 lb. ground beef
Olive oil
2 large onions, chopped
2 bunches celery, chopped
1 green pepper, chopped
1 Tbl. chili powder
1 large can tomatoes
1 can each of peas, lima beans, red kidney
    beans and mushrooms
1/2 lb. cheese-American
1 lb. spaghetti - broken, cooked and drained

Cook ground beef in olive oil until crumbled and brown. Add onion, celery and green pepper and sauté lightly. Add chili powder, tomatoes, cheese, peas, lima beans, red kidney beans, mushrooms and spaghetti. Mix all together and put in casserole. Lay slices of cheese on top and bake slowly at 350° for one hour. Better each time you warm it over. Will serve 10 to 12.

Molly Brown House Museum
Denver, CO

Scotch Shortbread

1 cup butter, softened
1/2 cup powdered sugar, sifted
2-1/2 cups sifted flour
1 Tbl. cornstarch

Cream butter and sugar, add flour and cornstarch mixed together. No liquid. Take a small piece of dough at a time, pat to about 1/4-inch thick. Run rolling pin over to smooth, using powdered sugar in place of flour, and cut with a small cutter. Prick each cookie four times with a fork. Bake on ungreased cookie pan at 350° until lightly brown.

Molly Brown House Museum
Denver CO

References:
1) Arnold, Sam'l P. • Eating Up The Santa Fe Trail • Colorado:
    University of Colorado Press, 1990 •
2) Krajeski, Anita • Coors Taste of the West • Des Moines, IA:
    Meredith Publishing Service, 1981 •
3) Wills, May Bennett • The Unsinkable Molly Brown Cookbook, 1966 •

Kylee Smylie, Wellington, Co.

COOKBOOK COMMITTEE

A special thank you to the volunteers listed on this page that made this book a reality!

Thank you to all the school volunteers across Colorado. Your help is so essential! If you'd like to volunteer, and haven't, contact your local school and see how your love and caring can make the difference!

Celebrity Search Team:
Connie McChesney
Ruth Smylie
Judy Stachurski
Jean Delaney
Becky Ostertag
Peggy Tarr
Frances Betts

Typesetting the book:
Argina Swenson
Becky Ostertag
Judy Stachurski
Sarah Clark
Renee Galego
Nan Zimmerman
Karen Tigges
Terry O'Donnell
Joyce Newcomb

Contests and Artwork in Book:
Nanci Jacobs
Connie McChesney
Frances Betts
Kim Nohava
Sarah Clark
Terri Westover

Contest Judges:
Cheryl Lynn Wallace
Steve & Cheryl Miller
Crystelle Mayeda
Terry Nash
Dale Rosenbach
Kathy Phifer

Recipe Test Cooks:
Jill Becksted
Connie McChesney
Judy Stachurski
Jean Delaney
Ruth Smylie
Ronda Koski
Becky Ostertag
Gloria Borensen
Mary Ann Fox
Veronica Kattnig
JoAnn Smith
Sarah Clark
Wendy Lanham
Gail Dionne
Robbyn Wood
Cindy Hayes
Shelli Johnson
Kati Brown
Jody Boatright
Peggy Tarr
Nan Zimmerman

Recipe Test Cooks (cont.)
Argina Swenson
Lori Haskett
Terri Gutierrez
Marilyn Hodges
Margaret Ritchey
Martha Allen
Judy Schnug
Lynette Boyd
Deanie Kelly
Lorraine Brandt
Margaret Ritchey
Martha Allen
Teresa Burns
Patsy O'Brien
Cheryl Groff
Linda Patzer
Karen Peter
Cheryl Stull
April Korby
Bob Marshall
Connie Matsuda
Patti MacDonald
Jan Lockwood
Amanda Keismetter
Carla Bredehoft
Jolene Wearrne
Debra Bishop
Gail Trlica
Ann Scott

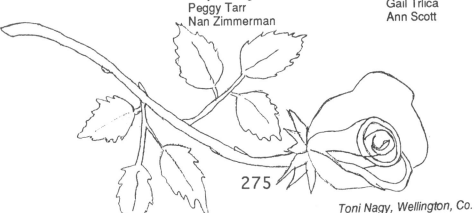

275

Toni Nagy, Wellington, Co.

CONTRIBUTORS INDEX

CONTRIBUTORS INDEX

CONTRIBUTORS INDEX

RECIPE INDEX

RECIPE INDEX

RECIPE INDEX

RECIPE INDEX

RECIPE INDEX

RECIPE INDEX

RECIPE INDEX

RECIPE INDEX

RECIPE INDEX

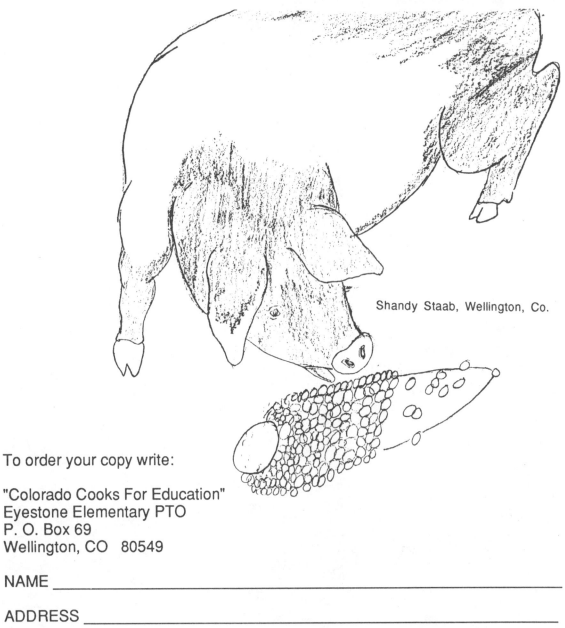

Shandy Staab, Wellington, Co.

To order your copy write:

"Colorado Cooks For Education"
Eyestone Elementary PTO
P. O. Box 69
Wellington, CO   80549

NAME _____

ADDRESS _____

CITY _____STATE _____ZIP _____

Enclose $15.95 plus $3.05 (shipping and handling) per book.

# of Books ordered _____ times $19.00 = TOTAL ENCLOSED$_____